Development Encounters

Sites of Participation and Knowledge

HARVARD STUDIES IN INTERNATIONAL DEVELOPMENT

Reforming Economic Systems in Developing Countries
edited by Dwight H. Perkins and Michael Roemer, 1991

Markets in Developing Countries: Parallel, Fragmented, and Black
edited by Michael Roemer and Christine Jones, 1991*

Progress with Profits: The Development of Rural Banking in Indonesia
Richard Patten and Jay K. Rosengard, 1991*

Green Markets: The Economics of Sustainable Development
Theodore Panayotou, 1993*

The Challenge of Reform in Indochina
edited by Börje Ljunggren, 1993

Asia and Africa: Legacies and Opportunities in Development
edited by David L. Lindauer and Michael Roemer, 1994*

Macroeconomic Policy and Adjustment in Korea, 1970–1990
Stephan Haggard, Richard N. Cooper, Susan M. Collins, Choongsoo Kim, and
Sung-Tae Ro, 1994

Building Private Pension Systems: A Handbook
Yves Guérard and Glenn Jenkins*

Green Taxes and Incentive Policies: An International Perspective (Sector Study Number
11)
Glenn Jenkins and Ranjit Lamech*

*Framing Questions, Constructing Answers: Linking Research with Education Policy for
Developing Countries*
Noel F. McGinn and Allison M. Borden, 1995

Industrialization and the State: The Korean Heavy and Chemical Industry Drive
Joseph J. Stern, Ji-Hong Kim, Dwight H. Perkins, Jung-Ho Yoo, 1995

Moving to Market: Restructuring Transport in the Former Soviet Union
John S. Strong and John R. Meyer, 1996

Economic Recovery in The Gambia: Insights for Adjustment in Sub-Saharan Africa
edited by Malcolm McPherson and Steven Radelet, 1996

The Strains of Economic Growth: Labor Unrest and Social Dissatisfaction in Korea
David L. Lindauer, Jong-Gie Kim, Joung-Woo Lee, Hy-Sop Lim, Jae-Young Son, Ezra F.
Vogel, 1997

Between a Swamp and a Hard Place: Developmental Challenges in Remote Rural Africa
David C. Cole and Richard Huntington, 1997

Getting Good Government: Capacity Building in the Public Sectors of Developing Countries
edited by Merilee S. Grindle, 1997

*Assisting Development in a Changing World: The Harvard Institute for International
Development, 1980-1995*
edited by Dwight H. Perkins, Richard Pagett, Michael Roemer, Donald R. Snodgrass,
and Joseph J. Stern, 1997

*Environment and Development in a Resource-Rich Economy: Malaysia under the New
Economic Policy*
Jeffrey R. Vincent, Rozali Mohamed Ali, and Associates, 1997

*published jointly by the International Center for Economic Growth

HARVARD STUDIES IN INTERNATIONAL DEVELOPMENT

Development Encounters

Sites of Participation and Knowledge

Edited by Pauline E. Peters

WITHDRAWN

Harvard Institute for International Development
Harvard University

Distributed by Harvard University Press

Published by Harvard Institute for International Development

Distributed by Harvard University Press

Library of Congress Cataloging-in-Publication Data

Development encounters : sites of participation and knowledge / edited by
Pauline E. Peters.
      p. cm. — (Harvard studies in international development)
      Includes bibliographical references and index.
      ISBN 0-674-00259-8 (cloth) — ISBN 0-674-00260-1 (paper)
      1. Economic Development. 2. Economic development—Citizen
participation. I. Peters, Pauline E. II. Series.

HD75.D4875 2000
338.9—dc21   00-040686

Editorial Management: Sarah Newberry
Editorial Assistance: Jolanta Davis
Copyediting: Hope Steele, Cambridge, MA
Design and production: Desktop Publishing & Design Co., Newton, MA
Printing: Maple-Vail Book Manufacturing Group, York, PA

TABLE OF CONTENTS

CONTRIBUTORS VII

ACKNOWLEDGMENTS IX

1   Encountering Participation and Knowledge in
    Development Sites 3
    Pauline E. Peters

2   The Micro Politics of Participatory Projects: An Anatomy of
    Change in Two Villages 15
    Ajay Mehta

3   Decentralization, Participation, and Representation:
    Administrative Apartheid in Sahelian Forestry 29
    Jesse C. Ribot

4   New Challenges for Alternative Ways of Development among
    Indigenous Peoples of the Amazon 61
    Margarita Benavides

5   Battlefields of Wits: Interface between NGOs, Government, and
    Donors at the Development Site 77
    Isaac N. Mazonde

6   The Routinization of Participation: Emerging Norms, Local
    Participation, and Conflict Management in Latin America 95
    Theodore Macdonald

7   Writing Against Hegemony: Development Encounters in
    Zimbabwe and Malawi 121
    Anne Ferguson and Bill Derman

8   Developing International Health Science Research: Measuring
    or Marginalizing Quality 157
    James A. Trostle

9   Rethinking the Role of Elites in Rural Development: A Case
    Study from Cameroon 175
    Paul Nchoji Nkwi

Bibliography 197

Subject Index 217

Author Index XXX

ACKNOWLEDGMENTS

The book's essays constitute a selection of those originally presented at two workshops held at the end of 1995 and mid 1996. I should like to thank not just the authors of the essays presented here but all the participants who attended the workshops. The lively discussions significantly influenced my own thoughts about development encounters, participation and knowledge, and also helped reshape the essays published here. Particular thanks are due to Frederick Cooper who first raised the idea of following up an earlier workshop series on the history and politics of development knowledge (see Cooper and Packard ed. 1997) with one on development encounters – the ways in which development ideas such as participation and indigenous knowledge are put into practice in specific sites. I benefitted greatly from working closely with him in the planning and running of the workshops. These workshops brought together people who work as practitioners in various types of development with those who work as academic analysts of development. Such encounters are not always easy but the participants jointly created an atmosphere that encouraged stimulating and challenging debate, even if we did not all agree with each other's interpretations or conclusions. The participants at the workshops on development encounters, including the essay writers, were the following: Bina Agarwal, the late Juan Carlos Aguirre, Arun Agrawal, Margarita Benavides, Miguel Gonzalez Block, Marty Chen, William Derman, Priyanthi Fernando, Ann Forbes, Julie Goldman, Allan Hoben, Anne Ferguson, William Fisher, Theodore Macdonald, Isaac Mazonde, Ajay Mehta, Hudita Mustafa, Andrew Mushita, Paul Nkwi, Lisa Peattie, Donna Perry, Dina Razon-Abad, Jesse Ribot, K. (Shivy) Shivaramakrishnan, Paul Smoke, Shiv Someshwar, James Trostle, and Shiv Visvanathan. In addition, thanks are due to Sarah Newberry and Jolanta Davis for their editorial work at the Harvard Institute for International Development as well as to the University Press editors. Finally, we all are very grateful to the

Rockefeller Foundation, particularly Joyce Moock, for funding the workshops and some of the publication costs.

CONTRIBUTORS

Margarita Benavides at the time of writing the paper was the coordinator of the Amazon Program of OXFAM America and, since 1999 has joined a nongovernmental organization called Instituto del Bien Comun in Lima, Peru. She is currently the coordinator of a project that helps Amazonian groups map their communal lands.

Bill Derman is Professor of Anthropology and African Studies, Michigan State University, whose most recent research concerns the social organization and politics of water resource management in Southern Africa.

Anne Ferguson is Associate Professor of Anthropology and the Director of the Women and International Development Program in Michigan State University, USA. Her research focuses on natural resource management and gender, particularly in Malawi and Zimbabwe.

Theodore Macdonald is an anthropologist and the Associate Director of the Program on Nonviolent Sanctions and Cultural Survival (PONSACS) at the Weatherhead Center for International Affairs of Harvard University.

Isaac Mazonde is senior research fellow and acting director of the National Institute of Development Research and Documentation (NIR) in the University of Botswana. His research addresses appropriate technology, agriculture, food security, and minority groups.

Ajay Mehta is the Chief Executive Officer of Seva Mandir, a nongovernmental organization based in Udaipur, India.

Paul Nkwi is Professor in the University of Yaounde, Cameroon, and the President of the Pan African Association of Anthropologists.

Pauline E. Peters is a Fellow at the Harvard Institute for International Development and a social anthropologist whose research concentrates on Southern Africa and on the topics of the social dynamics of agricultural commercialization, land tenure, poverty and gender, and who has written on various dimensions of the society-policy nexus.

Jesse Ribot is a Senior Associate in the Institutions and Governance Program of the World Resources Institute, Washington D.C. He is currently coordinating on a comparative research program in Mali, Cameroon, Uganda, and Zimbabwe exploring the local dynamics of natural resource decentralization policies.

James Trostle is Associate Professor of Anthropology at Trinity College, Hartford, Connecticut. From 1988 to 1995 he was Senior Social Scientist in the Applied Diarrheal Disease Research Project at the Harvard Institute for International Development. His recent research interests include studies of research and policy-making, and the social factors in recent Latin American cholera epidemics.

1 ENCOUNTERING PARTICIPATION AND KNOWLEDGE IN DEVELOPMENT SITES

Pauline E. Peters

INTRODUCTION

Participatory development and indigenous knowledge are said to be among the current "buzz-words" of development (Pottier 1993:13) and to reflect a "new orthodoxy" (Stirrat 1996:67).[1] Fashions may move faster in the field of development than in academic social sciences, but both fields experience the paradigm shifts described by Kuhn (1962) for science. These shifts are products of interactions between changing ideas (theories, models, frameworks) about social processes and changes in those processes themselves. In a period when new paradigms—such as indigenous knowledge and democratic participation—are becoming the focus of development thinking and practice, it is especially important to examine in a systematic way the front lines of the development process. Over the half-century in which development has been a central theme of global politics, paradigms have come and gone, and it is crucial to understand the conditions that separate a dynamic and productive initiative from one that proves to be more of the same or regressive. How are local knowledge and participation being defined and practiced by different groups engaged in various development activities in a range of countries? It is crucial to understand what sort of ideas and projects "take" and are produced within developing countries themselves, how development ideas are appropriated within local political and institutional frameworks, and how institutional capacity is built up that allows for a fruitful combination of local knowledge and action with initiatives from national and international development agencies.

This volume is a product of two workshops held in 1995 and 1996 where participants from Africa, Asia, Latin America, and the United

States with direct experience in development as organizers of non-governmental organizations (NGOs), program managers, policy researchers, activists, and scholar-practitioners met to address the issues of "Knowledge, Ideas and Practices in Development Sites" and "Participation and the Micro-Politics of Development Encounters."[2] The volume includes a selection of the papers that were given at those workshops. The workshops and the volume are companions to an earlier series of workshops on "Development Knowledge and the Social Sciences" that looked at the production and transmission of development ideas[3] and the subsequent volume, *International Development and the Social Sciences*, edited by Frederick Cooper and Randall Packard (California University Press, 1997). The latter was a project in the history and sociology of knowledge. This volume focuses on the development field itself and the multiple ways in which development knowledge and practice are constituted, adapted, and contested within development sites. The emphasis here is not on development as merely an external project that is accepted, adapted, or resisted in a local setting, but on a more dynamic view of interaction, in which the development apparatus is examined at the same time that the complex social and economic contexts into which it intervenes are explored.

The most important theme that emerged from the earlier series of workshops and that framed the two on Development Encounters was that development over the past fifty years has had shifting meanings but has been continually a site of contestation. Development is one of the most powerful intellectual constructs and political slogans of the past half-century, giving order and purpose to a world in which colonies disappeared, in which virtually everyone acquired citizenship in a sovereign state, but in which profound inequality remained. The concept of development was invoked in the 1940s by colonial powers seeking to reassert imperial hegemony in what proved to be the waning days of colonial rule. The very ambiguity of the notion of development, however, has led to its providing a basis for radical critique as well as for policy orthodoxy. Development became a mobilizing concept for nationalists in Africa and Asia as well as for Latin American economists seeking to counter North American economic and political dominance. The universalistic aspirations at the heart of development—of improving standards of living and eliminating poverty—had a radicalizing potential, specifically as a counter to the racial construction of colonization. Universalistic language also provided a basis for challenging local elites as well as colonial powers and subsequent neocolonial endeavors.

Today, debates about development are truly globalized. Across a wide range of countries and regions, disagreements among development professionals and struggles among social groups not only turn on competing definitions of development but also, increasingly, insist on distinguishing development from modernization and westernization. Strategies for lobbying powerful agencies of national states or international donors are hammered out not only in highly localized arenas but also in international meetings and in internet communications that link representatives of groups previously isolated. Such multiple "takes" on development lead the authors of this volume (cf. Cooper and Packard) to depart from the overly deterministic vision of development as a new imperialism projected by such critics as Escobar, who describes "development discourse" as having "created an extremely efficient apparatus for producing knowledge about, and the exercise of power over, the Third World...that ensures certain control over it" (1995:9). Recent attempts of development agencies and donors to link democratization and participation to development are a response to the growth of social movements and of debate among policy makers, public intellectuals, and widely dispersed groups about the shape and process of development. They also create new arenas for debate and confrontation. These are the focus of this volume. The chapters consider the multiple faces of development revealed in development encounters: How do participatory approaches help disadvantaged people to improve their lives, and where do they facilitate their coming under intensified control by a state or groups within it? How is participation differently defined and practiced? Do the purveyors of different forms of knowledge engage together to solve problems, or is one type of knowledge deemed superior and so serves to downgrade or erase another? In what ways are participation and knowledge productively joined?

KNOWLEDGE AND KNOWLEDGEABLE PRACTICE

The notions conventional in modernization theories of development about the universal applicability and objectivity of scientific knowledge have been severely criticized on both theoretical and practical grounds. The "postmodern" challenges of the past decade or so have provided another basis of critique to longer-standing debates within

development studies that draw their inspiration from radical traditions of thought (for example, those of Paul Streeten, Colin Leys, and
Andre Gunder Frank) as well as those by anthropologists that draw
on ideas of cultural difference. The growing attention paid to "indigenous" knowledge is one outcome of these multiple critiques. The
groundbreaking volume, *Indigenous Knowledge Systems and Development*, edited by Brokensha, Warren, and Werner (1980), has been
followed by a flood of theoretical and methodological writings and
practical applications. These have been closely allied with approaches
promoting "participation." Among the best known are the works of
Robert Chambers, Gordon Conway, and others on "participatory"
appraisal methods, the large body of literature on participatory research
on farming systems, and certain approaches in rural development.
All of these incorporate ideas of indigenous knowledge and participation.

Insisting on the situated character of all knowledge has proved to
be a positive influence in development as theory and practice. There
are now many demonstrations of the ways in which activities in farming, animal husbandry, resource management, health care, education, and other fields gain from incorporating relevant indigenous
knowledge. Convincing claims have also been made that indigenous
knowledge is central to both equity and sustainability. Yet the approaches
in development that privilege indigenous or local knowledge, in their
turn, have become subject to criticism. One basis for critique is the
overdrawn separation of indigenous or local knowledge from so-called
scientific and Western knowledge. By definition, indigenous knowledge premises an opposed "other" knowledge that replays the dicho-
tomies of traditional versus modern, folk versus scientific, and rest
versus West (Agrawal, workshop paper; 1995).[4] More usual and more
interesting is the interplay, even mutual constitution, of different
forms of knowledge generated and practiced in different sites. Notions
of eclecticism, bricolage, or creolization have recently been invoked
to describe the kinds of combination that take place. The critiques,
then, do not deny the multiple sources of knowledge but the presumed isolation of "indigenous" or "local" knowledge from other (scientific, Western) knowledge. The dynamics of these encounters can
be better illuminated, however, if one does not start with a premise
of total separation.

Another criticism is that notions of "systems" of indigenous knowledge reify and oversystematize specific "local" ways of knowing and

doing. They tend to privilege stasis, coherence, and conservatism over adaptation, experimentation, and opportunism. James Fairhead shows that this tendency to reify knowledge abstracts particular types of knowing (e.g., in farming) from their "social and political context," and leads analysts to impute unconscious forms of knowledge to farmers' actions that may be "fortuitous side consequences" (1993:198). He also points out that rendering virtually everything done by farmers or others as forms of knowledge ends up as a topsy-turvy version of the notion that indigenous peoples lack (appropriate) knowledge and need to be educated out of their ignorance (cf. Agrawal 1995; Hobart 1993). To conflate practice with either ignorance or knowledge is the same analytical error. Fairhead and others stress that many forms of practice are not comprehensible in terms of articulated statements of knowledge, and that knowledgeable "performance" may be a more insightful way of understanding what people do and why rather than premising a body or system of knowledge (cf. Richards 1993).

The critiques of the overseparation of indigenous or local knowledge from other forms of knowledge are not to be taken as denying the importance of recognizing how different sources of knowledge figure in social interaction. Calls for more equitable development or more participatory approaches cannot proceed without paying close attention to whose knowledge is at play—who is defining the "problems" and the proposed "solutions"? The twinning of local knowledge and local action in participatory and related approaches parallels the more theoretical and abstract debates influenced by Foucault on the mutual constitution of knowledge and power. Despite the institutional separation of academic theory and applied practice, the parallelism of Foucauldian emphases on addressing knowledge/power and those in development on knowledge/participation indicates the lack of permeable barriers between the worlds of thought and action. One of the shortcomings of a complete isomorphism of knowledge and power is the failure to recognize the work of knowledgeable actors in changing and (re)producing differentials of knowledge and power. The writings of Foucault and many of those inspired by him have been criticized for allowing abstract "forces" and "discourses" (of, say, modernity, capitalism, or development) to obscure the ways in which knowledge and power are deployed by specific socially and historically situated actors. Current discussions of the role of knowledge in development suggest a preferred focus on knowledgeable agents. The knowledge/power link revealed by Foucault may be more effectively grounded in social action through Giddens' formulation of knowledgeability and capability as defining agency. Norman Long, whom several of the authors of this volume invoke, has continually stressed the need to attend to agency: "knowledge encounters involve the struggle between actors who aim to enroll others in their 'projects', getting them to accept particular frames of meaning" (1992:27). The resulting negotiation of definitions and meanings; the success and failure in claiming priority for one type of knowledge; and the multiplicity of interests, maneuvers and strategies underlying these are the subjects of several of the following chapters.

PARTICIPATION

Participatory approaches to development have become de rigeur once again in recent years. Popular in the community development schemes of the 1950s and 1960s, and again in the 1970s turn to "basic needs" and "bottom up" philosophies of development, participatory approaches have been resuscitated yet again in a current context concerned with human rights, democratization, civil society, and popular social movements. Some claim the superiority of "local" accountability and authority in managing resources and guaranteeing security; others promote participation as doing more with less in a situation of economic strain and dwindling foreign aid. Although *participation* and *participatory* are ubiquitous terms in current discussions of development, especially in natural resource management projects, their meanings and practical embodiments are so various as to be in danger of being just another development fad.

Participation ideally connotes the ability of people to share, influence, or control design, decision making, and authority in development projects and programs that affect their lives and resources. In a participatory environmental management project to rehabilitate a watershed, for example, this should translate into people who live in the area being fully involved in defining the problems and the feasible solutions, and in selecting the chosen remedies, designing the work, allocating responsibilities, and sharing in the benefits. All too often, however, participation has been part of the rhetoric of governments and private agencies without the reality of involvement and influence (Gatter 1993, Mosse 1996). State-organized "participatory" development initiatives may be mobilization by another name, and "participatory" projects may resemble old-style corvee rather than people's empowerment (Hoben et al. 1998; Ribot, this volume). Much of the time, the situation is ambiguous, with partial participation, degrees of participation, and thus disputes over when "real" participation occurs. The aim, however, is clear. As David Maybury-Lewis states, "Obviously, not any kind of participation will do. Forced or directed participation is not acceptable, so it is democratic participation that is being sought" (1996). The chapters collected here suggest some answers.

Belief in the advantages of participatory development in the last decade has produced a large number of manuals for facilitating community participation and for conducting participatory research. These can be extremely useful and have generated a search for new ways of conducting development and political organizing. It is essential, however, to remember that participation is a political process involving contestation and conflict among different people with different interests and claims, rather than merely a methodology or a set of facilitating techniques. Moreover, particular forms of participation are highly variable across groups, cultures, and regions. To assume that participation is new, that it is absent from local communities, and that it needs to be taught ignores the vigor of social associations that exist in most communities and, more critically, obscures the ways in which the latter are affected by national and international political processes. The tendency to separate participation from politics is just another reflection of the widespread tendency in development discourse and practice to bracket off politics. Yet participation or the lack of it is fundamentally a political process, and only a political analysis can reveal what does or does not take place and why. This is demonstrated clearly in the following chapters. The cases reveal some answers to these questions: What constitutes participation? Who participates? Whose voices are heard and whose stories are accepted? Such questions raise for the authors issues of representation and accountability of individuals and organizations as spokespersons, to an inquiry into the phenomenon of the "nongovernmental organization" (NGO), and to a debate on the myriad meanings given to the terms *community* and *local* in participatory development approaches.

There is a need to look inside the "black box" of NGOs, especially those espousing participation as a means or an end: How do they define themselves? What connections do they have with other NGOs within and outside a country? What constitutes the accountability of an NGO as spokesperson? The current love affair of aid donors with NGOs, often in the name of cutting back the state to size and encouraging "civil society," and the subsequent flow of aid to NGOs have led to the proliferation of new organizations. Some of these organizations are, or strive to be, representative of the people for whom they serve as lobbyist or intermediary with state and other powerful agents. Others are opportunistic attempts to benefit from aid flows, and are little more than "briefcase NGOs." Some organizations act as catalysts, able to mobilize resources to lever change on behalf of and with the participation of certain sectors of a population. At other times, however, an NGO becomes a new type of patron with all the problems of dependency this entails. Even if an NGO facilitates a change in the distribution of rights and privileges to benefit an excluded group, to what extent can such a change be sustained if the NGO leaves? Lasting change requires institutional procedures being put in place. Here, the negative descriptor—nongovernmental organization—obscures the critical point that consideration of what NGOs do is impossible without inquiring into the relations between the NGOs and the state.

The chapters presented here also interrogate *local* and *community*, both common terms in discussion of participation. Although much participatory development is assumed to take place among local populations, the authors consider that a single focus on the local is itself a problem. Action, whether participatory or not, in any locale, has its own dynamics peculiar to that place and time; these dynamics are also part of wider processes over space and time. The need to trace connections, linkages, and flows is recognized in several chapters. Similarly, use of the term *community* should be carefully examined. Participation is usually assumed to concern a community. Yet several of the authors show how internal differentiation (of class, caste, ethnicity, or gender) renders participation difficult to achieve. In showing the danger of assuming an unproblematic community, they echo the cogent conclusion of anthropologist Peter Little: "community is commonly misused to invoke a false sense of 'tradition', homogeneity, and consensus...[whereas] most rural communities are not free of conflict, nor are they homogeneous" (1994). Just as "community is not a place but an ideological construct," as Silverman and Gulliver (1992) remind us, so the following chapters show that participation is not a technique but an ideal.

THE CHAPTERS

From his vantage point of long experience working in Seva Mandir, a major NGO in India, Ajay Mehta has seen villagers seeking to improve their lives through patronage rather than lobbying the state to create entitlements. In this context, the role of NGOs is to help poor and politically powerless groups to participate in the sense of gaining more direct access to the political process, and to help them devise ways of developing communal and other resources. Definite successes have been the result of collaboration between the NGO and marginalized groups, both in relation to strategies of managing resources and to political processes of representation. Given the considerable inequities in Northern India, where the projects are situated, Mehta points out that "the politics of cooperation" achieved with the NGO's help is not guaranteed to last, and that "the odds are stacked against" the poor. In fact, some of these difficulties have also been described in another paper by someone who worked on the same project (Ahluwalia 1997). Mehta's chapter does more than show how an NGO may be able to help shift the political balance, even for a while. He also is anxious not to let the NGO remain a black box. Seva Mandir has been developing a self-reflective procedure to deal with the "internal contradictions" of an organization dedicated to helping the poor yet vulnerable to its staff becoming part of the collusive oppression of villagers or diverting resources for private gain. Just as the villagers' full participation in beneficial development depends on ensuring accountability of their leaders, so an NGO has to find ways of making itself and its staff accountable to their clients.

The chapter by Jesse Ribot considers the example of participatory forestry management in West Africa. Ribot shows how one has to take careful account of the political structures and processes in place to assess the degree to which West African states' policies and projects undertaken in the name of "participation" actually translate into real benefits for a wide range of people. What is being devolved and to whom? What can different categories of local people participate in? How is a community defined and by whom? How are decision making and rights over resources actually distributed? In several of the West African countries discussed, participation takes place without locally accountable representation. One has to inquire into the relation between spokespersons and those for whom they speak. Participation without locally accountable representation becomes charity at best and indirect rule at worst. When decision-making authority over valuable resources is devolved to nonrepresentative groups, "participatory" approaches facilitate private monopolies. The key issues to be faced, then, are the nature of representation, the role of governance structures, and the constitution of community. Similarly, Sivaramakrishnan argues that the participatory "joint forest management" program in Bengal should be seen as part of a process of "state-making," and that participatory development is both a global discourse embodied in internationally funded development and the outcome of local politics and national state-making (Sivaramakrishnan 1996).

Margarita Benavides describes how Amazonian indigenous groups' experience of colonization has included loss of territory, exploitation, and subjection to cultural imperialism. In the face of these threats, new types of indigenous political organizations have arisen, especially national and international federations. In lobbying for greater participation in the decisions over the use of the natural resources from which they live, the indigenous groups have developed the idea, new to them, of "territory." Like the Basarwa organization described by Mazonde, the Amazonians insist on the equation of cultural identity with territory in defining their separate but equal status in a state. Like the Basarwa, they also experience tensions of internal differences—relations between the groups and various outsiders have been through young men with some education and/or familiarity with the wider society, and the distinct opinions of women or elders without such exposure may go unrecognized. The role of NGOs such as OXFAM, for which Benavides works, is to help indigenous groups and subgroups to find ways of improving their organization and of resolving some of the tensions and conflicts that threaten them, as well as to mediate, where appropriate, in the groups' dealings with external agencies. The political dynamics internal to a nationwide coalition of political and voluntary organizations formed to lobby the Philippines state on land reform described by Dina Razon-Abad provides a similar example. Consensus- and coalition-based politics, through which participation of the powerless is channeled, are vulnerable to both internal conflict and external destabilizing forces (Razon-Abad 1996).

Isaac Mazonde's chapter on the Basarwa (their adoption of this label, long considered pejorative in Botswana, recalls other examples of appropriation and valorization of negative terms such as *black* and *queer*) discusses a group at a much earlier stage of political organization than the Amazonian indigenous federations discussed by Benavides and Macdonald. Nevertheless, the Basarwa, like the Amazonian groups, are struggling to define their fuller participation in their respective countries' policies. In doing so, they are engaged with debates and negotiations among themselves, with groups within Botswana and with groups in Africa and Europe. Moreover, both the Basarwa and the Amazonian groups face similar questions: How representative are their spokespersons, the leaders of the organizations formed to lobby for their members' rights? How real is a people's participation if their spokespersons and/or leaders are not accountable? How does a group ensure that financial and other aid from external organizations does not smother rather than enhance a group's agency? For the Basarwa, the formation of lobbying organizations has facilitated their political visibility. The question remains, however, whether structures of patronage and donor funds determine leadership and agendas rather than these emerging out of a representative community politics. Finally, both Basarwa and the Amazonian groups are faced with the task of ensuring their full "integration" into the political economy of their countries but not at the cost of sacrificing their separable identity. Here, surely, is a dilemma at the heart of "participation."

Theodore Macdonald discusses two ongoing conflicts over rights to resources in Colombia and the Galapagos Islands and the ways in which participation is being defined in each. The cases differ profoundly in some ways: the Colombian dispute sets up the U'wa, a tiny indigenous group, against an alliance of powerful oil companies and state interests—a real David and Goliath story, as Macdonald notes. In the Galapagos, the conflict takes place among a multiplicity of groups with differing, often competing, interests in the rich resources of the area. In both cases, however, the reality of a participatory process for resolving the disputes turns on hammering out an institutional procedure that seeks to provide those currently excluded from existing authority with the political power essential for participating with parity. In this, Macdonald's chapter complements those by Benavides and Mazonde. Participation as a right rather than a favor or privilege occasionally extended by those in authority entails change in administrative procedure and legal frameworks. As Macdonald stresses, meaningful and sustained participation requires not only attention to the "rules" themselves but to the processes for "rule-making." In all these cases, this translates into political action at some level.

Anne Ferguson and Bill Derman show the inextricable interplay between knowledge and participation in their discussion of how scientific knowledge is constructed and used in development projects. They challenge Escobar's proposition that "development" is a single hegemonic paradigm through which knowledge about and in the developing world is produced. Through close examination of several development projects in Malawi and Zimbabwe in which they were directly involved, both individually and together, they show how the use of particular knowledge changed over time and from project to project, in response to changes in personnel, political climate, and research methodologies. The shifts in the types of knowledge drawn on also entail shifts in levels and forms of participation by national researchers vis-à-vis foreign researchers, university vis-à-vis government institutions, farmers vis-à-vis project managers. As the authors point out, despite the shortcomings of "participation" in many development sites, in three out of four projects discussed local people were treated as knowledgeable agents. The difficulty lay and still lies in the ways in which this recognition is translated into practice. In all cases, interactions among diverse knowledgeable agents took place in political arenas where some actors, some knowledges, some ideas have greater pull than others. But each case also showed new openings and departures, leading the authors to insist on a greater open-endedness than notions of hegemonic development knowledge imply.

James Trostle's story of a very different type of development project—the funding of biomedical research—reveals a picture of gains and losses with similarly intricate nuances. Although today we have become nervous about the commodification of knowledge, Trostle reminds us of Socrates' reference, well over two thousand years ago, to "various subjects of knowledge" being peddled "from city to city." From Trostle's account, biomedical research knowledge seems particularly well armored against criticism and new ideas and methods that depart from quite antithetical premises. Once again, we are reminded of Kuhn's work on the conservative function of paradigms. The "capacity-strengthening" approach of facilitating applied biomedical research in developing countries contrasts with that of participatory research approaches advocated by Chambers and Uphoff. The former invokes universal standards of proof and identifies capacity and needs according to universal, scientific standards; the latter promotes the identification of local capacity and needs through a combination of local and external resources. Through careful scrutiny of particular instances of proposed research and researchers' practices, Trostle shows that although the project helped many researchers and institutes to get their research underway, it also, willy-nilly, replicated some of the current foibles of the Western scientific community (such as privileging empiricist over interpretive methods, measuring researchers according to numbers of citations in international journal indexes, and "salami publishing"—the division of research into as many publishable slices as possible).

Paul Nkwi's chapter reveals how knowledge and participation have been productively joined in Cameroon but also casts the role of elites in a different light from some of the other chapters. In many instances, elites stand in opposition to local participation, whether overtly so, as in the villages described by Mehta, or more subtly, as in Ribot's case. In other cases, such as those discussed by Benavides and Mazonde, a potential threat to meaningful participation by local residents occurs when representatives and spokespersons develop interests and positions at odds with those of their erstwhile peers. The provocative message of Nkwi's description of the NGO he has helped establish is that elites do not always or necessarily siphon off resources and power. He argues that the Kom elite, of which he is a member, has acted as an initiator, "energizer," and "catalyst" for development to be taken up by local hands. The elite have used their own extensive knowledge—of local sociocultural organization, symbols, and political process, and of national politics and development rhetoric—to work with rural people in Kom to develop projects that benefit them. The ways in which local politics and local development are caught up in national politicking and personal rivalries provide a fascinating account that, although in some ways a special case, also reveals the obstacles and the potentials for self-directed, participatory development by local groups in alliance with elites who operate through national and international networks.

The writers quoted at the beginning of this introduction, on participatory development and indigenous knowledge being "buzzwords" or a "new orthodoxy," labeled them in this way to signal neither wholehearted embrace nor dismissal but rather a call for careful examination of these purportedly new approaches. The present volume contributes to this endeavor and, in particular, to the ways in which participation and knowledge are defined and used *in the practice of development*. The authors base their examination of how different types of knowledge are deployed and whether and how participation occurs on their direct experience in development encounters. There have been many shifts in the definition of what constitutes development—so many, in fact, that writers often refer to fads and fashions rather than paradigm shifts. The lesson taken from the instability in preferred approaches in development by the authors of this volume is not to lapse into cynicism or despair but rather to see that the practices of both theorizing and action warrant a fairly constant critical reflection, whether one reflects from a position in an NGO, a government agency, a university, or a farm.

NOTES

1   The introduction draws, in part, on workshop commentaries by Frederick Cooper and the author, and the section on participation draws on a piece published in *Cultural Survival Quarterly*, 1996, by the author.

2   The workshops were held at HIID, organized by P. Peters and F. Cooper (University of Michigan), and sponsored by the Social Science Research Council. Funds were generously provided by the Rockefeller Foundation.

3   These were held during 1993–1994 and sponsored by the Social Sciences Research Council and funded by the National Endowment for the Humanities.

4   Arun Agrawal presented a version of his paper at the first Development Encounters workshop.

2   THE MICRO POLITICS OF PARTICIPATORY PROJECTS: AN ANATOMY OF CHANGE IN TWO VILLAGES

Ajay Mehta

The record of development and democracy in the Indian context presents a paradox. Rather than empowering poor people over time, the national forces for democracy and development frequently have enfeebled the poor relative to other social groups in society. In particular, the processes of development and poverty alleviation have shifted the balance of power in favor of development functionaries vis-à-vis the poor, while certain aspects of democratic government have attenuated the extent of social cohesion amongst the rural poor.

This chapter describes the efforts of a nongovernmental organization (NGO) called Seva Mandir (for which I work) to countervail the debilitating aspects of development and democracy. It also considers some inner contradictions in voluntary action intended to empower the rural poor. The context for the work described here are the groups living in the hilly tracts of Aravalli range in southern Rajasthan, a state in northwestern India. The largest section of the populace consists of poor tribal peasants, although people of other low and high caste denominations also live in the sparsely populated villages of this region.

THE POLITICS OF CONTROL AND CO-OPTATION

After independence, the Indian State took on responsibility for enhancing the well-being of rural communities. Over time, a large bureaucratic establishment was created to serve the health and schooling needs of these communities. As a consequence of public pressure, substantial resources were also allocated to alleviate poverty and bring about rural development. At the political level, *Panchayati Raj*, or village-level democracy, was instituted to give villagers a voice in governance and to provide a forum for self-governance and some control over government bureaucracy. Despite significant allocation of resources and the creation of institutions for self-governance, these interventions have not succeeded in either empowering the poor or enhancing their well-being. If anything, they have strengthened the ability of more powerful and more affluent segments of society to control and co-opt the poor to serve their interests.

Before independence, this area was ecologically rich and well endowed with forests. Although the feudal system was far from just, the rural people benefited from a well-preserved environment. In the postindependence period, these resources were ruthlessly commercialized and over-exploited. The development of an organized industrial sector did not benefit the rural poor significantly because they lacked the social and economic means to take advantage of the opportunities that were being created as a result of national economic growth. Rather than entitle the rural poor to resources that could improve their livelihoods, the state continued the colonial/feudal policy of a custodial approach to forest and land management. Villagers were denied secure entitlements to large tracts of forests and revenue lands vested in the state. Although, legally, people were denied access to land belonging to the state, in practice these lands were systematically privatized by certain groups on an informal basis through collusive alliances with state functionaries and with the active support of elected public representatives. Even as this pattern of land tenure and management selectively benefited some villagers, it had the perverse consequence of making rural people increasingly obligated to state officials and politicians.

Moreover, conflicts emerged between and among villages when the process of de facto privatization happened to override the longstanding customary claims of user groups. Since people gained access to resources through patron–client relations and collusive politics, compared with the better-endowed and more powerful elements in rural society the poor were disadvantaged in terms of the amount of land to which they could lay claim. Additionally, these ad hoc land tenure arrangements had an adverse effect on land productivity.

The overall effect of such development processes was to generate pathologies of disempowerment, inequality, and inefficiency. The use of state subsidies, bank credits, development projects, and so on gave officials immense power over the poor. It also intensified the need for the poor to search for powerful patrons at the expense of forging ties of solidarity among themselves. The consequence, then, was to reduce the ties of horizontal solidarity among rural people and to reinforce vertical ties of dependency with powerful patrons and power brokers. Rather than expanding entitlements to public goods, development and democracy were successful in making people dependent on external patrons, whose stake in enhancing the well-being of the poor is equivocal at best.

SEVA MANDIR AND VOLUNTARY ACTION

In the early phase of Seva Mandir's work, around three decades ago, the focus for the NGO was on promoting adult literacy among poor peasants. It was believed that, through literacy, the poor would become more aware of their rights and entitlements. They would therefore be more effective in achieving their well-being and getting the state and society to be more accountable to their needs. With experience, Seva Mandir realized that this single-minded stress on literacy was not enough to bring about significant improvements in the well-being of villagers through their own capacities or through putting pressure on the state. Seva Mandir therefore extended the scope of its work to include developmental programs that would benefit people in economic terms. Agricultural extension work and infrastructure development activities (such as building link roads and improving people's access to water for irrigation purposes) were introduced alongside the work of literacy. This combination of activities was strongly welcomed by the people.

Throughout the 1970s, village people who were associated with Seva Mandir programs became popular and well respected within their communities as a result of the development-cum-literacy promotion activities. Some of these people successfully competed for elected office in the Panchayati Raj institutions (the grassroots tier of Indian democracy). Seva Mandir at that time felt that these developments were encouraging and would lead to improvements in the functioning of the village councils (*Panchayats*) and also in the functioning of government agencies responsible for development and welfare services in the rural areas. The experience of these elected representatives subsequent to gaining office, however, belied our expectations. Most of them, albeit sponsored by and belonging to the community of poor peasants, proved unable to make the village councils and the government bodies more responsive to the needs of the poor. Their ineffectiveness within the power structure had to do with the fact that these institutions were embedded in structures dissociated from the interests of the poor. The new representatives were thus caught in a dilemma. By not conforming to the existing patron–client basis of local development, they ran the risk of losing what little support and patronage were available for the poor, whereas if they conformed, they became indistinguishable from the people they had replaced on the grounds of those people being co-opted and corrupt.

Considering the limitation of mere representation in the institutions of political democracy, Seva Mandir tried to overcome this constraint by organizing poor peasants into village-based groups. The intention behind this was to get villagers to demand accountability from their representatives in the village councils and to pressure the government to expand the scope of people's entitlements to public goods. Thus, during the early part of the 1980s, helping organize activist village groups became the major thrust of Seva Mandir's work. It was felt that this process of organizing village people to demand their entitlements from the state was a critical step in getting development to happen. The experience of this activist approach to development did not prove wholly satisfactory. The factors preventing these village groups from influencing the state agencies included poverty, ties of dependency, and dispersed settlement patterns (all of which divided villagers), as well as the very nature of the state agencies of development.

As a consequence of the limitations of this approach and certain favorable developments in the level of governmental support for the voluntary sector, in the mid-1980s Seva Mandir made a paradigm shift in its thinking and approach. It decided that instead of depending only on the state to provide development, capacity for development should be created at the level of village people and civil society at large. This strategy came into being around 1987 to 1988. Programs concerned with health, education, soil and water conservation, afforestation, and women's issues were initiated, and village committees were set up to manage and monitor these programs.

As part of this strategy to create capacity at the village level to serve people's development needs, a cadre of village-based professionals called *paraworkers* was slowly raised and trained in the disciplines of health, education, forestry, women's issues and child care, community organization, and so forth. They were given modest stipends to make it worthwhile for them to serve their respective communities. Professionals were recruited by Seva Mandir to develop programs designed to enhance the ability of the village people and Seva Mandir jointly to bring about development. The shift in the locus of authority and resources for development from the state to institutions of civil society created an agency that could address the deeper constraints of development and bring about changes in social relations and values necessary for poor people to benefit from and be empowered by development and democracy.

THE POLITICS OF COOPERATION

In this section, the experiences of two village clusters (out of the 450 in the Seva Mandir area of engagement) are described. These experiences are exceptional in terms of the degree to which people have been able to cooperate and to gain distinct political authority. They are in no sense, then, "typical" of participatory development projects. The purpose of choosing these villages is to suggest that the principles underlying the transformation of these villages are available to the region as a whole. The villages represent a promise and hope rather than a formula.

The Story of Nayakheda Village

Nayakheda is a hamlet, comprising about 30 households, of the revenue village of Usan, some thirty kilometers north of Udaipur. It is part of a belt of seven multicaste villages consisting mostly of poor peasants and a small minority of landlords. Seva Mandir had been working in this area for over two decades. In the 1970s, Seva Mandir had worked to promote adult education and agricultural extension work. Toward the end of the decade, it had tried to help villagers form groups to negotiate their entitlements from the state. Unfortunately, the expectations from group formation and awareness-raising work were not realized. The failure of the groups to influence government systems and officials led Seva Mandir, in the mid-1980s, to focus on creating capacity among local people, as well as within Seva Mandir, to service some of the development needs of the people. The choice of programs to be supported was weighted in favor of cooperative efforts. Despite having created this capacity, no headway on development could be made in Nayakheda because of the nature of local politics. The alliance between the local landlord, officials, and elected village council representatives was so powerful and self-serving that they refused to provide space for the poor to undertake development activities with the help of Seva Mandir.

Not only were the local landlord and his coterie resistant to the idea of people's lands being improved, but also, with the connivance of the police and revenue officials, the landlord had occupied a substantial part of the village pasture lands for mining purposes. Another segment of the village commons was monopolized by other powerful people in the village, thereby leaving no stake for the ordinary villager to benefit from or invest in the improvement of these lands. This stand-off in terms of development ended with a bizarre incident in 1990: the landlord and his two sons were sent to jail for the suspected murder of eleven people belonging to the family of a political and economic competitor. He remained in jail for three years before being released by the High Court. It was during his absence that the people were able to organize themselves and take advantage of the support that was being offered by Seva Mandir. They were familiar with the ideas of working as a group and the advantages of being transparent in their dealings with each other and with Seva Mandir. From a situation of few development successes, much was achieved.

The people were able to recover the usurped common lands, though it meant spending a lot of money in courts to disprove the claim made by the landlord's family that the land was legally theirs. The success of this recovery created the social climate for projects addressed to the entire watershed of the area. There was palpable enthusiasm on the part of the villagers for these works because they felt that they were fully involved in the planning and execution, and would share in the final benefit of the development programs. Even though the remuneration for land development works supported by Seva Mandir was lower compared with remuneration offered by government through a World Bank–funded project, people were drawn to these works because they felt they had control over the process of development and because they knew that Seva Mandir was accountable and accessible to them on an ongoing basis. This mobilization for comprehensive land development involved the entire multicaste population in the 150 households in seven hamlets, including that of Nayakheda. By recovering from the landlord the village commons, and by successfully challenging the unfair use of common property resources by other powerful people, a stake had been created among the people collectively to improve productivity of their resource base.

Initially, people came together in relationship to the development works supported by Seva Mandir, but subsequently this solidarity developed a life of its own. This became manifest at the time of village council elections and then continuously in their daily struggles against the landlord's desperate efforts to regain control on his return from jail in 1994.

In the early part of 1995, election to the village councils was held under the new constitutional amendment, where affirmative action in favor of women and members of the tribal and other disadvantaged groups was introduced for the first time. In Nayakheda, Shiv Lal, a tribal person associated with Seva Mandir for many years as a forestry paraworker, stood for the office of *sarpanch* (village council head). Since he was highly respected and popular with the people because of his work in watershed and land development, offers were made to him by the mainstream parties to stand as their candidate. In response, village group members persuaded Shiv Lal to stand as an independent candidate, unattached to any political party.

For the campaign Shiv Lal had no funds. The task of matching the Congress Party/landlord candidate appeared to be daunting. It is alleged that the mainstream (Congress) party candidate spent close to $1000 plying voters with gifts and liquor. Among the Congress Party candidate's active campaigners was the local government agricultural supervisor. Such partisan behavior by officials, although forbidden by service conduct rules, is not uncommon in practice. The group members assured Shiv Lal that they needed no funds to persuade people whom they should vote for. They did spend $60 hiring transport and buying apples to popularize their election symbol. This money came from voluntary contributions. After the polling was over and the votes had been tallied, it was clear that Shiv Lal had won with a large majority. An attempt was made to manipulate the results in favor of the Congress/landlord nominee, but the supporters of Shiv Lal were able to thwart these efforts with a display of public strength at the voting center.

Gaining political office has made life difficult for the leaders of the movement such as Shiv Lal and also for the Seva Mandir field staff because they have become subject to harassment, even involving threats of bodily and other harm. At another level there has been a marked change in the power relations in the area. Some of the close allies of the landlord switched allegiance to Shiv Lal's camp and prevented the landlord from becoming deputy head of the village council. There is also growing support for a people-based approach to development on the part of the neighboring village people. Villagers from distant villages regularly attend the Nayakheda Seva Mandir meetings. Whether the politics of cooperation will survive and grow into a widespread movement is difficult to predict, since, at present, the odds are stacked against them. What is clear, however, is that by having gained control of a Panchayat, they have entered a new phase in terms of their political standing and power base.

The Story of Shyampura Village

The experience of another village called Shyampura (consisting of 100 households), located seventy kilometers southwest of Udaipur City, echoes the Nayakheda experience of the power of people coming together. It also shows, however, how constraints to development lie not only in dealing with powerful vested interests, but also in overcoming constraints internal to the community, such as insecure land tenure, social conflict and lack of cohesion, and political leadership unable to build consensus for common action.

Seva Mandir started working in Shyampura in 1982 with a program to promote adult literacy among the poor peasants. Later on, Seva Mandir encouraged villagers to form groups as a means to lobby for entitlements from the state. A component of the group-building program was to encourage people to take more responsibility for trying to solve their internal problems. In the mid-1980s, Seva Mandir expanded its role to help villagers service their individual and collective development needs.

The lack of adequate response from the state, despite repeated efforts by the groups to claim their attention, made Seva Mandir realize that people would lose faith in themselves and the value of coming together if they did not experience some positive outcomes. With this idea in mind, Seva Mandir developed a major program to help villagers to afforest their degraded private and common lands and to build dams for storing water for local use. In 1987–1988, Seva Mandir built a substantial water reservoir in Shyampura village. The District Magistrate had promised the villagers a dam in 1985, but nothing had happened. The successful completion of the dam created good will for and confidence in Seva Mandir among the people. It also greatly enhanced the confidence and prestige of the core village group that had lobbied for and negotiated consensus among the villagers for this Seva Mandir project to go through.

The watershed of the reservoir was highly degraded on one flank. Because the land belonged to the forest department, it was not possible for the people to treat the problem even though they realized the need to do so to prevent the siltation of the reservoir. Because the Forest Act proscribed people's management of forest resources, no action could be taken. Although officially people could not develop the land, individual farmers had settled parts of the watershed with the informal consent of forestry officials. The most active and influential members of the Shyampura village group were precisely those responsible for encroaching on the reservoir's watershed. This fact effectively undermined the ability of the group collectively to put pressure on the forest department to treat the lands, since their leaders stood to lose their access. These kinds of internal contradictions are symptomatic of the social context and prevent people from coming together to create entitlements of sustained benefit to the larger group.

In 1991, there was a change in forest policy by the state. For the first time in a hundred years of forest policy, local communities were given the right to protect the forest and in return also to share in the benefits generated from the land. This Joint Forest Management (JFM) policy gave the Shyampura community a chance to develop the watershed with the permission of the forest department. After elaborate preparations, a contract to improve fifty hectares of the watershed was signed between the forest department and an elected committee representing the community. The leaders of the group who stood to lose access to their encroached lands in the watershed were persuaded to agree to this venture with the promise that Seva Mandir would build them a lift irrigation system downstream to compensate them for the loss of their access to forests. The decision to convert forest into a joint property of the village was initially not appreciated by all the villagers; for some it meant that the option to privatize the land was foreclosed. In fact, people from the neighboring village of Amlia immediately started to make their own encroachments when they heard about the JFM contract being signed. Through protracted efforts on the part of Seva Mandir and the Shyampura group to resolve conflicts and doubts amongst the potential stakeholders, the project made headway. The prestige gained by Seva Mandir and the local group in building the dam played an important role in getting the people to agree to this project.

These developments set the stage for a political transformation in the area, similar in some respects to that in Nayakheda. Prior to the village council election of 1995, the BJP, an important political party at the state and national level, approached Nathu Lal, one of the leaders of the Shyampura group, to become their nominee for the post of the village council head. Nathu had stood twice for the post of village head in the past and had lost. Knowing that Nathu had good standing in the area on account of all the work that he had helped initiate there, the BJP saw him as a winning candidate. Nathu agreed to be their nominee. Although confident of getting votes from rural people, he was not confident of getting the votes of the urban people in the constituency. It was because of this that he also needed the BJP.

Nathu won the election by defeating, for the first time in five decades, the Congress Party candidate of the area. From all accounts, the victory of Nathu is connected to his being perceived by the people as being capable of engendering broad-based cooperation as a means of bringing about development in the area. Now that Nathu holds elected office and commands authority, his rural supporters will expect him to facilitate the development of common property resources, things that they have experienced positively. They would also expect him to continue to be honest and transparent, and use his authority to direct government functionaries to be more accountable to the people. Yet, as part of the power structure and as part of the BJP, there will be pressures on Nathu to conform to expectations of people in authority. It will be interesting to see whether the politics of cooperation are reinforced as a result of Nathu having gained public office, or whether he will be marginalized or co-opted by the power structure.

There is evidence of growing interest in cooperation on the part of people and disenchantment with the patronage mode of seeking individual benefits. This trend seems also to invite a reciprocal interest on the part of leaders such as Nathu to reinforce cohesion and community-based approaches to development. In April of 1995, after the Panchayat elections, people of four villages in this area came together to declare as sacred about seven hundred hectares of forest. They did this to protect these lands from being encroached on and overexploited.

The commitment of the more powerful in the community to promoting solidarity was made tangible after the elections when Nathu and some twenty-seven members of his clan agreed to make an annual contribution to the village fund. The donation would come from the additional earnings they were going to make from operating the lift irrigation scheme downstream of the water reservoir. The commitment to build a lift irrigation scheme had caused resentment among people of a neighboring hamlet because they had felt left out. This contribution to the fund is a gesture to make amends and cement ties of solidarity. These events at a micro level, although small in scale, suggest that it is possible to challenge the politics of control and that the ingredients of doing so can be identified.

THE POLITICS OF NGO SECTOR INTERVENTION

In this final section, I consider the contradictions endemic to development organizations such as Seva Mandir, which are made up of middle-class people attempting to empower village people. People who work in Seva Mandir on a full-time basis can be broadly categorized in the following way. Some are professional and administrative personnel who have retired from positions in government or the private sector. These people bring with them a great deal of experience and skills at the same time that they are steeped in the values of hierarchical systems of management. Another distinct category of personnel is that of young professionals who choose to work in NGOs. Although potentially very capable and less rigid in their management styles, these professionals in general have not been able to make a long-term commitment to working with Seva Mandir. Low emoluments, more attractive career prospects elsewhere, and changing personal commitments are some of the reasons for the high turnover of these people. The biggest group in Seva Mandir consists of people who are local residents and initially came to work for Seva Mandir because it offered them a job. Their economic backgrounds tend to be modest and their skills of limited market value. They are strongly wedded to their traditional identities and draw confidence from a firm sense of belonging, but, at the same time, they are not immune to the revolution of rising expectations characteristic of the middle class in Indian society. Around 80 percent of Seva Mandir's total staff of 225 people come from such backgrounds. There is irony in the fact that they initially took on the work as a source of income rather than out of a specific commitment to the type of work Seva Mandir does, whereas most of these employees spend long years working in interior villages with growing competence and engagement in the idea of making development meaningful for local people.

In general, it can be said that the people who work for Seva Mandir come from the spectrum of the middle class and are not very different in background from the people who work for the state. The challenge for Seva Mandir, as a result, becomes one of creating structures and processes that will safeguard the goals/values of the organization against the strong pressures on middle-class people to become self-serving and patronage-minded. Different kinds of ambivalences and anxieties characterize the behavior of the different social groups in the organization. The local staff members, notwithstanding their competence, secure traditional identities, and solid contributions, have deep-seated anxieties and self-doubt about their professional self-worth and also about the viability of the voluntary sector and therefore their vocation. They are often threatened by the presence of Western-educated professionals who have the mobility and authority that are associated with higher education and fluency in English, the language of the elite. Their modest levels of emoluments aggravate their economic and social anxieties. As part of a slowly homogenizing middle class of our society, they feel deprived.

For those who come to this work from professional backgrounds and have held positions in government, the emphasis on transparency and nonhierarchical modes of management can be frustrating. Accustomed as they are to the exercise of authority, the temptation to subvert democratic and egalitarian values is considerable. For young professionals who come to this sector out of choice and interest, the slow rhythm of work and outcomes and the incipient resistance to their presence, by their local counterparts on the one hand and senior mentors on the other, can be debilitating to their enthusiasm for development work. Their lack of personal maturity and experience makes them vulnerable to these professional hazards.

For an NGO the size of Seva Mandir, there are strong internal contradictions with respect to the agenda of empowering the poor. The experience of Seva Mandir over two decades shows a tendency for staff members to form small groups to serve their narrow interest at the expense of other well-motivated members of the staff and the people they are supposed to serve. The fact that people working at the grassroots level, with modest levels of remuneration, lose heart in the difficult enterprise of people's empowerment is to be expected. Before they can share power and authority with the poor, they need to feel worthwhile themselves. This is something for which larger society does not prepare people. They are undermined in their self-confidence when they cannot get jobs commensurate with their expectations and social needs. Most people who work in the field are people with this background. It is only slowly that they discover the value of their own skills and ideas and develop self-esteem in doing development work. The psychological and cultural need for them to exercise power and patronage is as strong as it is with people of similar backgrounds in government.

Changing this orientation takes time. Meanwhile, it becomes important to ensure that there are systems of power sharing within a development NGO, as well as between the organization itself and the rural poor whom the organization is supposed to help. In the case of Seva Mandir, one experiment that has shown some promise is establishing a cadre of village-based professionals, trained to serve the needs of the community. These people are remunerated and provided a long-term stake in serving the community. They are also supposed to be accountable to the village group, though in practice this happens only once the group becomes strong and experiences the value of coming together and exercising control over their representatives. The village paraworkers, as they are called, grow into leadership roles and develop the confidence to hold the institution to some extent accountable. Not to have secure and well-informed people among the poor is to centralize leadership roles outside the community of the poor. The newly elected public representatives in Nayakheda and Shyampura are both paraworkers—Shiv Lal in forestry and Nathu in literacy. Some seven hundred trained villagers exist in Seva Mandir's area of operation. One of the most critical factors in the process of change is that of leadership. The fact of having provided some exposure and financial security to village people has allowed some of them with leadership skills to remain closely associated with development works that serve the interests of the poor.

At the level of Seva Mandir as an organization, there is an effort to disperse authority, create multiple centers of initiative, and encourage diversity in terms of the backgrounds of its staff. All the operational units of Seva Mandir, such as forestry, women's work, health, and literacy, are required to develop direct links with the rural people and create an organizational structure at the village level for villagers to service their own development needs. This system, besides making villages self-reliant in skills, also encourages multiple points of initiative within the organization. The need for transparency in relations between the NGO and the villagers and within the NGO is critical, but extremely difficult to achieve. The fact that the NGO has elaborate financial procedures, hierarchy in management levels, and multiple centers of initiative makes it easy to have an alibi for something not being done. Taking issues such as openness and transparency seriously and encouraging initiative at all levels does incrementally encourage staff to internalize these values and react when these values are violated.

The experiences of Nayakheda and Shyampura suggest that NGOs have a role to play in empowering people. NGOs doing development as a means of promoting participatory development and of engendering social cohesion can go a long way in enabling people to gain political authority. Although development and democracy on their own in India have not served the interests of the poor, they do provide space where power can be contested and these very forces turned to the advantage of the poor. Institutions of civil society such as Seva Mandir have a role to play in changing the circumstances of the poor, especially looking to the fact that the poor themselves can, with a little bit of support, become the custodians of their own interests. The challenge before NGOs is to overcome their internal contradictions and keep pace with people at the grassroots level who are able to show the way to empowerment, provided the others in society are willing to contribute. Participation in development can be achieved only by recognizing the need to foster the politics of cooperation.

3

DECENTRALIZATION, PARTICIPATION, AND REPRESENTATION: ADMINISTRATIVE APARTHEID IN SAHELIAN FORESTRY[1]

Jesse C. Ribot

As a form of rule, apartheid is what Smuts [1936] called institutional segregation, the British termed indirect rule, and the French association. It is this common state form that I call decentralized despotism.

Mahmood Mamdani, *Citizen and Subject*, 1996:8.

Participatory natural resource management and rural development build on existing forms of rural administration and representation. This chapter explores the formal political-administrative structures used and created by community-based participatory forestry projects in the West African Sahel. Without some form of locally accountable representation, these projects, despite their good intentions, do not create an autonomous domain of community decision making. Although they may be local, they are not community projects. Rather, they take on the contours of their state-centric political-administrative base. Although participatory forestry may involve local populations, currently it gives them few powers of decision and few substantial benefits from what is a potentially lucrative forest trade. It could, however, do much more. This chapter examines representation and the devolution of benefits in participatory forestry approaches in Burkina Faso, Mali, Niger, and Senegal, while exploring what decentralization and participation currently are and could become.

DECENTRALIZATION AND COMMUNITY PARTICIPATION: IF EVER THE TWAIN SHALL MEET

In the 1980s, the developmentalist view flipped from seeing the African state as a progressive force for change and modernization to that of a primordial arena of greed that hindered development (Ferguson 1996). In parallel, the assumptions about the undifferentiated category of "civil society" as primordial and backward reversed, so that it was seen as the source of creative energy for modern market-oriented change-if only the state could be rolled back. This curious reversal of state-society polarities invigorated decentralization and participatory development movements and policies. Participatory development has become a means to incorporate civil society into the decisions formerly reserved for state agents. Now that the state is bad and civil society is good, decentralization and participation are ostensibly avenues by which control is being transferred from one to the other.

Participatory approaches to development got a great boost from this reversal in developmentalist perspectives. Participatory approaches emerged from a long history of frustration with failed top-down development, and they now sit comfortably at the intersection of indigenous rights movements, anti-statist sentiments of both the left and right, fiscal crises of post-cold war Third World states, and structural adjustment agendas. The privileging of civil society, of "indigenous" institutions, and of the "local" supports a participatory approach that has been promoted by both outside and local agents.

Decentralization, which includes participation, has become a primary means in promoting this approach. *Decentralization* is the devolution of central state assets and powers to local or private decision-making bodies (representative local government, local administrative branches of central government, community organizations or private individuals, and corporations).[2] When the decentralizing is to *community*[3] and representative local government, it can be a mechanism of community participation. When it is to local branches of the central state, it may be called *deconcentration*—bringing the state and its services closer to the people. When it is to nonstate bodies (NGOs or other private groups or individuals), it is *privatization*—indeed it is a form of enclosure when it involves privatization of community or public resources.[4]

As part of a reaction against state-centered top-down development approaches, aid organizations are introducing participatory forestry (and natural resource management) around the globe on the basis that it can improve forest management, boost economic and administrative efficiency, address equity problems, foster development, and help "save" the environment.[5] Participatory forestry is viewed as a way of achieving forest management while drawing on the skills, knowledge, and proximity of local populations with the added benefit of encouraging local autonomy and increasing local income. In many projects called "participatory," however, it is not clear that any of these goals are, or can be, achieved.

Involving communities in decisions and benefits is predicated on the existence of some structure for community decision making that is locally accountable and representative. Participation without locally accountable representation is simply not community participation (cf. Ribot 1996). Even if it is "local," it may not involve the community as a whole. The inadequacy of collective representation not only makes it difficult to define participation as being a community matter, but also undermines many of the ostensible goals of involving local communities. Whether, for example, costs, benefits, and equity considerations are internalized in decision making depends on how community representation is organized.

Participation also, of course, depends on the devolution of decisions over valuable resources (natural and financial) to local representative structures. In the West African Sahel, however, the instruments through which communities are being involved or represented in decisions do not constitute participation by the community. Locals who do "participate" (whether or not they represent the community as a whole) are not allowed an active voice in many of the critical decisions over the disposition of forests and forest products. Community "representatives" are not locally accountable, and no significant decision-making powers are being devolved to them.

Decentralization and participation projects currently practiced in the Sahelian countries do not necessarily devolve central state powers or create truly community institutions. Many apparent decentralization efforts re-centralize with one hand what they devolve with the other. In the following cases, I show that when local structures have an iota of representativity, no powers are devolved to them, and when local structures have powers, they are not representative but rather centrally controlled. In the legal maze of decentralization and participation, "participatory forestry" efforts often create centralized control articulated right down to the local level through the intermediary of nonrepresentative local, state, and non-state authorities. Indeed, many projects are extending the state's powers into everyday decisions-by making detailed rules and contracts for participation, and by policing the actions of those who get involved (Ribot 1995a;1995b;1996; Schroeder, forthcoming).

Although the current donor preference for civil society is a new context for fostering participatory approaches to rural development and administration, the form that community-based participatory projects is taking may not be so new. Much of what took place in the colonial period laid the groundwork for the current movement. Indirect rule and *association* policies under the British and French aspired, in anthropologist Lucy Mair's (1936:12–14) positive assessment, to develop "...an African society able to participate in the life of the modern world as a community in its own right." Although colonial policies now look brutish in hindsight, they were supported by idealist justifications in which their purveyors believed (Alexandre 1970b:65–68; Buell 1928; Perham 1960), and which do not sound very different from today's ideas about local participation.[6] In addition to the ideology of indigenous-based development, today's participatory practice has important structural similarities to colonial rural administration.

Africans have been infantilized and naturalized since the earliest part of the colonial period to justify their subjugation through separation from Europeans.[7] Policies of indirect rule under the British and *association* under the French created an institutional segregation in which Europeans and urban citizens obeyed civil law and most Africans were relegated to live in a sphere of customary law, an administratively state-ordained regulation. In 1936, the British colonial officer Lord Hailey wrote that "...the doctrine of differentiation aims at the evolution of separate institutions appropriate to African conditions and differing both in spirit and in form from those of Europeans" (in Mamdani 1996:7). Mamdani points out that the "emphasis on differentiation meant the forging of specifically 'native' institutions through which to rule subjects." He continues:

> ...although the bifurcated state created with colonialism was deracialized after independence, it was not democratized. Postindependence reform led to diverse outcomes. No nationalist government was content to reproduce the colonial legacy uncritically. Each sought to reform the bifurcated state that

institutionally crystallized a state-enforced separation, of the rural from the urban and of one ethnicity from another. But in doing so each reproduced a part of that legacy, thereby creating its own variety of despotism. (Mamdani 1996:7–8)

Participatory projects parallel the colonial experience not only in context, but also in practice when they appeal for their legitimacy to local, indigenous, non-state authorities, legitimizing these authorities in the process. Participatory approaches to rural development are in a bind. They must use or construct community representation if they are to proceed. But they must do so under conditions where locally accountable representative bodies do not exist and representative alternatives are difficult to construct beyond the temporary legitimizing presence of outside development agents. Although so-called participatory development projects bring some benefits to rural West Africa, they cannot be widely transformative while embedded in the current bifurcated political-administrative context. Without great care they may reinforce the very structures of unequal privilege they seek to upset.

The following discussion of participatory forestry projects and policies in Burkina Faso, Mali, Niger, and Senegal explores participatory development in its political-administrative context. The main focus is not the parallels with the past, but the practices that leave today's rural populations without representation in decisions affecting their everyday lives and with little control over the valuable subsistence and commercial resources around them. The chapter is divided into six more sections. The first broadly examines the role of the state in community participation. The second briefly describes current institutions of rural representation. The third analyzes participatory forestry policies and projects in the four case countries. The fourth presents an analysis of the distribution of decision-making powers and benefits from participatory forestry. The fifth section compares participatory and colonial approaches, and the final section concludes.

Rather than opposing state and civil society, this chapter ends by attempting to bring the state back in as a legitimate representative of community-if and when local governance is reformed. In this view, community participation is not set in opposition to the state but concerns the appropriate structure and role of local state formations. One has to ask who is represented and served by local governance bodies-the central state or their local constituencies? Representation is ostensibly a role of the state: a downwardly oriented state accountable to and legitimated from below, not the upward and outwardly oriented colonial and postcolonial states accountable to colonial rulers and the international aid and financial institutions. Decentralization with participation requires a switch from the decentralized despotism of administrative apartheid in indirect rule or *association* to autonomous forms of rural, representative governance—locally accountable bodies with real powers of decision over financial and natural resources. This chapter casts local representation as a problem to be addressed so that inequitable forms can no longer be relied on in an uncritical manner. If decentralization and participation are to converge it will be through a generalized participation in some form of rural democracy.

LOCAL ADMINISTRATION AND REPRESENTATION

In the Francophone countries of the West African Sahel, decentralization and popular participation both rely on at least three sets of laws. First are the *organic codes*, which set up the levels of governance (national, regional, and local) among which powers and responsibilities are divided. These codes determine the actors present at each level of government, which of these actors are to be elected and appointed, and the relation between appointed and elected officials. The second set of laws are *electoral codes*, which shape who is represented by elected officials and how accountably. These laws determine the frequency of elections, who can run, and who can vote. The third set of laws are *technical codes*. These are the bodies of law concerning specific sectors of society and economy such as traffic laws, land tenure, forestry and pastoral laws, and specifying who gets to make which decisions over the sector in question—as in appointed officials, elected bodies, technical services (such as the forest service), corporations, cooperatives, NGOs, or private citizens.

Who decides the disposition of trees and forests is circumscribed by these bodies of law and upheld by judicial and enforcement bodies. In this section I briefly describe the current structure of local authorities typically involved in the forestry sector. These are the authorities that organic and electoral codes set up. In the following section I examine the specific division of "technical" powers as spelled out in new "participatory" forestry projects and laws.

Participatory development and natural resource management projects usually rely on village chiefs or rural councils to represent rural populations-when they are attempting to be representative at all. The degree to which chiefs or councilors represent or are accountable to the populations for whom they ostensibly speak is, however, questionable. Chiefs are often seen by outside actors as a kind of authentic, primordial, precolonial, indigenous, local, and therefore appropriate, institution of community representation. A brief look at chiefs indicates that their representativity and accountability is very problematic. Rural councils, which are elected official representative bodies, are also quite problematic since these institutions are structured in a way that does not accountably represent local populations.[8]

Chiefs

In the West African Sahel, villages are the most common unit of social aggregation around which local use and management of woodlands are organized both by local populations and by outside agents. Each village, roughly 100 to 1500 people, typically has a chief; some have specialized chiefs overseeing forest use. There are also other poles of authority within villages, such as Imams, marabouts, sorcerers, non-village-based pastoral chiefs, griots, merchants, heads of certain castes (hunters in Mali), and "chiefs" of the young (*maasamari* in Niger) (see Ouédraogo 1994; Mamdani 1996; Spierenburg 1995). Colonial rulers, however, relied on village chiefs, disproportionately shifting power to the village chief and away from these other authorities (Alexandre 1970a, 1970b; Buell 1928; Cowan 1958; Deschamps 1963; Perham 1960; Suret-Canale 1970). These other figures are involved in resource management, but most state and outside organizations still privilege chiefs as their primary village authorities. Although the authority of current chiefs is in many ways a product of the colonial period, the great majority of rural West Africans see the village chief as a principal authority (Alexandre 1970b:24; Fisiy 1992; Ouali et al. 1994:16).[9]

In the countries of the West African Sahel most chiefs gain their position through inheritance via a patrilineage tracing back to warriors, the founding family of the village, or families chosen by colonial powers to replace antagonistic local leaders.[10] In the early colonial period, chiefs were chosen—"as far as possible"—by "custom." In 1934, a decree covering Guinea required that village chiefs be "(designated by the authority of family chiefs [heads of household])"

(Alexandre 1970b:52–53).[11] Then, in 1947, the colonial government issued a decree on "Indigenous Rule in Senegal," stating that "Village chiefs and commissions are elected by direct universal suffrage by the electors, male and female "…for a four-year term (Alexandre 1970b:58)."[12] In 1957, however, the colonial government introduced legislation again limiting suffrage to household heads (as in 1934) and a specified list of notables, while limiting candidacy for the position to those from "…families who have a right to the chieftaincy…" (Alexandre 1970b:61). No limits were set on their terms.

In independent Senegal, Mali, Niger, and Burkina Faso, there are still state-structured processes for choosing village chiefs (BKF 1993d; Ngaido 1996; RdM 1995; RdS 1972). In Senegal, village chiefs (usually the head of the hereditary male line) are elected by heads of households, who are virtually all male (RdS 1972:968). This system is identical to the colonial system first instituted in Guinea in 1934 and later throughout the French West African colonies under the policy of *association* (Alexandre 1970b:52–53). In Mali, under the new laws of decentralization, village chiefs are selected by a village council (of five to seven members) elected by universal suffrage in each village, but from a list of candidates selected by the appointed state administrator at the level of the *cercle*. The village council is presided over by this same state representative (RdM 1995:art.62,70). The term of the village councils, and presumably of the chief, is five years (RdM 1991:art.171).

In Burkina Faso, each village is divided into committees of youths (men eighteen to fifty), elders (men over fifty), and women (over eighteen). At national elections, each committee elects its representatives and these representatives constitute a village council. The village council then elects from its members a village council president (BKF 1993d). In Niger, "traditional chiefs" have been officially recognized since the mid 1970s and their current status is laid out in a 1993 Ordinance (93–028 in Ngaido 1996), according to which (art.7) only those "…of a given traditional or customary collectivity can be candidate to the chieftaincy of the considered collectivity, if he has customary right to it." As Ngaido (1996:19) points out, chieftaincy effectively becomes a caste for birth members only. Chiefs have the status of "administrative magistrate," allowing them to preside over local customary, civil, and commercial matters. "Traditional chiefs" also preside over a village council "elected or designated" by "local structures of participation," which include youth associations, cooperatives, socio-professional groups, Islamic associations (the Imam), and so on. The village council advises the local state administrator. "Customary and traditional communities are hierarchically integrated in the administrative organization...placed under the tutelage of administrative circumscriptions and territorial collectivities..." (art.2) (Diallo 1994:12–13; Ngaido 1996:17–20).

These village chiefs are not necessarily representative of or accountable to the people over whom they preside. The official processes in Senegal and Burkina Faso systematically underrepresent or exclude women, but this occurs to a much lesser degree in Burkina Faso where women have one third of the village vote. In Niger and Senegal, chiefs hold their positions for life. They neither represent nor are they systematically accountable to the village as a whole. Further, in Niger, only members of an elite line, or "caste," can run for the office of chief. In Burkina Faso and Mali, the process for choosing village council presidents and village chiefs appears more accountable due to regular periodic elections. In Mali, however, under the new decentralization laws chiefs are effectively administrative appointees confirmed by periodic local elections.

Aside from the systems of chief selection, there are various social mechanisms of local accountability (see Fisiy 1992:213; Mamdani 1996; Spierenburg 1995). These mechanisms, however, do not guarantee the accountability of chiefs. Some are despots and others are responsive community leaders, depending on the personality of the chief, the specific history of the village in question, and its location in a larger political economy.[13] For example, in a 1994 forest rebellion involving thirty villages in Makacoulibantang, Eastern Senegal, about half of the chiefs acted in line with the wishes of villagers who by-and-large were against commercial woodcutting in their area. The other chiefs were "bought for a few sacks of rice" by the wood merchants (Ribot, forthcoming).

Councils

Since independence from France in the early 1960s, Burkina Faso, Mali, Niger, and Senegal have created elected units of local government.[14] In Senegal, one express purpose of these councils was to facilitate "participation" by local populations via direct suffrage (Hesseling n.d.:15; RdS 1964; RdS 1972). Participation and local autonomy are also express purposes in Burkina Faso's and Niger's decentralizations (Diallo 1994:ff6; Ouali et al. 1994; RdN 1992). In all four countries, the smallest units of rural governance constitute five to fifty villages. Their spatial jurisdiction is called the *rural community* (similar in scale to U.S. counties). These local governments have both elected governance bodies, called *rural councils*,[15] and a central government administrator, the *sous-préfêt* (sub-prefect), appointed by the minister of the interior.

In Burkina Faso, the rural council is constituted from elected representatives of village committees. These representatives form a council and elect a president from among themselves. In the other three countries, the candidates for rural councils are presented for election by nationally registered political parties. Each party presents a slate of candidates for the council, and the elected councilors elect a president from among themselves. In Senegal, the slates fill three fourths of the council while one fourth is chosen by a general council of producer and marketing cooperatives and associations (such as youth and women's associations) for a five-year term (RdS 1972; 1993a:art.185-195). In Mali, the councilors of the rural communities (*Communes Ruraux*) are presented by party list, in a system of proportional representation, elected by universal suffrage for a five-year term (RdM 1995:art.4,7; RdM 1991).

In Niger, a series of coups d'état has periodically halted decentralization efforts since independence. To this day, only about 10 percent of the rural administrative units planned since independence have been established.[16] The structure of representation in rural administrative affairs was first organized (1961) through appointed chiefs, who presided over elected councils in each administrative district.[17] In 1983, a system of representation based on village councils composed of members elected or appointed by "structures of participation" (those cooperatives and associations mentioned above in the discussion of village chiefs) that were under the supervision of executive appointees. This system was eliminated in 1991, when appointed state administrators ran rural affairs in consultation with political parties and other organizations (Diallo 1994:4,16). Prior to the 1996 coup d'état, Niger had planned to create elected representatives at the level of arrondissements. The elections were to be by party list, as in Senegal and Mali.[18]

Although there is universal suffrage in elections in Mali and Senegal and in those proposed in Niger, independent candidates cannot run for election to local councils (nor can any individual or group present slates without a party's endorsement). Since villagers have little influence over national political parties and lack the resources to form parties, they are unable to choose their own candidates. Indeed, villagers in Eastern Senegal, where I conducted my field research, often told me that rural councils do not represent them, they represent political parties and the cooperatives.[19] As one villager explained, "the Councilors are chosen by Deputies in the National Assembly. Deputies choose people from among those who support them in their elections. The Councils are chosen by the parties" (Koumpentoum June 1994). As Hesseling (n.d.:17), based on her research in Senegal in 1983, says of councils "They are at times nothing more than sections of the Socialist Party." Further, few parties have the resources to organize local government slates, so there is little competition in local elections.[20] In 1977, when Senegal's rural council system was just being established, it was already evident to one researcher that party politics would undermine popular participation:

> The Rural Community could be a body that would organize and steer desired auto-centric development. But for this, it must be removed from political controversies. Unfortunately, it is already becoming a stake for the political parties who are trying to control its executive institution. A politicized Rural Council is at risk of not serving the interests of the community, but those of the party(ies) from which its members are derived. In this manner popular expression is at risk of being strangled, one more time. (André Carvalho, 1977, cited by Hesseling n.d.:43)

Apart from rural councils not being openly elected, they are not independent decision- making bodies. Like the councils of the colonial era, the official role of Rural Councils in all four Sahelian countries is merely to advise and assist the sous-préfèt on political and administrative matters. Decisions of the rural councils of local governments must be approved by the sous-préfèt and préfèt. So, even in Burkina Faso where rural councils are relatively representative of local populations, they are simply not autonomous decision-making bodies. They are administrators for the central government, in the same way as were the colonial village and canton chiefs. Today's rural councilors, like colonial chiefs, are upwardly responsible to their administrative officers rather than to the local population. So, on two counts-the administrative system of control or "tutelage" under the préfêts and the electoral system of party politics-their accountability is oriented upward toward the central state.

In all of the cases, chiefs and councils are set up to be administrative organs of the central government. Although some may be representative, they are not independent. They are advisers to administrative decision-making bodies, but do not officially hold decision-making powers themselves. In some cases they represent rural populations, but they do not have an independent domain in which to make that representation meaningful. The rural world in these cases is administered from above through variously constituted local bodies with differing degrees of local accountability. Even where the representatives are locally accountable, the decisions being made are not theirs. They ultimately must be approved from above.

Despite official structures, in practice village chiefs and rural councilors do take and hold some decision-making powers. The Burkina Faso case provides one illustration of village chiefs overriding official project rules (rules, as always, are only part of any local dynamic-see Ribot 1998). Rural councils, village chiefs, and market elites take many unofficial powers in Senegal's forestry affairs. Chiefs also, at times, represent villagers fairly (Ribot, forthcoming). The cases presented below illustrate that although the policies and laws are designed to devolve powers to local authorities and to ensure local community participation, they do not do so in practice. They are simply not structured to do so. This simple fact brings into question the intentions behind what is called decentralization and participation.

Two Cases

Given the limitations on existing forms of representation, how do "participatory" policies and projects construct local control? Who makes decisions and who benefits? The thumbnail sketches of participatory approaches that follow are now being promoted. In Burkina Faso and Niger, projects are creating village-level participatory structures through committees. Mali and Senegal are using local government as the basis for participatory forestry. The details of participation in decisions and benefits in Burkina Faso provide an example of participation by committee, and Mali provides an example of the reliance on local government (summaries of this case material were first presented in Ribot 1996). I comment briefly on how these policies and projects compare with those of Niger and Senegal in the following section.

Participation by Committee in Burkina Faso: The Forest of Nazinon

Institutional Structure of the Project

Burkina Faso's 1991 forestry code outlines extremely broad management guidelines (BKF 1991). Specific management rules will be detailed in an application decree that is yet to be drafted (BKF 1994; Tavares de Pinho 1993). Within Burkina Faso, woodfuel production practices range from uncontrolled production by the military to highly managed woodfuel production projects such as the joint United Nations Development Program (UNDP) and Food and Agricultural Organization (FAO) project in the Nazinon forest 30 miles south of Ouagadougou. In this section I focus on the Nazinon project. The new forestry policies to be detailed in the application decree of the forestry code are likely to be modeled after the practices in Nazinon, which are considered cutting-edge participatory forestry. In 1994, such managed forests supplied on the order of 5 percent of urban woodfuel demand. These project-based practices are also being proposed for more general application across Burkina Faso (BKF 1993c).

The Nazinon scheme creates cooperatives (called *groupements*) in villages surrounding the forest of Nazinon and a union coordinating the cooperatives. In each village, the UNDP/FAO project organized villagers interested in woodfuel production into a cooperative responsible for forest management. Each cooperative elects a president, secretary, treasurer, and manager. A Union of Nazinon cooperatives with a general assembly is constituted of all managers, secretaries, and treasurers of the village cooperatives. The union's administrative council is constituted of the cooperative managers and a president elected from the general assembly. The administrative council is empowered to make daily administrative and business decisions of the union and is responsible for surveying the implementation of all laws concerning the union and forest management (Nazinon cooperative statute, BKF 1993b,c).

The national forest service set up a technical office of the union to develop forest management plans in collaboration with the administrative council. These plans direct the union's management and use of the forest. The plans must be approved by the forest service, after which the manager from each cooperative is charged with ensuring its implementation under the guidance of the technical office. In addition, a control committee (which includes representatives from the national government's control service, the minister responsible for cooperatives, the minister of territorial administration, and a village council representative, surveys the union's and cooperatives' accounts.

Each union also has a management fund, co-managed with the forest service, fed by woodfuel taxes and fees, gifts, inheritances, or loans (BKF 1993c:art.16–17). In Burkina Faso, all firewood prices (producer, wholesale, and retail) are fixed by the Minister of Commerce (BKF 1993a:10). The producer price of firewood (the price at which cooperatives can sell to merchants) is fixed at 1610 FCFA[21] per *stère* (one cubic meter of roundwood). The entire fixed amount is paid by merchants to a local control post of the forest service, which is monitored by a representative of the union. Each cooperative gives the buying merchant a ticket identifying the cooperative from which the wood was taken, and the cooperative keeps a stub for their own records. The merchants truck the wood to the local forest service control post where they turn in their ticket, pay the 1610 FCFA per stère, and receive a transport permit. They are then free to take the wood to Ouagadougou.

Officially, the 1610 FCFA is divided four ways. The cooperative's woodcutters receive 610 FCFA per stère. The Forest Management Fund receives 500 FCFA; 200 FCFA funds the treasury of the cooperative; and 300 FCFA pays for the cutting permit (i.e., a forest service tax). The funds that enter into the cooperative's treasury are earmarked to finance forest management activities, credit for cooperative members, and public works serving the larger village community. There are, however, several ways by which merchants circumvent the fixed local and producer price, and by which village notables and even non-village-based woodcutters have made claims on cooperatives' resources. Village cooperatives have had trouble keeping urban woodcutters (brought from the cities by their merchant patrons) out of their forests. Wood cut in one village is often sold by these woodcutters through the tickets of another cooperative, channeling the funds for management and other purposes to the latter cooperative's account. Merchants at times pay their woodcutters directly, paying less than the 610 FCFA (the producer share of the 1610 local price) in the forest and then arrange with cooperatives to receive back the 610 FCFA earmarked for the woodcutters. In this manner they undercut the fixed price. Foresters also engage in woodfuel commerce themselves.

All this occurs under the surveillance of project coordinators and agents.

There are also problems arising with the disposition of the funds in the cooperative's treasury. According to cooperative members, they have had problems with the chief and Imam. "The notables asked for a loan for a sacrifice in the name of the whole village, but they did not pay it back. We gave them 35,000 FCFA for a cow and 5000 for a sheep. They sacrificed at the chief's house. They ask each year, it's a sacrifice in the name of the village before the harvest. The cooperative is obligated to pay out. We cannot refuse."

"Last week," one cooperative member recounted, "the chief and préfêt came to ask for money to complete the building of a schoolhouse. The cooperative had already given 300,000 FCFA to the project. The cooperative will have to meet to discuss this. In any event, the 300,000 was not paid back."

The members of the cooperative said they feel these uses of their funds are wrong. They feel that the fund is for them and that the village is stealing from them. The fund, however, was set up for the village. The cooperative has some control over it, but it is intended for public works, since the forests ostensibly belong to the village as a whole.

The powers of the village elites are nevertheless somewhat tempered. According to a forestry extension worker with the project,

> The cooperative cannot be denied its existence by anyone in the village since the préfêt in Léo [capital of the Department] has officially recognized it. The government is in agreement with them [the cooperative members] because the government knows that this affair is profitable for the government. So, even if the village chief is against this project, he cannot say anything. There are two reasons he cannot be against it now. First, he agreed to allow the project in the beginning. Second, he took money from the project that he cannot repay. If he goes against the project he will be biting himself since he is now in debt to the project, which is the government.

Village authorities are not paying back what are supposed to be loans from the forestry fund, and cooperative members feel robbed. The distinction between project and village is blurred, not because of misunderstanding of rights, but because of competing loci of power. This split is between the village chief and the project, which derives its backing from the préfêt in Léo and the forest service. The cooperative members know their rights over the fund and have explained the rules to the chief. The conflict between the project and chief reflects a lack of legitimacy of these rights for the chief as well as the inability of the project to enforce them in the face of the chief's powers.

Representation in Popular Participation: Who Makes Decisions?

Members of Burkina Faso's National Commission on Decentralization expressed concern that representation is lacking in natural resource management project committees:

> When the members have been regularly elected, they have a legitimacy and therefore represent all of the village in matters concerning this sectoral aspect of local development policy. If one considers that the management of the commons policies is in the end a global [or overall] policy of local development, one would thus be cautious when considering the commons management committee as the structure that can represent the village in all instances responsible for management of local development. (Ouali et al. 1994:21)

The commission goes on to say that, since the beginning of participatory efforts in the 1960s, little real participation had been effected. Rather, local populations have been viewed as "objects of development" to be educated, informed, and guided. The only participants in development have been "...international experts, politicians, and national technocrats often located in urban areas...." (Ouali et al. 1994:21–22).

The management structures being created in Nazinon are not representative. They are not participatory in any inclusive or community sense. The new policies place some responsibilities for and powers over woodfuel management into the hands of a group of self-selected economically interested individuals (cooperative members). Decisions over the disposition of forests (embedded in management plans) and over the revenues from forest exploitation are taken by these private individuals in conjunction with the forest service. But, ultimately, the forest service maintains complete control of all production and management decisions through required approval and through control of the rules by which production and management can take place. A local representative (from the village council) is brought only into the national Control Committee where he or she is just one member among many.[22] Further, the Control Committee makes no decisions over forest use.

In short, little control over forest disposition is devolved to local authorities-despite the fact that they take more control than they are ceded. Control remains officially located with the forest service and private groups. Even these private organizations, however, are given little say in forest management. No realm of autonomous decision making is specified-that is, written into law-for the cooperatives or union. The creation of such a realm is left to the forest service. So, although foresters *may* decide to cede important decisions to the union and its cooperatives, it would be as a privilege at the whim of foresters rather than a right.

Participation Through Local Government in Mali: Decentralization After Revolution

In 1986, Mali's President Traoré began stringently implementing co-lonial forestry laws (RdM 1996). In order to show foreign donors that Mali was serious about environmental protection, fines for break-ing branches, cutting trees, or starting forest fires were raised well beyond the average annual income. In the following years fining binges by the forest service became routine (RdM 1994d:3). After good har-vests, foresters went so far as to set fires so they could fine surround-ing villages. When no one would admit to the crime, villagers (in-cluding village chiefs) were thrown in jail. Reports of beatings and extortion came from around the country.[23] Those fined appealed to their deputies in the national assembly who thrived on the arrange-ments. Deputies could intervene to free the villagers, getting local political credit and often payoffs in the process.[24] The foresters, who were entitled to 25 percent of fine revenues, raked in profits. The brutal years of fining, taxation, and extortion paid off. By 1988, Mali's forests were virtually paved with international forestry projects, sup-porting various forest service activities.

The years of forest service oppression had their backlash. During Mali's 1991 revolution, foresters-the most salient state presence in rural Mali-were reportedly attacked and almost all foresters were chased from the countryside.[25] In the national conference to recon-stitute the government after the revolution, one of the first demands of the rural representatives was the *elimination* of the forest service (and of the *Commandant de Cercle*). This did not happen, although the forest service's activities were curtailed for a few years. With the support of international donors, the forest service is now being retrained and reintroduced as an extension service agency—rather than a paramilitary force. Mali's foresters are now implementing the new participatory forestry policies.

The Institutional Structure of Participation

Mali's 1994 forestry laws assign responsibilities for forest management to local government (called Decentralized Territorial Collectives). The new laws give local governments a forested domain within their territorial jurisdiction and the right to protect or conserve part or all of their forested domain. According to the new laws, any individual or group of individuals wishing to cut commercially for woodfuels within the forest domain of a local government must organize a Rural Wood Management Structure (WMS-Structure Rurale de Gestion de Bois). A WMS can be a cooperative, corporation, association, or any other form of organization recognized by the state. In practice (as in Burkina Faso's and Niger's committees), these are groups of private individuals interested in practicing or investing in commercial woodcutting.

Before a WMS can begin using the forest, the forest service must propose a management plan for approval by the local government. This plan includes an annual woodfuel production quota that, according to forestry officials, is to be determined by the sustainable potential production of the forested domain of the local government in question. The annual quota will be set by an ad hoc commission composed of two representatives of the WMSs, one from local government, and one member of the forest service. Recognizing the contentious political nature of quota allocation, the new laws also create a regional commission to resolve conflicts over the fixing and distribution of quotas. This commission is to be organized by the minister responsible for forests. Once a management plan and quota have been established and approved, a cutting permit can be delivered by the forest service upon the payment of a forest exploitation tax.

Mali's new participatory forestry laws, replacing a system in which the forest service delivered permits to whom, where, and when it chose, give local governments considerable power over the disposition of forests. Indeed, Mali has developed the most progressive forestry laws in the Sahelian region. Local government representatives can decide to protect the forests by decree, or they can control exploitation through approval or rejection of forest management plans. They can also use these powers to control which WMSs can exploit local forests. The forest service, however, has maintained control over how much wood can be cut, where, when, and how (via quotas and management plans).

Representation in Popular Participation: Who Makes Decisions?

As in Burkina Faso, Mali's local government representative on the quota committee is only one among four members and is not guaranteed a controlling role. The "...mode of allocating the quota..." in this committee is left to the order of the regional governor (a central government appointee). The forest service has also reserved the role of quota dispute resolution for itself, a role better fit for an independent judiciary. Some significant decisions have been devolved to local government bodies, but two factors cancel the most progressive aspects of these new policies. First, since independent candidates cannot present themselves for local elections, local government is not necessarily representative or locally accountable-thus these "local" decisions are not necessarily community decisions. Second, jurisdiction over forests may not be devolved to local government, but rather to intermediate-level governance structures such as cercles and regions (many forests will also remain under central government control). These governance structures, which are also not representative, cannot even be considered local.

In short, Mali's system places decisions over the disposition of forests in the hands of local government. It also gives local government control over labor opportunities and revenues from commercial forestry-for those local governments that choose not to reserve their forests. Unfortunately, local government is still responsible to political parties and under the tutelage of the sous-préfêt and préfêt. The forest service still retains control over the allocation of commercial rights in the form of production quotas.

PARTICIPATION BY WHOM IN WHAT?

Who participates in what benefits? The benefits in these cases include labor opportunities in woodcutting, income from these labor opportunities and from woodfuel sale, and some role in forest decision making. Labor opportunities are important since this work often has gone to migrant or urban workers from outside the woodcutting area.

Integrating local labor increases village income. There is also profit from the sale of wood. In Burkina Faso, firewood prices fixed by the minister of commerce keep prices in participatory projects above those received by independent woodcutters. These opportunities and profits go largely to the private individuals who make up management committees and woodcutting organizations. Membership is self-selected or influenced by foresters and village elites-these are effectively private organizations. In addition to private income and profit, some benefits are directed at the community as a whole in two countries. In Burkina Faso, each cooperative has a fund fed by a firewood tax, part of which is earmarked for public works serving the larger village community. In Niger, 10 percent of nontax revenues from woodfuel sales go to the village chief (a hereditary power in Niger)—this too is ostensibly to benefit the community as a whole.

Although some villagers benefit from labor opportunities, local woodfuel sale, and fees collected for community funds, most of the profit in West African woodfuel markets accrues through access to transport and urban trade (Ribot, forthcoming). Unfortunately, the forest services in all of these countries have maintained tight control over the delivery of transport permits and have refused to assist woodcutters in gaining access to transport or merchant licenses. This legacy of the colonial apartheid has been strictly maintained. Villagers in all four countries have expressed their desire to operate in transport and urban markets. This most lucrative segment of the woodfuel sector is currently dominated by urban merchants and truckers. In short, villagers are permitted to "participate" in forest labor but only in a limited portion of forest-based profits.

Who participates in decisions? Management plans and quotas reserve decisions over where, when, and how much wood will be cut for the forest services. In Mali and Senegal, local government representatives participate in the daily decisions of plan implementation and have some control over the plans. In Burkina Faso and Niger, it is the village-level committees of cooperatives and unions that can make daily implementation decisions. But the rules of cutting and management that they must follow and the quantities they can cut are defined by the forest services-based largely on questionable ecological grounds.

The most critical decision-whether forests surrounding a given community will or will not be cut-has been reserved by forest services in all cases but Mali. In Mali's new forestry laws, rural councils have the definitive right to protect all or any of their forested domain (although the proportion of forests in the local domain will be determined by what a national committee decides is in the national interest) (RdM 1994a:art.18, 53; RdM 1994b). In Burkina Faso, Niger, and Senegal, however, the forest service can give woodcutting rights in any forest to anyone they choose, regardless of local wishes.

In these latter countries, local communities have no legal mechanism for protecting local forests. Foresters can allocate exploitation rights via parastatals, concessions, state sale of parcels, and the delivery of exploitation permits. Communities in project areas who choose not to accept the conditions of "participation," and those simply not chosen for projects, have no legal control over the disposition of forest resources: forest services can sell the forests out from under them. These local governments and village communities simply do not have the right to say "No" to forest service-sanctioned cutting in surrounding forests. This is hardly participatory forestry.

In short, participation in such projects amounts to the forest services managing forests with the assistance of private groups within local communities, with increased labor opportunities and profit for these private groups, and with some income earmarked for whole communities. Critical decisions over forest disposition are devolved into "local" hands only in Mali. Even in Mali, however, these decisions are restricted to the limited area of forests assigned to local governments by a national committee.

THE EXTENSION OF INDIRECT RULE

Participatory projects reproduce some colonial relations of rural administration. Like *association* and indirect rule, participatory projects rely on administrative bodies to control the use of local labor and resources, legitimated by quasi-representative local appointed or "customary" authorities. In this manner, participatory projects micromanage valuable resource and rural populations rather than creating an autonomous local domain (Ribot 1995a; 1995b; 1996).

Starting in 1917 there have been several decentralizations in Francophone West Africa (Buell 1928:929–930; Cowan 1958:60; Diallo 1994; Gellar 1995:48; Hesseling n.d.:15; Ouali et al. 1994:7; RdM 1977; RdS 1972; Schumacher 1975:89–90). Each has created geographically smaller units of governance, appointed administrators to manage these units, created councils to advise these structures, devolved responsibilities to these new governance structures, and centralized approval of all decisions in a hierarchy now stretching from the sous-préfêt of the arrondissement (also overseeing the rural community and villages), préfêt of the department and governor of the region, to the minister of the interior and president at the federal level. Before independence this hierarchy stretched up through the lieutenant-governor of each colony, the governor-general, and the minister of colonies, to the president of the French Republic. These administrators are all appointees of the federal government. Each decentralization devolved responsibilities such as public works and schools while strengthening central controls over decision-making processes and local budgets.

Control over land allocation plays an important role in these changes. Local land control played a central role in maintaining the administrative apartheid that Mamdani (1996:140) described, fortifying the position of "native" authorities (see Bassett and Crummey 1993; Downs and Reyna 1988; Hesseling n.d.; Watts 1993). In more recent reforms, land control is strengthening the legitimacy of the new state-organized forms of local governance, as land allocation functions are being slowly transferred from "customary" authorities to state-structured representative bodies (cf. Fisiy 1995), both of which remain under tight administrative control. In turn, with land control and state backing, "customary" authorities and the more recent rural councils are empowered to manage rural life. In both cases, almost every decision must be approved by an appointed administrator of the local state.

The present decentralization and move toward participation follows the pattern of past policies. Obligations, in a process called *responsibilisation*, are being devolved to more local units of rural administration. In forestry this devolution of responsibilities is accompanied by a devolution of a tighter and closer *tutelle*, a tighter and closer regulation of obligations by local bodies, and a tighter and closer monitoring of local actions by both administrative and technical services of the central government. Rather than carving out a realm of local autonomy, the process is one of stretching the tentacles of central government further into rural life. As in the colonial period, rural populations are administered from the center as dependent subjects. Whereas obligations of the past involved taxes in kind and labor, today they involve tax and labor responsibilities in ecological management.

Under colonial rule, the councils of the lieutenant-governors and the governor-general were created to advise, rather than to decide on, policy matters (Buell 1928:930; Von Vollenhoven 1920:189–257). Indigenous authorities were included in these councils as a minority. The official role of today's rural councils and chiefs is to advise and assist the sous-préfêt. Similarly, the role of the committees set up in "participatory" forestry projects is to advise officials of the forest service. To ensure the subordinate role of these committees to the forest service, the forest service officials preside over the committees and must approve their decisions. In addition, local "representative" authorities (chiefs and councilors) are included only as a minority of members on these committees, just as "native" representatives were included in the colonial councils, which prevented any possibility of there being an African majority (Buell 1928:927–930). As in colonial times, government administrators (along with commercial interests) ruled the rural world. What is ensured by these structures is that no decisions are in local hands except as a privilege allocated by administrative authorities.

A related parallel between participatory approaches and the colonial policies is an emphasis on community. Africans were "to be civilized 'not as individuals but as communities', to be subject to a process that one-sidedly opposed the community to the individual and thereby encapsulated the individual in a set of relations defined and enforced by the state as communal and customary...." (Mamdani 1996:51; cf. Vaughan 1991:11–12). As "communities," Africans were effectively isolated into manageable groups or tribes, each under the rule of its "native" authority. Participatory projects also have this tendency to view rural Africans as communities. Without questioning the integrity of the groups being engaged, these projects construct representations-in both senses of the word-of community through committees and both customary and state structure local authorities, without evaluating whether the individuals that constitute the local population are empowered in the shaping of these representations. Participatory community development projects are based on the most convenient management units. This continued micropartitioning of rural Africa isolates communities and subjugates individuals to ostensibly community goals under ostensibly community leadership.

Both the policy of *association* and recent participatory approaches also follow economic necessity of the central state. French colonial authorities moved from direct rule to *association* because, with the advent of World War I, they could not afford to extend management down to the village level without local assistance (Alexandre 1970a; Buell 1928:983; Suret-Canale 1966). They created a situation with sanctions-at times draconian ones-for local populations to "participate" in the colonial project. With the fall of the Berlin Wall and the withdrawal of international interest and funding in Africa, there is a new move back to relying on local authorities to carry out the tasks of outside agents-this time, independent states and the international community.

In a form of economic apartheid, continued urban-centric control over marketing is a direct result of the earliest laws giving commercial licenses only to French citizens who generally lived in the four communes (urban centers). Today licenses and permits are still under urban control, while rural populations are relegated to the residual category of usufructuary "rights," inferior to commercial rights since they are valid only so long as urban merchants and the forest service do not decide to cut the forests out from under them. Village subjects can effectively use forests-as long as they do not diminish their commercial value—until merchant citizens come to take them away. Although participatory projects claim they aim to increase rural benefits, no project has dared to increase access by forest villagers to the lucrative forestry markets from which villagers are systematically excluded by government policy-supported merchant oligopolies (see Ribot 1995a; 1998; forthcoming).

CONCLUSION: PARTICIPATION AND DECENTRALIZATION— IF EVER THE TWAIN SHALL MEET

The apartheid of colonial administration, relegating rural populations to the status of subjects, is reproduced when rural populations live under administrators rather than representative governance structures; when they are allocated privileges rather than given rights; when rural governance structures have no domain of autonomy from their administrative superiors; when there is a lack of access to judicial recourse for the rural poor; and when, as is the case today, urban elites lobby for independent candidates in municipal council elections, but not for rural councils. Administrative apartheid is also reproduced in the insufficiently critical humanitarian ideologies that see rural Africans as ignorant, lacking capacity, and a threat to the forests, as well as needy, dependent objects of assistance and development. West African states are still effectively divided into citizens and subjects, the first with rights and the latter privileges. Rural rule is still under the authority of rural chiefs and "elected" councils who have little role other than to advise their administrative supervisors.

In participatory forestry, this apartheid takes the form of technocratic paternalism. Forest villagers are seen as hungry peasants, incompetent to make but a few highly monitored technical decisions over the disposition of forests, which they would destroy if not constrained (see Fairhead and Leach 1996; Ribot 1995a). This view justifies an administratively driven directing of villagers into forest labor activities defined by the technical decisions of the forest service. The villagers are given the opportunity to cut and sell forest products under the strict financial and labor supervision of their forest service superiors. Participatory projects and laws create privileges, often with burdensome responsibilities, rather than rights. These responsibilities and privileges are distributed among those within local communities through nonrepresentative bodies and chiefs.

Although the language of decentralization and participation is often of local control, autonomy, and benefits, the new structures being introduced in their name afford little. Local populations are still relegated to a carefully circumscribed set of roles and relations with the forests, little autonomy is created, and few new benefits are devolved. As before, rural populations are limited to usufructuary rights and the local sale of wood products. Locals—in the form of advisory committees—have better control over who gets labor opportunities, but they still are systematically excluded from the most lucrative part of commerce, since a system of licenses and permits, originating under colonial rule, still places trade and transport in the hands of urban elites. The new projects and laws of decentralization and participation examined in this chapter do not at all weaken this most economically significant part of the colonial bifurcationist legacy.

Participatory projects take on the contours of their political-administrative context. They create nonrepresentative committees at the subvillage or subrural council level. These committees are under the direct tutelle of the central forest services. They are advisory rather than legislative or decision-making bodies. These committees include the quasi-elected advisers-councilors and chiefs-from the local communities in question as minority members. The other members are

appointed or self-selected. The resulting committee is an administrative unit of the forest service. Even if the local authorities were
independent, they have no binding say in decisions. In a system of
profoundly central control extended into the countryside in succes-
sive "decentralizations," it is hard to see the new participatory approaches as more than just another wave. This form of participatory
project entails the micromanagement of forests by the state with some
privatization, not "community" management or decision making, not
democratic or popular participation.

Locally accountable representation is one prerequisite to generalized rural participation. Such accountability could be based on ad-
mitting independent candidates in local government elections, making suffrage universal at the village level, giving women an equal vote
in the choice of leaders, and creating specified term lengths. Perhaps
there are better (electoral or non-electoral based) indigenous, local,
or even exogenous means for structuring local representation and
accountability (cf. Ouédraogo 1994; Spierenburg 1995). The current
powers of both chiefs and rural councils are structured by current
laws with antecedents in the colonial period. The exclusion of women
and central control are explicitly written into law. The current governments could change these laws, but resist doing so.

As this chapter illustrates, the political, economic, and social significance of any act of decentralization depends on what is being devolved and to whom. There are many powers and resources that can
be decentralized to many different entities: service provision responsibilities, assets of the state, regulatory powers, and decision-making
powers all can be decentralized to local branches of the central state,
autonomous local state governance bodies, nongovernmental organizations, individuals, and so on. The political and economic meanings of a given act of decentralization depends on *what* is devolved to
whom. The political valence of decentralization cannot be assumed.
Each act of decentralization must be scrutinized to understand its
implications. In some instances it can be the extension of the central
state, the shedding of what should be central state responsibilities,
privatization, or enclosure. Decentralization can also be the creation
of local autonomy under locally accountable representation when the
right powers are devolved to the representative groups. In that case it
can be a powerful form of community participation.

Whether participation and decentralization shall meet pivots
partly on the question of locally accountable representation. There

are also many other factors involved. Below are some of the questions we need to ask about projects of participation and decentralization to determine whether they are serious efforts to include rural populations in the powers and benefits of the state.[26]

1. Are there locally accountable representatives? To determine this, the system of election (or selection) must be scrutinized.

2. What are the types of tutelage (or administrative oversight) built into representative structures? When central administrators must approve decisions, tutelage is a centralizing force. When it is to ensure that decisions are within the jurisdiction in question, it is simple oversight.

3. What are the powers, if any, being devolved to these bodies (adjudication, decisions, resources, finances)? Are these powers devolved as discretionary privileges to be allocated by a higher authority or as rights?

4. What are the structures of redress? Where are courts located and are they independent from administrative and political branches of the central state? Is there an accessible independent judiciary?

5. What size are the local jurisdictions? Are they too big to be local or too small to have any significant powers?

6. How many layers of "decentralized" government (region, cercle, arrondissement, canton, district, rural community, village, etc.) are there? More layers means that the powers of the state are diffused among them, providing a more powerful formula for central control.

7. Are responsibilities being devolved that increase local burdens disproportionally to the benefits and powers being devolved?

8. What decision-making powers and assets are being devolved to private bodies? Do the decisions and assets concern public or community resources? Depending on which decisions and assets are being privatized, the process can be a form of enclosure and exclusion, not of participation.

9. Are powers of decision that should be kept central being devolved to smaller units of government? These would include, for example, setting policy on welfare, health and safety, taxation, and some

environmental protection standards for which devolution to smaller jurisdictional units could cause competition among those units leading to the minimization of these essential government functions.

In short, decentralization of different powers and resources to different bodies serve very different agendas. We need to examine what they are and how they function *case by case*. Bringing decentralization and participation together through the intermediary of empowered, locally accountable governance structures-that is, through local enfranchisement-provides a foundation for a generalized form of rural popular participation.

ACKNOWLEDGMENTS

Many thanks to Louise Fortmann and Michael Watts who provided critical and encouraging comments on a draft of this chapter at the 1997 African Studies Conference in San Francisco. I also thank Allyson Purpura, Matt Turner, and the members of the CCACC seminar on Nature and Culture (particularly Sheila Foster, Neil Smith, and Peter Taylor) for their insightful comments on drafts and Pauline Peters for her careful reading and detailed constructive suggestions.

NOTES

1   This chapter is based on material from my article "Decentralisation, Participation, and Accountability in Sahelian Forestry," which appeared in Africa vol. 69, no. 1, pp. 23–65, 1999.

2. *Decentralization* has been defined in numerous ways. I follow the very broad definition provided by Cohen et al. 1981:17–32. For a more in-depth discussion of decentralization, see Adamolekun 1991; Cohen et al. 1981; Conyers 1984; Leonard and Marshall 1982; and Thomson and Coulibaly 1994.

3. Despite its problematic nature, I use the term *community* to mean the ensemble of the local population. In the West African Sahel, I use it to refer to the village, which is the most common unit of social aggregation, or the population under the smallest unit of local government (discussed later).

4. Although the World Bank (1996) calls inclusion of private citizens, NGOs, and corporations "stake-holder participation," this is simply a way of in-

cluding privatization (of assets and decision-making powers of the state) under the banner of participation. When I use the term *participation*, I am referring to *community participation* unless otherwise indicated.

5. In theory, participation can increase economic and managerial efficiency by (1) allowing the local populations who bear the costs of forest-use decisions to make those decisions, rather than leaving them in the hands of outsiders or unaccountable locals; (2) reducing administrative and management transaction costs via the proximity of local participants; and (3) using local knowledge and aspirations in project design, implementation, management, and evaluation. Participation can redress inequities by helping to retain and distribute benefits of local activities within the community (see Baland and Platteau 1996; Cernea 1985; Cohen and Uphoff 1977; National Research Council 1992:35; Peluso 1992; World Bank 1996). Aid organizations and national forest services also often assume that community participation in resource management results in better environmental practices. Although such a claim has some logical underpinnings, it is not a demonstrated fact (see Little 1994).

6. For example, in 1922, Yves Henry, the agricultural inspector general of French West Africa, argued for a participatory model of development: "To educate the peasant, give him the means to work well, then progressively bring to his land tenure improvements without which any program would be but in vain...." With Henry's plans, the administration of French West Africa created an agricultural policy it believed was based on the specificities of African peasants (Chauveau 1994:32).

7. See Governor-General Von Vollenhoven, who said in 1917 that "The native of French West Africa is a child; he loves to live under his chiefs, as a child loves to live with his parents..." (quoted in Buell 1928:996). Also see Megan Vaughan, who writes of the "politics of difference" in which European colonizers produce "Africans" as "other" through various means, including association of Africans with nature and beliefs in the "'childlike' qualities of 'savage races'" (1991:13,20).

8. Many projects also approach subvillage groups, such as fishers, woodcutters, pastoralists, farmers, and women's or youth associations. These groups, whether unions, cooperatives, NGOs, or associations, however, do not necessarily reflect the concerns of a village as a whole-particularly in matters concerning public resources such as forests, streams, and pastures. Although they are often treated as if they were representative, they are not. They represent their particular interests and their representatives or leaders are accountable to their particular constituencies-often only to themselves. There is no systematic basis for them to represent the community as a whole. In Senegal, for example, cooperative presidents-usually powerful notables-treat their cooperatives as private property, often

filling them with family or dummy members to obtain state services to which cooperatives are entitled (Cruise-O'Brien 1975:128; Ribot 1993). Spokespersons for various local movements or organizations are often self-appointed or sponsored by outside aid agencies or NGOs and are nonrepresentative (Guyer 1994:223; Mazonde 1996:56; National Research Council 1992:35). Since my concern in this chapter is on the ostensibly accountable and locally constituted structures of rural representation (rather than on various types of NGOs), I do not examine these latter groupings in any further detail.

9. Cowan (1958:186) remarks that the *évolué* ("evolved"—meaning the French educated youth) were aware that chiefs were often creations of the administration and therefore caused "the *évolué* to look upon the chief, not as a representative of a way of life which is essentially African, but as a tool in the hands of the administration."

10. Precolonial chiefs derived their authority from a variety of sources: rights of conquest, control over land, direct descent from great ruling ancestors, membership in a particular ruling family, and so on (see Alexandre 1970a; Crowder and Ikime 1970:xi; Fisiy 1992; Fortes and Evans-Pritchard 1987[1940]:10–11; Schumacher 1975:87; Spierenburg 1995).

11. Governor-General J. Brévié proposed such a policy for the West African colony in 1932 (Cowan 1958:44).

12. It would be worth digging through the colonial record to find the types of problems that emerged under this short reign of universal suffrage and limited terms at the village level.

13. The notion that indigenous African chiefs were despots was used during the early colonial period to justify subjugating them to European standards of conduct (see, for example, Buell 1928:987; Suret-Canale 1966).

14. These units are specified in "organic codes," which shape the ministries and their organization and the appointed officials that will represent different central government agencies within the various spatial territorial divisions, such as regions, departments, circles, cantons, arrondissements, communes, rural collectives, and rural communes. Since the names of the most local units vary among the countries, I call all of them *local government*. As such, these laws shape who (elected and appointed) will be present within the rural areas, and at what level of administration, to make decisions over natural resources.

15. The most local level of administrative council goes by different names in each country. I will use the terms *rural community* and *rural council* to refer to the jurisdiction and its representative body, respectively.

16. Niger's indigenous population is organized into "Customary Collectives" (Collectivités Coutumières), including 10,000 villages and 200 cantons and groupements (the equivalent of cantons for nomadic populations). Niger's 17 July 1964 law on decentralization legislated the repartition of Niger into 200 communes, but indigenous village and canton chiefs have retained their power and only 21 of the 200 expected communes were ever established (Diallo 1994:7).

17. "The district chiefs had no powers at all" (Diallo 1994:4).

18. A report on a proposed integrated rural land management law (the Rural Code), now in a pilot phase (see Elbow 1996), described the current state of rural administration: "Despite the expansion, diversification and specialization of deconcentrated structures...the sous-préfecture effectively presents the same institutional core bequeathed by colonization" (Diallo 1994:19). An integrated system of rural management is also being developed under the title "Rural Code." This code proposes to establish committees representing local communities based on traditional chiefs and representatives of various associations and cooperatives.

19. Cooperatives in Senegal are usually dominated by a few powerful notables (Cruise-O'Brien 1975:128; Ribot 1993).

20. The role of political parties in local government needs to be examined in greater detail. At the end of the colonial period, the question of whether parties should be introduced into local government was being contested (Cowan 1958:221). Those against party involvement argued "...that the matters dealt with in local councils are essentially *local* in nature and that therefore the major parties whose differences may be on matters of national policy have no place in purely community problems" (Cowan 1958:221). Clearly, in French West Africa those against party involvement lost the debate. Further, it is questionable whether parties are appropriate in a context where they can hardly afford to organize down to the rural community level. Two problems are introduced. First is that of being unable to chose candidates who are appropriate to the local community and second is that of having no competition among parties at the local level (since so few can afford to propose candidates), thus eliminating the competition necessary among candidates to produce locally accountable representatives (Schumpeter 1943). In Senegal, over 300 of the 314 rural councils are organized by the Socialist Party.

21. Francs of the Francophone West African Community. During the fieldwork for this chapter in 1994, the exchange rate was approximately 350 FCFA per U.S. dollar. The FCFA is pegged to the French Franc at 100 FCFA per FF.

22. For a similar case in Cameroon, see Fisiy 1992:227–228.

23. Interviews with international aid workers and researchers in Bamako.

24. The above story was recounted to me by a high official in the forest service. The story is consistent with other reports by researchers and with forest legislation.

25. One forestry researcher (who did not want to be identified) explained foresters were killed, "necklaced," but forest service officials told me that there were just threats. Another said, "In 1991, I was told by a number of foresters that at least one forest agent was shot and killed in Kayes area. Also I know that one was very badly beaten by herders in the Bankass area in April 1991."

26. Joel Barkan's comments on a decentralization panel at the annual meeting of the African Studies Association, San Francisco, CA, in November 1996 were helpful in the formulation of this list.

4 NEW CHALLENGES FOR ALTERNATIVE WAYS OF DEVELOPMENT AMONG INDIGENOUS PEOPLES OF THE AMAZON

Margarita Benavides

The incorporation of Amazonia into national and international economies has been mainly through colonization, either spontaneous or directed flows of migrants, and through several extractive and production booms that responded to the fluctuations in market demand (Barclay 1991, Ribeiro 1975, Chirif 1983, Davis 1978). The impetus behind most colonization has been the chimera of the "great Amazonian emptiness." Amazonia has been seen as uninhabited, or if indigenous peoples have been deemed present, they are assumed to have no rights to their territory (Smith 1983).

As a result, indigenous inhabitants have lost significant parts of their territories, have been removed by bosses or "patrones" from their original places to other areas, or concentrated in missions. They have been devastated by epidemics and semi-slavery and, in some cases, have been forced to abandon their territories and seek refuge in areas less accessible to the colonizers. On numerous occasions, however, indigenous groups have responded with acts of resistance that have taken on a warlike or messianic character. The most famous among these were the rebellion of Juan Santos Atahualpa in 1742 in the central rain forest of Peru and the march in search of Loma Santa of Moxenos of the Beni in Bolivia during the late nineteenth century.

Since the 1960s, new forms of indigenous political organization have emerged. Community and intercommunity political organizations arose with the purpose of reclaiming indigenous territorial rights. In this process, indigenous peoples who formerly were dispersed came together to form ethnic and inter-ethnic federations. These were then consolidated into national confederations, which in turn formed an International Coordinating Body.[1] As a result of these political efforts to reclaim territorial rights, the Amazonian indigenous peoples have obtained legal recognition over important territorial areas. At present, apart from the task of defending these territories, they are taking on the challenge of producing alternative modes of development suitable for the particular environments they inhabit.

Two tasks, in particular, claim the attention of indigenous organizations and their allies among NGOs at this stage. The first is to strengthen their organizations through greater participation by community members and to improve the forms of representation and expression at different levels of organization (community, intercommunity, national, and international levels). The second is to develop proposals and programs that will manage the existing contradictions between the market and the indigenous economy and satisfy the economic expectations of indigenous people without jeopardizing the sustainable use of their natural resources over the long term.

THE EMERGENCE AND SPREAD OF INDIGENOUS ORGANIZATIONS

Traditional Political Organization

Although there is sociopolitical variation across Amazonian ethnic groups (Santos and Barclay 1994), it is possible to state some general principles shared by all. Traditionally, these groups have lived in dispersed settlements composed of residential units or compounds comprising several nuclear or extended families, each functioning as an independent productive group with its own hearth (COICA, OXFAM America 1996). Considerable exchange of produce and work took place within and across the productive units that constituted residential compounds, although the individual settlements could be separated by minutes or hours of travel. The physical spaces and the resources used by a settlement for agriculture, gathering, hunting, and fishing were recognized and respected by other groups with the possibility of shared use among allied groups. Human beings were conceived as "owners" only of what they produced. Everything within nature, including the land itself, had its own "spirit owners," with whom it was necessary for humans to create a relation of ritual exchange before taking anything.[2]

These settlements generally had a chief or "group head" with religious and political power. The authority of these chiefs was based on their ability to communicate with the spirits who, according to indigenous conceptions, inhabit nature, and to maintain the exchange relations with them in accordance with ancestral norms. Thus a good chief guaranteed harmonious interaction with the beings of nature and, consequently, the security of the group's supply of sufficient resources for subsistence. According to traditional thought, the health of human beings and the supply of natural resources depend largely on the good will of the beings of nature, which can be obtained through upholding the norms of generosity and exchange among people, and between people and the "owners" of natural species. A good chief must be able to ensure that members of the group duly observe these norms, and to organize the festivities and rituals that mediate exchange with the various owners of natural species. The chief also represents the group in the relations of exchange, alliances, and conflicts with other groups. Socially and politically, these residential cum territorial groups remained dispersed. They came together only on festive and ritual occasions when exchanges occurred between allied households, or on occasions of conflict when a warrior leader might arise to bring the conflict to resolution.

Political Changes in the Wake of Colonization

With the colonization of Amazonia, the settlement patterns of indigenous groups have changed from dispersed to nucleated.[3] Crucial influences in this process have been persecution and displacement by slavers and epidemics, causing both the abrupt declines in population levels and the dispersion and factionalism of traditional settlements. In this context, the missions became a kind of refuge for people. Also, in recent decades schools have acted as poles of attraction for dispersed settlements. In this fractioning of traditional settlements and their re-concentration in missions or community towns, different factions of different clans have been grouped in the same settlement, and traditional chiefs have suffered a significant loss of authority in the new and disrupted context. The constituent families of the residential groups have come to feel like "orphans," deprived of the daily spiritual leadership of traditional chiefs, while the chiefs have felt demoralized by the loss of their social base and followers (Gasche, 1982).

In the towns and missions, new external agents such as missionaries, bosses, merchants, and school teachers began to exercise authority over this period. Some indigenous chiefs also allied themselves with bosses or merchants to extract natural resources or recruit laborers. Frequently, authorities of the new communities represented political interests of the colonialist state or of the church, which has often been closely linked with the state, especially where the latter has had a weak presence. Some traditional leaders have maintained internal legitimacy over a part of the community, a situation that has provided them with the opportunity to rebuild a "modern" kind of clan, in which they could occasionally play their ritual roles. But their power has been weakened. The articulation of indigenous peoples with the market economy and the growth of nucleated settlements require a more intensive exploitation of natural resources. In this context, the traditional rules of ritual interchange with the "owners" of nature, which tended to limit the extraction of natural resources and to maintain an ecological balance, have been relaxed. Some indigenous peoples have explained the crises in which they find themselves as the result of the violation of traditional rules of behavior regarding nature and society.

With the colonization of the Amazon, many ethnic groups have lost possession of significant parts of their traditional territories, although during recent decades indigenous rights over communal land have been recognized by states. Since the 1960s, new types of political centralization have begun to appear. Indigenous organizations were created with the main objectives of defending indigenous territories and increasing their participation in decisions about development in indigenous areas. Standing up for their culture and identity, they deployed the concept of "autonomous development." At the same time, collaborative relations between indigenous groups and the representatives of non-indigenous NGOs were common.

In the case of the Peruvian Amazon, some of the indigenous federations were organized at the local level with the help of anthropologists and other professionals who had entered indigenous areas with the purpose of carrying out development projects. With the help of these professionals, some of them from nongovernmental organizations, the few federations that existed at the time gradually became interconnected, giving birth to a national confederation.[4] National organizations in turn encouraged groups who were not organized to form their own federations.[5] Through the actions of these federations, often in concert with their non-indigenous collaborators and NGOs, legal recognition of important territorial areas has been obtained from national governments. At first, these areas were called *tierras* (land), but toward the mid 1980s the term and concept of *ter-*

ritory began to be used, highlighting the particular relation between indigenous peoples and their environment (forest, rivers, lakes, etc.), and proposing the idea that "the indigenous people and their territories are one" (Chirif, Garcia, Smith 1991).

The strategies and mechanisms employed to obtain legal recognition of land have varied, depending on each country's administrative and legislative structure.[6] In the case of Bolivia, no legislation recognizing the territorial rights of indigenous peoples existed until 1996. There is an Indigenous Law proposed by CIDOB (Confederación Indígena del Oriente Boliviano), which has been awaiting approval in the National Parliament since 1994. Some communities have obtained property titles through the agrarian reform policy, which recognizes family plots in a joint way (as in the case of the Chiquitanos of Lomerio in the Department of Santa Cruz, Bolivia). Some territories have been recognized by supreme decrees, especially during the government of President Jaime Paz, obtained through such public pressure as the sacrificial march by indigenous groups from Beni to La Paz in 1990. A march of indigenous peoples from the East of Bolivia to La Paz in August 1996 achieved the recognition, through the INRA (National Institute for Agrarian Reform) Law, of indigenous territories as "original communal lands." In May 1997, the Bolivian government granted eight titles for territories in eastern Bolivia.

At the international level, several important advances have been effected in recognizing the rights of native communities as possessors of territories within national states. Among the most important is Agreement 169 of the International Labor Organization, signed by Peru and Bolivia, and thus recognized as law in both countries. This agreement includes the recognition of collective rights of indigenous peoples over their traditional lands and the requirement that the states consult them about development initiatives that can affect them or their territories. There are also important advances at the level of the United Nations regarding the rights of indigenous peoples (Stavenhagen 1994). Since 1995, the Open Working Group of Human Rights from the United Nations has been discussing a draft of the Declaration of Indigenous People's Rights, which has been elaborated in consultation with indigenous representatives.

In spite of these achievements and the international and legal recognition of Amazonian ethnic groups as indigenous peoples, much remains to be done. Even in those countries with more advanced legislation in this area, native rights to the subsoil are not recognized. In

Peru, Ecuador, and Bolivia, the new oil boom is placing at risk both the environment and the rights of indigenous peoples to make decisions about the use of their territorial areas. In Brazil, the approval of Decree 1775 could be an important setback to the rights of Amazonian peoples over their territories. In the case of Peru, the Constitution of 1993 excluded the previously existing exemption of indigenous lands from seizure for unpaid debts and the prohibition of the sale or separation of land from indigenous control.

In the development of political organizations at the local, national and international level, the concept of "indigenous" has taken primary place, and an ideology has been constructed to support it. The foundational claims of the ideology of indigenous status have been the rights of ethnic groups in the Amazon (as of groups in other parts of the world) to the territories and natural resources they use, and the right to participate fully in making decisions about development in indigenous areas. Indigenous organizations insist on their participation in both public and private development initiatives affecting indigenous areas. They also insist on their right to have their own vision of the future incorporated.

This vision of the future is under construction. Indigenous groups have suffered greatly in the wake of colonization and related changes. Through their political organizations, they are trying to understand their situation and to create a vision of their future in which they are integrated into the global society but maintain their own identity and culture. They propose that their identity and culture maintain roots in the traditional indigenous society, but they also respond to the new context and demands of the modern world. As one response, indigenous groups and allied NGOs have been developing new programs of intercultural education, health services, and natural resource management that attempt to integrate traditional and modern values. Only a few of these programs have achieved official recognition.[7]

New Challenges for Indigenous Organizations

Building Mechanisms to Create Cohesion in Indigenous Organizations

Greater cooperation has to be achieved at the communal and intercommunal levels by overcoming clan and ethnic factionalism and cultural/generational gaps among indigenous peoples. The central role played by indigenous organizations in promoting the recognition of the rights of Amazonian peoples cannot be doubted. Problems with this role have been identified, however, and pose the following challenges for the new organizations. Because a main purpose of indigenous organizations is to achieve recognition of people's rights in local, national, and international arenas, leaders have to be able to communicate with representatives from other groups. They should be able to speak Spanish, be able to read and write, and have some knowledge of the cultural codes and behaviors of non-indigenous groups. Individuals who have acquired some of these skills are usually those who have attended schools, usually outside their communities in non-indigenous areas. This experience has tended to lead them away from their own traditional modes of knowledge transmission, especially knowledge of the natural environment, which is an important referential basis of indigenous culture (Chapin 1994). At the same time, their acquired skills and knowledge from school or other contacts give them a better understanding of the mechanisms used by the national society to dominate indigenous peoples and to deprive them of access to land and natural resources. It is unsurprising, therefore, to find many leaders of the indigenous organizations to be skilled but also somewhat separated from the majority of the members of their organization.

This situation expresses a cultural/generational gap within indigenous peoples that is derived mainly from the kind of education to which they have access and the limited number of people who are able to take full advantage of these opportunities. Normally these communities have only primary schools; very exceptionally they have secondary schools. But the main problem is in the kind of formal education that they receive, mainly in Spanish and with a colonialist content, which alienates them from their own culture and identity. This situation needs to be changed rapidly. There have been some attempts to develop alternative forms of education. The most outstanding of these is the Program for the Formation of Bilingual Teachers of AIDESEP, which proposes an intercultural and bilingual education. In this program, teachers are trained simultaneously in modern, Western knowledge and in traditional, ethnic knowledge and helped to develop a good command of Spanish (the national language) and of their own ethnic language. The expansion of high-quality intercultural and bilingual education in indigenous communities is crucial for reducing the widening cultural/generational gap in those communities and for creating conditions that will allow indigenous peoples to enter the national and global society with strong cultural identities, but also with the ability and skills to act in the non-indigenous world. This will also improve their ability to generate appropriate proposals for the development of their communities and peoples, responding to their social needs and environments and building a more equitable relationship with the surrounding world.

With the appearance of modern political organizations, new forms of organization and decision making have appeared in a process that is yet to achieve maturity. In the traditional context, when important decisions have to be taken, consensus is searched for amongst the men who constitute a settlement or compound, normally in a ritual context designed to achieve the vision necessary to make a good decision. This kind of decision making is still in effect, for example, among the Bora and Huitoto on the Ampiyacu river in the Peruvian Amazon for carrying out their traditional feasts. Among these same groups, the communal assembly, comprising the heads of constituent nuclear families who belong to different clans, makes the political decisions. This is a new organization for making decisions about the relations of the community with the non-indigenous world. Among indigenous peoples, both "traditional" and "modern" ways of decision making co-exist, but in different contexts. The communal assemblies do not always foster widespread participation. This is mainly because of a lack of information and understanding among members about the problems discussed, which may have to do with state policies or economic issues that extend far beyond the community. The community assembly also elects the community's representatives, who are usually selected on the basis of clan membership, following traditional alliances. Such decisions often hinder decision making on behalf of the entire community represented by the assembly.

Similar divisions also appear at the level of the federations or confederations, where leaders tend to give priority to their ethnic groups' problems, making it very difficult for them to act as a cohesive unit working toward common objectives. Some people think that other forms of representation, more in accordance with traditional ways, should be explored. The problem is that the traditional way of organization and decision making has been continuously violated by the colonization process, so it has frequently become compromised. On the other hand, political organization today has to respond to a different context, representing indigenous peoples' interests in the face of powerful agencies of the state or national and transnational enterprises interested in exploiting their natural resources. Thus, very creative efforts are needed to build institutions that can generate the levels of participation, representation, and accountability adequate for the complexity of today's reality.

Managing International Aid and Indigenous Development

The appearance and growth of indigenous organizations and national NGOs are closely connected to international aid. Prompted by their concern about individual and group rights, social justice, and the role of civil society in democratization, many northern NGOs since the 1970s have begun to support indigenous movements and their collaborating local NGOs. Most of the indigenous organizations, especially the regional and international federations, receive external funding from development agencies. Some of the agencies have failed to ensure the effective supervision of the management of funds and to require the clear accountability of leaders to both the groups they represent and to the donors. As a consequence, leaders have often been free to act in their own personal interests rather than in the interests of the organization and its members. This situation is so widespread that many organizations have suffered crises and institutional breakdown.

The managerial and leadership crises have led some development agencies to withdraw their support from particular organizations, or to decide not to work directly with indigenous organizations in general any longer but rather to work through NGOs that are presumed (sometimes erroneously) to have better institutional and administrative capacities. Some agencies continue working with the indigenous organization but support them in developing their institutional capacity. Although this last alternative seems by far the best route, there are, unfortunately, agencies that, apparently unaware of previous problems, fund organizations without evaluating their institutional and administrative capacities. The usual result is to deepen the crisis.

One positive outcome of these crises has been that the subject of leaders' lack of accountability, which remained taboo for a long time, is now being debated openly with the objective of finding solutions. Thus, those leaders and NGOs with a more political vision are engaged in attempts to rebuild their organizations from the grass roots. Until now, most organizational and development initiatives have been taken by the leadership, with the majority of community members themselves remaining mostly passive in looking for solutions to the problems of their organizations. The prevailing tendency has been to expect solutions to come from outside, an attitude often encouraged by the leaders themselves and by development agencies (Viteri, 1997). The belief that a project that provides funding will also resolve any problems is none other than the continuity of older patterns of dependency established by patrons and missionaries. Now some leaders see that they have to break with this kind of thinking and create spaces for discussion and reflection in the communities themselves, which could be conducive to developing organization and decision making for action. In such cases, outside funding would be only a complement or an aid to locally generated initiative and actions.

Indigenous Organizations and Gender Relations

In the indigenous organizations formed in recent decades, men have occupied leadership posts at community and intercommunity levels. This reflects, in turn, the fact that men have more access to formal education and to non-indigenous society, so that the relations between indigenous and non-indigenous societies have been mediated primarily through men. It is not clear whether this situation has arisen because of relations imposed from outside, because the colonizers (missionaries, patrons, and development agents) have pursued connections with men; or because of practices within indigenous society that determined that the interlocutors with non-indigenous society should be men, generally the heads of families. Probably all are involved.

Research on gender relations in indigenous societies is lacking. Existing ethnographies may not be very reliable sources because, often, the researchers have gathered information mainly from men. More research is needed in order to have a clearer idea on this subject. In my conversations on this topic with indigenous leaders and members of NGOs, two general hypotheses are posited: first, that indigenous men have traditionally managed knowledge, political power, and relations with outsiders and hence relations with non-indigenous society were established through men; and second, that there have traditionally been male and female domains of knowledge and power, with men and women acting in complementary ways, but that the fact that non-indigenous society has given priority to relations with men has diminished the authority and power of indigenous women.

For whatever reason, with few exceptions men hold the posts in the new political organizations. Women are able to gain some political influence through their access to new knowledge such as reading, writing, accounting, and training in activities directed to the market such as handicrafts. Although women need to acquire new expertise in order to gain access to political posts on equal terms with men, work on gender issues should not be limited to this latter goal. Women in indigenous society and economy have their own field of knowledge that needs to be appreciated and reinforced. Already some initiatives in this area are being carried out by different development programs, such as working with women in strengthening their traditional role in cultivating medicinal plants in their gardens.

Finally, one should note that men often resist attempts to incorporate women into organizational activities on the grounds that such involvement could lead to disruption within family and community, which need at present to be united in their joint struggle in, for example, the defense of territory and natural resources. Yet work to reinforce women's potential contribution to making decisions in community and intercommunity organizations does not necessarily lead to conflicts in the family or in the community. Many challenges remain here.

ALTERNATIVE FORMS OF DEVELOPMENT FOR INDIGENOUS AREAS

Having achieved some legal recognition of indigenous territories, indigenous peoples and the NGOs working with them have taken up a new challenge: to formulate development approaches that benefit indigenous peoples, that facilitate the sustained use of natural resources in the long term, and that reduce the contradiction between a market economy and indigenous economies.

The Clashes Between Indigenous and Market Economies

In the process of colonization, indigenous and market economies have come into contact, creating a series of clashes because, in many ways, these economies are organized according to opposing values (COICA-OXFAM America 1996). The indigenous economy is organized around family production for subsistence and exchange within and across settlements. It is based on the use of a great diversity of natural resources and a distinct sexual division of labor. As noted earlier, nature is understood to be inhabited by spiritual beings, "owners" of the different species with which relations of exchange are established according to ancestral norms. The use of resources is determined by a family's needs and their exchange obligations with others. There is neither the need nor the technology to accumulate goods. Nature and its resources are the "larder" from which one takes one's necessities. Individual prestige is based on generosity: the more generous the person, the greater the prestige acquired within the society. Relations of exchange and reciprocity create cohesion within the settlement and with allied groups. These values of generosity, exchange, and reciprocity underwrite a strong sense of material equality among all. A person who has something and does not share it is regarded as stingy or "mezquino" and is criticized and ostracized (COICA-OXFAM America, 1996).

The articulation of the market economy with the traditional indigenous economy marks the tendency toward a more intensive and selective pattern of production, with a more utilitarian use of nature and more specialized, less diversified work. Important values of the market economy, however, such as saving, accumulation, and investment, have not been internalized to the same degree by all. The majority act with greater assurance when practicing exchange, reciprocity, and generosity. On the one hand, the use of diverse resources for subsistence has been reduced as a result of people having to dedicate more time and energy to activities oriented toward the market. With this, the exchange of subsistence goods within indigenous society is reduced. On the other hand, market goods and money enter into and circulate through the network of exchange and reciprocity through long-term loans, which in turn inhibit savings, accumulation, and investment. The result is often contradiction and conflict. Indigenous people commonly assume that goods need to be distributed, not saved or accumulated. Those who adopt the market values and practices of accumulation, savings, and reinvestment and thus do not share what they have are seen to threaten material equality within the community. One pervasive form of social control that impedes economic differentiation within indigenous society is the use of rumor and envy, which are believed to unleash harmful consequences of magical origin. Two cases illustrate the process.

In one community of the Peruvian Amazon, a program of small loans had induced a group of households to breed pigs and to grow sugar cane on a very small scale for the production of molasses, which had a ready sale in the community because it was cheaper than sugar. The work party was organized according to the traditional framework of relations and decision making. The molasses found a good market in the community and the pigs began to reproduce. After three years, the group began to show signs of success and a capacity for saving and investment. Then, when all was going well, the five-year-old son of one of the partners died suddenly after a crisis of vomiting and diarrhea. The work-party families became generally demoralized and abandoned the cultivation of sugar cane and the manufacture of molasses. They claimed that they had been the objects of criticism by other members of the community, whose envy had generated harm or "dano," which had caused the child's death.

In Bolivia, an indigenous organization in partnership with an NGO has been carrying out a project for the management of a forest and a sawmill. After nearly ten years, the sawmill is still not self-financing. Although some reasons for this include poor market prices, the quality of the wood, the technological over-capacity of the sawmill, and so on, a critical contributing factor is that the sawmill is continually expected to make "loans" to community members. The loans are for a range of occasions, from emergencies, such as sickness, to the general support of community social activities. As a member of an indigenous community, the sawmill's manager is involved in networks of exchange and reciprocity and placed under considerable moral pressure to extend loans to the members of his community. The low circulation of money in the area means that loans are difficult to recover and this, in turn, reduces the sawmill's capacity for capitalization.

In recent decades a number of projects instituted by government, NGOs, and indigenous organizations have been aimed at improving local people's direct access to markets and at cutting out middlemen. The main argument has been that middlemen monopolize profits, taking advantage of the indigenous producers' needs or their ignorance of real prices. Most of these projects have failed. Many were not based on prior feasibility and market studies. In practice, indigenous areas usually are located very far from markets, with transportation costs often exceedingly high; within indigenous society there are very few people trained in enterprise management; and the communal pressure for the distribution of goods creates problems for capitalization. Furthermore, many of the projects were founded on assumptions of communal property, whereupon the project came to be the property "of everybody and of nobody"—that is, everyone wishing to obtain benefits and none willing to take on responsibilities (OXFAM-COICA 1996; Benavides and Pariona 1995). In retrospect, the failure of many of these projects has revealed the complexity of affairs. If community initiatives have shown problems of viability, individual or family initiatives have had their own limitations because of the strong sense of equality in the communities. At present, the groups formulating development programs and projects are experimenting, trying to find a balance between community norms and business interests in indigenous communities.

New Perspectives of Development: In Search of a More Integrated Vision of Indigenous Society and the Sustained Management of Natural Resources

In attempting to create conditions suitable for development in indigenous areas, some key principles that must be taken into account include both support for the family economy based on subsistence and market activities and a broad diversity of economic activities based on the sustainable use of natural resources in accordance with indigenous cultures and practices. The rules for the management and use of resources at the family, communal, and territorial levels should be made explicit and established through a wide participatory process, incorporating the forms of traditional regulation and adapting them to new contexts. This process will have to be complemented with a more systematic knowledge of the territory's characteristics, its natural resources and its capacity for use. The direction of development initiatives should be in the hands of indigenous leaders (in coordination with traditional authorities) and indigenous technicians, NGOs, and scientific specialists. There is a need to open up a wider space at the community level for men and women to express themselves and to participate in the decision-making process.

Such initiatives in alternative development are taking shape throughout the Amazonian region, even though they receive far less funding than mainstream governmental and private enterprise activities. They require time to show results, and they also need to be studied. These alternative development programs are constantly threatened by new policies and by public and private economic initiatives that do not respect indigenous rights over lands and natural resources, and that do not create effective mechanisms for participation by indigenous organizations in their development plans. A main challenge today for indigenous organizations is to confront these threats by creating alternative forms of successful development in their communities, and by gaining wider recognition as the representative organizations of the indigenous peoples.

Notes

1. During the 1980s, the following organizations were formed: AIDESEP (Asociación Interétnica de Desarrollo de la Selva Peruana, or Inter Ethnic Association for Development of the Peruvian Jungle), CIDOB (Confederación Indígena del Oriente Boliviano, or Indigenous Confederation of Eastern Bolivia), CONFENIAE (Confederación de Nacionalidades Indígenas de la Amazonia Ecuatoriana, or Confederation of Indigenous Nationalities of Ecuatorian Amazonia), and equivalent organizations in the other Amazonian countries. All of these organizations form the COICA (Coordinadora de Organizaciones Indígenas de la Cuenca Amazónica, or Coordinator of Indigenous Organizations of the Amazonian Basin), an international entity representing indigenous peoples from the nine Amazon countries.

2. Jurg Gasche (1976) describes for the Huitoto the exchange of the products of agriculture (manioc and other garden crops) for those of nature (hunting, fishing, and gathering). Exchanges between households take place through feasts: the organizers of the fiesta offer the produce of the kitchen gardens and the guests offer the products of hunting, fishing, and gathering; the former offer the goods produced by humans and the latter offer the products given by the "owners" of nature.

3. Although nucleated settlements are now the norm, there are cases in which dispersed housing has been maintained due to the characteristics of extractive activity, as in the case of the Kashinahua of the river Yurúa in Brazil. With the crisis in rubber exploitation, nucleation is also taking place in this indigenous area (Valle de Aquino 1996).

4. In the 1970s, NGOs began to support Amazon indigerous peoples in the defense of their territories and natural resources. These NGOs have evolved and now some of them are also working in alternative development projects in indigenous areas. The funding of these NGOs usually comes from northern NGOs that also fund indigenous organizations.

5. This was particularly marked during the 1980s. In the 1990s, international coalitions are forming; some link indigenous people's organizations with

NGOs that defend the environment, such as OILWATCH, and some link countries of the south and north, such as the Amazonian Coalition.

6. In Peru, based on the Ley de Comunidades Nativas (Law of Native Communities), some native community titles have been granted in adjoining areas; and communal reserves have been created in areas that are uninhabited but frequented by natives for gathering, hunting, or fishing. This process has been effected principally by indigenous organizations and NGOs, with funding from international agencies. The Peruvian State has shown little will to facilitate the granting of titles to native communities, always alleging budget problems, and has been willing to sign ownership titles only under great pressure, nearly always delaying the process as long as possible.

    In the case of Bolivia, no legislation recognizing territorial rights of indigenous peoples existed until 1996. An Indigenous Law Proposal of CIDOB has been awaiting approval in the National Parliament since 1994. Some communities have obtained property titles through the Agrarian Reform policy (as in the case of the Chiquitanos of Lomerío in the Departamento of Santa Cruz, Bolivia). The recognition of territories was acheived during the Government of Jaime Paz only after a sacrificial march of indigenous peoples from Beni to La Paz in 1990. A march of indigenous peoples from eastern Bolivia to La Paz, in August 1996, achieved recognition (through the INRA Law) of indigenous territories under the status of communal lands of origin. In May 1997, the Bolivian Government granted eight titles for territories in eastern Bolivia.

7. One example of an attempt to create appropriate indigenous education from the intercultural standpoint is being conducted by AIDESEP in collaboration with the Pedagogic Institute of Loreto. It has had important results even in the short time it has been in effect. The Programa de Formación de Maestros Bilingues (Program for the Formation of Bilingual Teachers) of Peruvian Amazonia is also beginning to be seen as a model for bilingual and intercultural programs in other Amazonian countries.

5 BATTLEFIELDS OF WITS: INTERFACE BETWEEN NGOS, GOVERNMENT, AND DONORS AT THE DEVELOPMENT SITE[1]

Isaac N. Mazonde

INTRODUCTION

The challenge that contemporary scholars face with respect to explaining the complex notion of development in the context of social groups is not so much to give an account of the survival strategies of individual members of groups as to focus on and isolate the linkages that develop between the interacting individuals or parties concerned. More enlightenment can be gained from an analysis of interlocking intentionalities in which attention is drawn to the forces making for conflict or incompatibility between the individuals or parties under discussion. In this context, it may be misleading to assume that just because an individual represents a specific group or institution, or belongs to a particular social category, he or she necessarily acts in the interests or on behalf of these others (Long 1989:4). In the study of development within the context of the developing countries and especially the more marginal communities, the link between representatives and constituencies, with their differentiated membership, needs to be empirically established, and should not be taken for granted.

This chapter brings to the fore the inherent problem of variation in the perceptions of different actors at a development site and further shows that such variation may result in conflicts that negatively affect the community for whom development was meant. The chapter focuses on Basarwa, a marginalized minority ethnic group of people in Botswana. Basarwa are also known as bushmen, or, sometimes, the San. They insist on being called "Basarwa," which is the name given to them by the Tswana, because they are keen on maintaining their identity within Botswana. Basarwa are found in seven of Botswana's eight administrative districts. The area of focus for this chapter is the Gantsi district where Basarwa, who form 20 percent of the population of this district, are more concentrated than anywhere else in the country. In particular, focus is on Basarwa in the settlement of Xade, within the Central Kalahari Game Reserve.

For the past decade, a fierce war of words has been raging between the Botswana Government and the residents of Xade, all of whom are Basarwa. The government does not wish to bring any developments into Xade because it wants to develop the game reserve in line with its recently re-emphasized policy of promoting tourism in the country, in the wake of declining revenues from diamonds. There is another major reason for the government to want Basarwa to move out of Xade. For a long time, the policy of the government has been to bring "developments" to remote area dwellers, the larger portion of whom are Basarwa. The new policy is to integrate Basarwa into the mainstream tribes. The government sees such a move as the only way to improve the economic condition of Basarwa, who are perceived as the poorest ethnic group in the country by all the actors in the Xade matter. These actors include the government, NGOs, donor agencies, representatives of some foreign governments, and the Basarwa themselves. All of these actors attempt in their own ways to influence Basarwa in Xade to follow a certain model of development.

At the end of the story told here, Basarwa in Xade undergo some social transformation that brings them closer to the social structure of the mainstream tribes of Botswana. Yet, in this structure, Basarwa have become much more dependent on the government for their livelihood. Hence, whereas some commentators have viewed the social transformation as a sign of development, others have regarded it more as an exchange of one form of poverty for another.

Whatever the truth may be, my position is that it is more important to realize that the "development" path taken by Basarwa in Xade at the end of a phase of intervention from different actors is an outcome of struggles among those various actors, namely, the Basarwa representatives (about whom I shall say more later), the government, the representatives of donor organizations and NGOs that purport to support the cause of Basarwa, and the Basarwa themselves. In other words, the specific patterns and paths of change that emerge within the Basarwa community at Xade cannot be explained only by the intervention of public authorities or of powerful outsiders. They have to be seen also as a direct consequence of the interactions, negotiations, and social and cognitive struggles that take place between specific social actors. Such a development path is contrary both to the received notion that development occurs as a result of the implementation of development models, and to the idea that development is a single, hegemonic imposition.

Nor is the response of the Basarwa to outsiders always uniform, irrespective of whether these outsiders are the Botswana Government or NGOs. The response is differential according to the perceptions of various Basarwa groups in Xade. This differential response further complicates the notion of development by bringing to full view more of its varied faces. A fuller account of the lives of Basarwa in Xade and their resistance to the government's move to evacuate them from the settlement is presented later in this chapter.

THE BASARWA QUESTION IN BOTSWANA

Since the 1930s, the colonial government had been contending with the problem of the marginalization of Basarwa, and with the fact that they were not being accorded treatment similar to that given to non-Sarwa groups. Basarwa were virtually treated like the wild animals among whom they lived. In fact, in the 1930s, two special advisers who came at the invitation of the South African Government to ponder the fate of Basarwa suggested that Basarwa should be considered as fauna and not as natives (Hermans 1993:3). With time, and through efforts of more sympathetic and knowledgeable colonial administrators such as George Silberbauer, the colonial government accepted that Basarwa deserved a more humane treatment. In order to preserve both the Basarwa and the wildlife, the colonial government decided in 1961 to set up the Central Kalahari Game Reserve, which measures 561 square kilometers. Basarwa were to remain inside this game reserve, and in it fifteen boreholes, or deep wells, were to be drilled and equipped for their use and also for use by wildlife.

Certain restrictions were imposed on the way Basarwa were to hunt inside the game reserve. They were to use only their traditional weapons (bow and arrow) and hunting methods (mainly chasing animals into deliberately dug pits). The use of the rifle was expressly prohibited within the game reserve. In addition, Basarwa were to obtain special licences to hunt, even inside the game reserve. Hunting inside the Central Kalahari Game Reserve has been a source of intense conflict between Basarwa and the game wardens. Basarwa are frequently arrested for killing game without licences. For such offences, they are punished severely and, reportedly, have been tortured to divulge information about illegal hunting inside the game reserve by themselves and by the non-Basarwa who engage them to hunt on their behalf.

In 1993, the number of Basarwa in Botswana was estimated between 40,000 and 50,000 (Botswana Government 1993), forming 4 percent of the total population. They are spread out, the majority still living in cattleposts outside the game reserve where they are easily exploited by cattle owners for whom they provide cheap labor. Botswana has eight administrative districts, and Basarwa are found in seven of them, although their largest concentration is in Gantsi, where they constitute 20 percent of the district's population. However, everywhere in Botswana, Basarwa are the poorest ethnic group, few read or write, none of their number has entered the super-rich class of urban entrepreneurs, and none has been elected to parliament or promoted to a high civil service job since independence in 1966.

In 1974, in response to a proposal by anthropologist Liz Wily, the postcolonial government of Botswana established the post of Bushman Development Officer and appointed her to fill it. The post was eventually incorporated into a retitled Remote Area Development (RAD) Programme, in a bid to embrace non-Basarwa who lived in the remote areas along with Basarwa. Nevertheless, Basarwa remain the dominant ethnic group among those labeled the *remote area dwellers*. Like their Basarwa counterparts, non-Sarwa remote area dwellers are poor people, but even they are slightly better off.

The RAD program has been funded largely by the Norwegian Government through its former development agency, NORAD, which has just been disbanded. In 1993, NORAD provided P4 million (U.S. $1.5 million) for the RAD program. The stated concern of the Norwegians is the improvement of the welfare of Basarwa. There are other NGOs, both local and foreign, which also give various types of assistance to remote area dwellers in general and to Basarwa in particular. Like the Norwegians, these bodies all mention the improvement of the lives of Basarwa as their aim. It would appear that the desire for an improvement of the welfare of Basarwa provides a common ground for all of them. Yet the different donor organizations, NGOs, and the government all have a different conceptualization of the ideal pattern of development for Basarwa.

It may be necessary to begin with government's view, since the other benefactors have emerged with the aim of either complementing it in part, or, in some cases, of opposing it. Broadly, government's policy is to encourage and foster the integration of Basarwa into the mainstream Tswana communities. Government considers this to be the best way to address the question of marginalization of Basarwa. Consonant with this framework, the government took two steps with respect to Basarwa who have been living inside the Central Kalahari Game Reserve since 1961. The first step, taken around 1979, was to group all of them in one settlement called Xade, inside the game reserve. In this settlement, development infrastructure such as a school, a clinic, and other social amenities were provided for the Basarwa. Because the settlement is inside the game reserve, it had to be fenced to keep out wildlife. The purpose of grouping the Basarwa in Xade was to make providing services to them easier.

In 1986, government took the second step. It considered that there was a limit to the number of social amenities and development projects that could be provided inside Xade, since the settlement is inside a game reserve. A major component of the RAD program is the allocation of two heifers and two female goats to each household of remote area dwellers. In addition, the government allocates small arable fields to the remote area dwellers and ploughs these fields at no cost to the holders. The remote area dwellers outside the game reserve benefited from this package, but it was not possible to extend it to Xade residents. First, there was not enough land, as Xade had not been planned as an agricultural settlement. Second, cattle production could not be practiced within a game reserve, since cattle would be prone to infection with the foot and mouth disease that is endemic among the wild game.

Government then resolved, without consulting the Basarwa in Xade, that the best way out of the dilemma would be to relocate the Basarwa outside the game reserve, where they could have access to land sufficient to enable them to carry out the development projects that were being implemented by remote area dwellers in other parts of the country. Accordingly, all development projects have been frozen in Xade since 1986. The residents of the settlement were encouraged to find a suitable area outside the game reserve where they could be resettled. The government would help them find a suitable spot and also facilitate their movement from Xade into it.

Simultaneously with attempts to relocate the Basarwa outside the Central Kalahari Game Reserve, the Botswana Government has been planning to promote tourism vigorously, following indications that revenues from diamonds, the mainstay of the economy for the past two decades, would experience a slump in the 1990s. The government considered that the Central Kalahari Game Reserve stood a better chance of achieving its full potential as a game reserve if people could be removed from it. The government was open about this matter and publicized it through the media. Unexpectedly, the Basarwa representatives, NGOs who are working to improve the lives of the Basarwa, and some donor organizations sponsored by foreign governments interpreted the planned removal of Basarwa from the Central Kalahari Game Reserve as a ploy by the government to sacrifice the cultural values of the Basarwa, who are powerless, as part of the strategies to improve the livelihood of the politically powerful non-Basarwa, who are the overwhelming majority in Botswana.

The perception has created a rift between the government on the one side and the Basarwa and all their sympathizers on the other. Consequently, there have been accusations and counter-accusations from one side to the other. The thrust of the accusations by the sympathizers of the Basarwa has been that the Botswana Government is discriminatory against the Basarwa in at least two ways. First, the government has been accused of trying to "de-tribalize" the Basarwa (that is, deny them their right to a separate cultural identity) through its policy of integrating them within the mainstream tribes of Botswana, none of which has a culture similar to that of the Basarwa. Second, through its policy of moving Basarwa out of the Central Kalahari Game Reserve, the government has been seen to treat them as second-class citizens who need not be consulted about their own fate. It has been alleged that through these actions the government has violated the human rights of the Basarwa.

Ditshwanelo, a local NGO, and the Kalahari Support Group, based in the Netherlands, have worked with the Basarwa, sensitizing them to the need to stand up for their rights. The Norwegian Government, which provides the bulk of the funds used by the Botswana Government for the RAD program, has, along with these two NGOs and other sympathizers of the Basarwa, opposed efforts of the Botswana Government to integrate the Basarwa within Botswana's main tribes and the government's policy to remove them from the Central Kalahari Game Reserve. The main opposition political party, the

Botswana National Front, has also joined the sympathizers of the Basarwa and has used the rift to gain political mileage. In the paragraphs that follow, more is said about the Botswana National Front and the Basarwa problem. Meanwhile, Basarwa have now become vocal against the government over what they call the injustices it is perpetrating against them. There is now tension not only between the Botswana Government and Basarwa but also between the Botswana Government and the rest of the organizations and foreign governments that work closely with Basarwa.

In response to the accusations, the Botswana Government has placed all the blame on foreigners (ostensibly both the Kalahari Support Group and the Norwegian Government) and the Botswana National Front. For a reason that is not easy to understand, the government has avoided making any statements against local NGOs who are working with Basarwa in Xade and elsewhere in the country. It is possible that the government finds it politically imprudent to try to discredit Ditshwanelo, a local NGO, because it is run by Batswana who command great respect and also because they appear to be operating above politics.

Meanwhile, many events have occurred that seem to have had the effect of making Basarwa a community to reckon with. Between 1961 and 1986, Basarwa in Botswana have acquired considerable political experience. Much of it began as a corollary to the Tribal Land Act. The Tribal Land Act of 1968 vested certain land rights in members of the recognized tribes of the country and excluded Basarwa because they were not regarded as "tribesmen" by the Constitution of Botswana. The Act was silent about the right to forage. The inequity of the Tribal Land Act became glaring when the Tribal Grazing Land Policy (TGLP) was implemented seven years later, in 1975. This policy allowed ranches to be delineated on communal grazing areas in districts with enough land to provide for such demarcated "ranching areas." Large-scale cattle producers with over 400 head of cattle or farmers with fewer heads who could group themselves to make the required figure of 400 head of cattle were given the opportunity to apply through land boards of various districts for allocation of such ranches. Basarwa living on such grazing lands were evicted by the ranchers without compensation because, not being members of any tribe, they were regarded as having no rights to the land they had been occupying.

Yet Basarwa had been living on the land for ages, in fact pre-dating the Batswana settlement. The implementation of the TGLP sparked a land rights movement among them. Both in communal and commercial areas of Botswana, they protested the treatment they received and took their complaints to district councils and appealed against allocations of land made by the district land boards in what they had always considered to be their areas. Some of them talked to the media, arguing vociferously that they were not being treated fairly.

It was at this time that NGOs, both within Botswana and outside, came onto the scene on the side of the Basarwa, who, they contended, were manifestly being discriminated against by the Botswana Government and the dominant Tswana groups. With the help of some NGOs, some Basarwa requested that the matter be placed before the International Court of Justice with the hope that Botswana could be required to provide just compensation for loss incurred by the establishment of the TGLP ranches, many of which had been demarcated on land formerly occupied by them.

It is necessary at this juncture to bring into the discussion some of the ways in which NGOs have responded to the marginalization of Basarwa in Botswana, and also how the Basarwa themselves have learned to speak for themselves. Although it is the case that Basarwa have been empowered by NGOs in Botswana to stand up to injustice, it is perhaps the Nyae Nyae Farmers Cooperative (NNFC) in Namibia that inspired the Basarwa in Botswana to think more along the lines of combining advocacy with development. The NNFC was established in 1986 as a multipurpose organization involved in political and development activities such as education, a mobile shop, land use planning, and water provision. Through the help of the Kalahari Support Group, visits were arranged between Basarwa in Botswana and those in Namibia.

As Basarwa in Botswana were receiving information and help from Namibia, various organizations, some from within Botswana and others from without, were working hard forming pressure groups among Basarwa and carefully selecting leaders for these groups from among those Basarwa with the qualities to lead others. The Kalahari Support Group was among the first NGOs to work with Basarwa in Botswana. This group and another lobbying group formed outside Botswana known as the Kalahari People's Fund provide various kinds of assistance to Basarwa, ranging from small grants for community projects to technical advice to community organizations.

Many Basarwa have been able to increase their involvement with self-help activities through the efforts of the Kalahari Support Group, the Kalahari People's Fund, and the Nyae Nyae Farmers Cooperative. For example, by the 1990s, a number of Basarwa communities had formed their own Basarwa self-help organizations with the help of these foreign organizations. The Basarwa community in D'Kar in Gantsi district formed Kuru Development Trust, a multipurpose development organization that has its own horticultural and marketing projects. Furthermore, in 1992, Basarwa established, with help from the Kalahari Support Group and the Kalahari People's Fund, an organization called the First People of the Kalahari. First People of the Kalahari is basically a pressure group that aims to fight for the rights of Basarwa and it consists of representatives from the different Basarwa groups within Botswana.

The organization met with the Botswana Government in 1993 to outline what they said were important issues to their constituents. The issues embraced, first and foremost, land rights. Hunger for land has driven some Basarwa, especially those in Gantsi, to press for a separate Basarwa district. This is not a widely shared view among Basarwa, however. The majority of them will be content to have a Mosarwa councilor, a Mosarwa member of parliament, and a Mosarwa chief. A Mosarwa chief, they insist, must sit in the House of Chiefs, just like chiefs of the major tribes of the country. Third, Basarwa are demanding the right to education in mother tongue languages for their children. Botswana's official policy is that only Setswana is recognized and used as the vernacular language in schools. Basarwa argue that this policy puts their children at a disadvantage vis-à-vis non-Sarwa children who are taught in their mother tongue.

The leaders of the First People of the Kalahari were not elected by Basarwa; they were brought together by their sponsors who helped them form the movement. As such, it is more correct to describe them as Basarwa spokesmen, rather than leaders. These Basarwa spokesmen have been given prominence by their sponsors, who often send them to attend conferences at home and abroad where they speak on the injustice Basarwa suffer in Botswana.

In June 1992 and October 1993, the Basarwa spokesmen attended conferences in Namibia and Botswana, respectively, at which they spoke strongly on the plight of their fellow Basarwa. Both conferences were funded by the Norwegian Government, which also paid the costs of the Basarwa representatives. Basarwa spokesmen have attended congresses and symposia including one entitled "Voices of the Earth: Indigenous Peoples, New Partners, The Right to Self Determination in Practice" sponsored by the Dutch Centre for Indigenous Peoples, and held in Amsterdam, in November 1993. They also attended another one entitled "The Question of Indigenous People in Africa," which was sponsored by the International Work Group for Indigenous Affairs (IWGIA) and the Centre for Development Research, and held at Tune, Denmark, June 1–3, 1993. The last trip was made possible by donors and discount tickets from Air France.

Within Botswana itself, various organizations with their own objectives have also become active in the Basarwa question. The most prominent of them is Ditshwanelo, an NGO that, within the scope of its mandate, also addresses the question of the rights of Basarwa. For example, in 1993, Ditshwanelo was commissioned by the Botswana Christian Council to investigate an allegation of sexual abuse against Basarwa in the Gantsi district. The report, which was contested by the ruling party's member of parliament for the district, confirmed and publicized more instances of abuse than had been reported in the media.

A conspicuous consequence of the association that Basarwa have enjoyed with various organizations and the outside world is the heightening of their understanding of civics, which also manifests itself more clearly in their participation in party politics. Throughout the 1970s and the 1980s, there had been little evidence of any significant participation of Basarwa in Botswana's politics at national or local levels. There were no Basarwa councilors or members of parliament, even in the Gantsi district where they are mostly concentrated. One reason for the low level of participation in politics of the Basarwa around Gantsi is that for a long time white ranchers have refused opposition party members entry to their ranches in order to canvas for support.

In 1989, however, the pattern of the participation of Basarwa in politics changed dramatically in Gantsi district, due largely to stimulation from the Botswana National Front (BNF), the main opposition political party in the country. Voter registration increased by 67 percent, due to high participation by Basarwa. Out of twenty candidates in the district, seven Basarwa ran for office of councilor and all of them won. For the first time, seven Basarwa were elected councilors.

BNF leaders had decided to make a major push in the settlements of the remote area dwellers where Basarwa were in the majority. BNF leaders exploited the marginalized condition of Basarwa in Botswana and their denial of human rights by the government and non-Basarwa groups. It also highlighted the exploitation of Basarwa by the "cattle barons" (the large cattle-owners) and their neglect by government. The ruling Botswana Democratic Party (BDP) tried to counter with their own strategy of appeasing Basarwa by appointing Basarwa to district land boards for the first time. The ruling party tried further to woo Basarwa into its ranks by appointing a losing Mosarwa BNF council candidate. Apparently, BDP had woken too late in the day to the reality that times had changed.

On the strength of the all-round knowledge that they had gained over time, and also aware of the support they enjoy outside Botswana, the Basarwa spokesmen have become bold enough to oppose the government's move to remove their people from Xade. The argument of the spokesmen was that the Central Kalahari Game Reserve had been established for the benefit of Basarwa and wildlife. They claimed it was the right of Basarwa to live among wild animals and to hunt them for their subsistence without any restriction from the Department of Wildlife and National Parks, because Basarwa are not agriculturalists.

PROBLEMS OF REPRESENTATION IN DEVELOPMENT

The Central Kalahari Game Reserve affair provides an opportunity to analyze in depth a number of issues around the concept of development and the authenticity or legitimacy of representation. The aim of the analysis is to illuminate the connection or interaction between the two concepts, not to explain what each concept means to the parties involved.

As far as the government is concerned, Basarwa can only remain within the game reserve to their own detriment; it is in their interest that they should move out. The government has another reason for wanting Basarwa to relocate outside the game reserve. The country wants to make wildlife-based tourism a major industry in the next National Development Plan that is being currently proposed. In other words, government sees moving Basarwa out of the game reserve as something that will also be for the benefit of the entire nation.

There does not appear to be consensus on the part of Basarwa on the question of moving out of the Central Kalahari Game Reserve. This was revealed at a meeting addressed by the district commissioner of Gantsi at Xade, late 1995. The district commissioner stated the government's point of view and also elaborated the advantages to be gained by moving out of Xade. He then asked for an indication of how many people would like to move. About three-quarters of those present indicated they would like to move. The problem seemed to arise only in respect of agreeing on a suitable site for resettlement outside Xade. It seemed difficult for those who wanted to move out of Xade to agree on an alternative site. They ended up with two sites but without agreeing on which one would be acceptable to all.

Those who refused to move out of Xade re-stated the old argument that the game reserve together with the game in it were theirs. In this claim, they were strongly supported by one of the Basarwa spokesmen, Roy Sesana, who argued that it was unfair of the government to make them leave their fathers' graves for a settlement where they would lead a completely new lifestyle to which they were not accustomed. However, according to Roy Sesana, the underlying reason for the refusal of some Basarwa to move out of Xade is the fear of being integrated into other tribes that have their own culture. Such integration, he said, would mean that the Basarwa become "detribalized." Once they are detribalized, they would be weak as an ethnic group and would no longer be able to exert force as Basarwa, speaking with "one voice," something that they are doing currently, Sesana asserted.

The occasion was complicated by the presence at the meeting of government trucks that are normally used for ferrying cattle. On this occasion, these trucks were ready to carry people to a new settlement. Some Basarwa interpreted the presence of the trucks as an indication that government wanted to force them to move immediately. In response to that impression, which was voiced quite clearly by the ordinary Basarwa (not the spokesmen), the district commissioner explained that the trucks were there to take people to sites for inspection purposes only. In other words, people wishing eventually to move would use the trucks for inspecting sites tentatively identified by the government.

Notwithstanding the strides made by Basarwa in terms of their understanding of civics and particularly in demanding their rights, there is an obvious difference between the position taken by the majority of Basarwa on the one hand and their spokesmen on the other, insofar as the issue of moving out of Xade is concerned. Many Basarwa want to benefit from the government's package for the remote area dwellers. They appreciate the difficulty of giving them such benefits while they remain in Xade. The Botswana Government is capitalizing on the difference of opinion between the majority of Basarwa and their spokesmen and is projecting it as an indication that the Basarwa spokesmen do not represent the views of Basarwa but of themselves and their sponsors, the foreign groups.

In view of that, it becomes expedient at this stage to present brief profiles of the important Basarwa representatives so as to lay some foundation for testing the validity of the assertion of the government about whose interests each representative is likely to represent.

John Hardbattle, the most traveled and by far the best known of these Basarwa spokesmen, owned a freehold farm on which he produced cattle and goats in Gantsi district. Unfortunately, he died at the end of 1996, at the age of fifty years. His mother was a Mosarwa and his father an Englishman (his parents never married, neither did they live together). Hardbattle's lifestyle was very different from that of most other Basarwa spokesmen. Basarwa are the poorest ethnic group in Botswana; he was a rich man, even by the standards of the dominant non-Sarwa Batswana. Hardbattle was fluent in Sesarwa, English, and Afrikaans. He was literate; the overall majority of Basarwa are illiterate. The fact that he was a half-caste who had European blood raised his status significantly, hence he did not suffer the injustice that is suffered by ordinary Basarwa. This does not necessarily mean that he did not speak for Basarwa. It does mean, however, that he did not feel the pinch personally. Together with Roy Sesana, Hardbattle went to the UN High Commission for Human Rights in March, 1996, to appeal to this body against the forcible removal of Basarwa from Xade.

Komtsha Komtsha is the chairman of the Kuru Development Trust. He lives in the small village of D'Kar, where the trust is located, outside Gantsi town. His insight of civics is admirable and he has a good grasp of politics. Komtsha's lifestyle is less sophisticated than Hardbattle's, but he too is not poor. In 1993, the government suddenly issued a deportation order against Reverend le Roux, a foreign cleric who was the manager of the Kuru Development Trust, of which he continues to be chairman. No grounds were advanced by the government for its move. When Komtsha was challenged that they, as the Basarwa spokesmen, were being used by foreigners, he retorted: does the government think we are incapable of thinking for ourselves? Komtsha then solicited the support of foreign governments to pressure the government to reverse its decision to deport Reverend le Roux. The President of Botswana finally acceded to the plea and gave Reverend le Roux a last-minute pardon, although the reasons for threatening to deport him were never advanced, despite several inquiries from many quarters including Reverend le Roux himself.

Jim Morris is regarded as the firebrand of the First People of the Kalahari organization. He is an activist within the opposition Botswana National Front political party. Hence, he has spoken out against the government much more vigorously than any of his colleagues. He lives in Gantsi, where he is a councilor.

These are the three most prominent Basarwa spokesmen. There are others who are less prominent, such as Roy Sesana, who lives in Xade; Aaron Johannes, who lives in D'Kar town in the Gantsi district; and Hunter Sixpence from Tsabong, which is outside the Gantsi district.

It is not possible to establish whose agenda the Basarwa spokesmen are pushing solely on the basis of the brief profiles given above. It is clear, nonetheless, that they do exert pressure on the government through the clout that derives in part from the support they receive from outside sponsors. There is no doubt that the interests of the Basarwa sponsors are served well through the advocacy of the Basarwa representatives. What is not clear is the extent to which those interests coincide with those of the rest of Basarwa. The fact that over half of Xade residents indicated a willingness to move outside the settlement, however, suggests that at least on the point of refusing to relocate outside Xade the Basarwa representatives do not enjoy the support of the majority of the Basarwa.

The second issue is that of developing Basarwa as an ethnic group. A view that is shared commonly by the sponsors of the Basarwa spokesmen, especially the Norwegians, is that Basarwa should be developed as an ethnic group within their own natural environment. According to this view, Basarwa will be detribalized if they are taken out of this set-up, and they will cease to exist as an ethnic group. With specific reference to the Xade incident, the view can be said to have some merit because it was voiced by a resident of that settlement. When the same view has been advanced by Basarwa spokesmen who live away from Xade, ulterior motives have been suspected by the Botswana Government. It has been suggested that Basarwa spokesmen who live outside Xade are trying to use the plight of Basarwa inside the settlement for their own economic advantage. The publicity and economically advantageous foreign trips that the spokesmen enjoy can only last as long as the bulk of Basarwa remain backward and isolated. Hence, the allegation goes, such spokesmen are bent on doing everything in their power to keep other Basarwa in their current situation of deprivation.

Both positions appear valid; Basarwa subscribe to both. However, Basarwa have not gained from the discord between the different parties to this development dispute. For the past eleven years, since 1986, they have been waiting for developments that have not been forthcoming. This is how the interface between representation and development has given the Basarwa an empty promise.

This is not to suggest that all interventions meant to benefit Basarwa have failed. At least efforts to change the social organization of Basarwa have borne fruit. In Xade, as in other RAD settlements elsewhere in Botswana, Basarwa, over time and with the encouragement of the government and certain NGOs, have adopted a Tswana-type social structure that is centered around a formally appointed chief. In their natural social arrangement, they do not have chiefs, even though leaders of hunting expeditions were given some recognition as social authorities (Hitchcock and Holm 1995:9). Because the change is externally induced, some scholars have refused to regard it as being authentic. For example, Hitchcock and Holm have concluded that it is "foreign aid organizations, their academic advisers, NGOs leaders and top ranking civil servants who are actually deciding the substance and rate of social change among the San" (Hitchcock and Holm 1993:323).

In their efforts to appoint chiefs, however, Basarwa have often encountered problems with government regulations that require that chiefs should be literate in order for them to be recognized by law. This requirement has meant that non-Basarwa, who have the advantage of being literate, have sometimes been appointed chiefs over Basarwa, in those Basarwa communities where no Mosarwa satisfied the requirements for being elected chief. This is one of the things that First People of the Kalahari is strongly contesting. At least half to three-quarters of Basarwa communities still have no form of governance that is recognized by the government.

Government's inertia in establishing Basarwa headmen, apart from the reason given above, is partly explained by the belief of many government officials that Basarwa are ill adapted to participate in the governmental hierarchy because of a lack of experience with such a form of governance. Although there is some truth in this position, significant evidence to the contrary also exists. In some areas of Botswana, bands of Basarwa have participated in larger social units described as "group clusters" or nexuses based on kinship, marriage, and locational or totemic affiliation. Among the Tyua and Shua of northern Botswana, the position of headman was institutionalized to the point where it was passed down from one generation to the next, usually through the male line. These leaders had the authority to make binding decisions and to adjudicate disputes between bands. Some used to organize regionwide ritual activities, large-scale hunts, and even warfare (Hitchcock and Holm 1993:310)

The government's rationale for changing the social structure of Basarwa was to enable them to participate in the current development process. In other words, the government considers the change of the traditional Basarwa social structure to be a precondition for the management of development programs. Basarwa have experienced both gains and losses in the process. On the one hand, Basarwa may be said to have gained by restructuring their social organization along lines followed by Tswana societies because they are now better able to organize politically and they currently wield more power than before. Various governmental and nongovernmental organizations have helped settle, train, and organize the new lives of former forager populations.

On the other hand, some aspects of both the culture and livelihood strategies of the Basarwa are being changed. As they change from mobile to sedentary lifestyles, they are also becoming almost entirely dependent on the government. In this connection it is necessary to recognize that there was one major factor that catalyzed their becoming more sedentary. The last few decades have witnessed a substantial move among them away from foraging to domestic food production and wage earning. In the drought period of the early to mid 1980s, most Basarwa subsisted on maize meal, oil, and powdered milk, which they obtained from government drought-relief programs. Currently, some 80 to 90 percent of Basarwa are estimated to depend on government drought aid mechanisms (Hitchcock and Holm 1993: 310).

Such dependence would seem to question the validity of the assertion just made in the preceding paragraph, namely, that Basarwa have gained from restructuring themselves organizationally. What this reflects is the complexity of the notion of development, particularly that it is not linear. Government's intervention, through the drought-relief program, was aimed at redressing the economic exploitation of Basarwa by large-scale cattle owners. But with their mobility now reduced, the Basarwa are becoming more dependent on government than they ever were on cattle owners.

Consequently, government's intervention, with its announced purpose of bringing about "development," has not addressed the question of dependence and self-reliance, which is so essential to development. In the long run, the intervention has the effect of merely being an exchange of one form of domination for another, which is not development in any sense.

Conclusion

In this chapter, an attempt has been made to analyze contestation among different actors at a development site. It has been demonstrated how the "development" of Basarwa is hampered by conflicts that result from differences in the understanding of the term development by the different parties that are at play in the development field. A struggle then ensues, on the basis of that difference of opinion, and Basarwa stand to lose from the conflict.

All the above is a reflection of the complexity of development at a site. The development site, Xade, is a battlefield for different forces that oppose each other on some issues and support each other on others. Unfortunately for the Basarwa, the intervention of the Botswana Government appears to be an attempt to extend state control over them, and not completely an intervention for the purpose of bringing development to Basarwa. There are limited gains for the forces that fight each other at Xade. The delay in moving Basarwa out of this settlement provides a temporary gain for NGOs that are working to keep them inside the game reserve. By the same token, the restructuring of the social organization of Basarwa is one gain for the government and some NGOs, but is not seen to usher in any tangible development to the Basarwa.

Moreover, the government's gain also hurts it in that Basarwa, once they are consolidated into a group, are able to raise their political awareness significantly and to increase knowledge of their civil rights. On the strength of this position, they give political support to the opponent of the government, the Botswana National Front. In other words, Basarwa have in fact also gained from the conflict. However, the fact that at the end they have not received the development projects they had expected suggests that they have missed their prime goal, notwithstanding their accommodation of suggestions to transform their social organization in line with the desires of both government and some NGOs.

The case has demonstrated how complex representation can also be. The Basarwa representatives serve the interests of their sponsors. Although the issues for which the representatives stand are against the intention of the government, it cannot be said that the issues are entirely against the interests of the Basarwa, even though many Basarwa are ready to oppose them. Yet it is through the representatives that foreign powers fight the battle in Xade. It is through them too, that the unfairness of the government's dealings with the Basarwa is exposed and opposed. Notwithstanding that, there is justification in concluding that the representatives are responsible for the failure of development projects to reach Basarwa. In other words, representation, as a form of mediation, captures within itself a number of the contradictory angles that characterize development.

Note

1. This chapter was originally given as a paper at the Development Encounters workshop in 1996 and subsequently published in 1997 as Battlefields of Wits: Interface between NGO's, Government and Donors at the Development Site. PULA Journal of African Studies 11(1):97–107.

6 THE ROUTINIZATION OF PARTICIPATION: EMERGING NORMS, LOCAL PARTICIPATION, AND CONFLICT MANAGEMENT IN LATIN AMERICA

Theodore Macdonald

Local participation is generally regarded as somewhat of a "good thing." By contrast with the much maligned "top-down" planning, broad-based participation is seen as the way development, conservation, land reform, and similar projects should be done. The reasons for preferring participation include respect (people should be consulted when something might affect them), appropriate knowledge (people can provide information essential to good design), and tactics (people will be more likely to comply with a plan that they have helped to create). Recently, this simple logic has shifted from informal or occasional field practices to innovative policies and practices encouraged and/or mandated by agencies such as the World Bank and Inter-American Development Bank.

At the same time, participation and consent are becoming institutionalized through emerging national and international norms, conventions, and laws. This chapter reviews two high-profile, ongoing (mid-1998) conflicts over land/sea tenure and resource appropriation in Colombia and Ecuador. In each, progressive legislation has been used or invoked to focus attention on participation and consent, and in the future can support advances toward resolving these and similar disputes. The de facto relationship between law and order, however, is indirect in each case. The cases thus illustrate the critical reciprocal relationship between evolving norms that support and sometimes mandate local participation and consent, and the active roles that potential beneficiaries are playing, and perhaps must play, to secure that status.

In Ecuador, UNESCO spurred new legislation—the Special Law for the Conservation and Sustainable Development of the

Galapagos—when the organization expressed its concerns that, in light of a range of problems, UNESCO might have to re-categorize the Galapagos Islands as a "World Heritage Site in Danger of Extinction" (UNESCO 1997). The Ecuadorian Government's initial, uncoordinated responses provided an opening for a wide range of local people to participate, for the first time, in the development of the laws. Among many items, these laws provided formal recognition of and roles for broad-based local organization. Local participation and, as we will see, through it, a mechanism for conflict management thus became institutionalized within a pioneering piece of conservation law.

In Colombia, national and international laws rose to the fore in a dispute that, at its simplest level, involved an international oil company—Occidental de Colombia (OXY)—and a small indigenous group —the U'wa—in a debate over local participation in the process of consultation currently required for any "development" project. Efforts to resolve the conflict have become stalled, in part, by the Colombian Government's inability to define *how* to implement a process of "consultation," and by extension local participation. The process is mandated by Colombia's 1991 Constitution and that country's ratification of an international human rights convention (International Labor Organization (ILO) Convention No. 169). The impasse led to a request, formally by the government and informally by the national Indian organization, for an Organization of American States (OAS)/Harvard research project and subsequent report, "Observaciones y Recomendaciones sobre el Caso del Bloque Samore" ("Observations and Recommendations on the Case of the Samore Block") (Macdonald, Anaya, and Soto 1997).

Research into both cases has suggested ways to break common administrative log jams by working first to obtain participation and consultation by the affected stakeholders and, later, to seek higher-level approval for their involvement. Consequently, these highly visible cases of conflict analysis involving groups characterized by gross structural asymmetry serve as examples or precedent setters, rather than unique anomalies.

The response to the Galapagos and Colombia cases illustrates the approach to such conflicts taken by the Program on Nonviolent Sanctions and Cultural Survival (PONSACS) at Harvard University's Weatherhead Center for International Affairs. The program focuses primarily on applied research into conflicts involving ethnic minorities, indigenous peoples, and other groups who generally occupy such structural positions within a particular country or region. Research seeks to understand the interests, perceptions, and needs of these generally weaker or disadvantaged stakeholder groups. The program also tests and suggests broad strategies and specific tools that are or can be utilized by such groups to alter asymmetry as they confront threats or take advantage of opportunities presented by national and international groups, institutions, governments, and/or economic forces. At the same time, the program's research tools permit evaluation and framing of local conflicts within the larger national, regional, and global social, economic, and political context.

In several cases like the Galapagos and Colombia ones, debates between stakeholders over property rights and access to resources often do not respond to any of the more powerful stakeholders' initial efforts toward "resolution." In each case the issues are complex and the stakes may be high, so the weaker stakeholders cannot be expected to respond to any efforts for a rushed resolution. In both cases the conflicts have been exacerbated, if not caused, by structural asymmetry and thus weak or at least questionable "working relations." Power differences alone do not explain a stalemate that, by definition, assumes a desire to advance. In such situations, however, and in light of the varied and poorly understood needs and concerns, the program initially focuses on research and analysis, rather than moving toward a search for a negotiated solution or some similarly inspired form of intervention. The research outlined here first asks: "What is needed to produce good working relations?" In view of a crowded and self-defined multi-stakeholder stage, we thus ask: "Between whom?" and " With regard to what?"

Current research in Latin America suggests that the ability of "weaker" stakeholders—in these cases Indians and artisanal fishers—to engage traditionally "stronger" actors—in these cases the national government and international oil companies—over a period of time provides them with a fulcrum from which they can catapult themselves into larger, ongoing debates over human rights, access to natural resources, and/or their status within civil society. Maintaining that leverage, therefore, is one of their goals. Yet, if the weaker stakeholders do not move forward on some actions, they will be regarded as intransigent and thus weaken their ability to remain within the arena. Debates over "participation" and required "consultation" often meet the weaker party's desire to remain within the larger arena while permitting some visible local advances.

This chapter reviews the program's research methods through the lens of the ongoing applied research projects. That research has focused on issues of participation, consultation, and asymmetry, and it draws on methods from anthropology, development planning, and international law to assist the work of

1. A series of interests associated with a UNESCO-recognized World Heritage Site

2. A multistate organization, the Organization of American States, where the program not only responded to a request for assistance by the general secretariat of the OAS and its Unit for the Promotion of Democracy (UPD) but also helped to inform the OAS's Inter-American Human Rights Commission.

The cases illustrate a current dilemma. Emerging international and national legal standards support the needs and rights of minorities and indigenous peoples to participate in development decisions that directly or indirectly affect them. The needs and related requirements can be extended to groups such as the artisanal fishermen on the Galapagos Islands. Yet many of their prescribed rights and related requirements remain untested or contested in local settings. Thus, although the cases reviewed here involve single conflicts in single countries, the underlying issues reflect and foreshadow regional land and natural resource disputes. Similar conflicts already exist and others will surface quickly and frequently. Local groups are pressing national governments to ratify ILO #169, one of the few international conventions that speaks to group rights. Meanwhile governments continue to encourage international private sector investment, and both hemispheres may enter into a proposed "Free Trade in the Americas" in 2002.

CASE I, GALAPAGOS: LEGISLATION THROUGH PARTICIPATION

Background

In 1995–1996, a series of protests erupted in Ecuador's Galapagos Islands. Tensions between the fishing community and the science/conservation community had first arisen in the early 1990s when the Ecuadorian Government tried to control, initially through a complete ban then through a series of moratoriums, the archipelago's lobster fishery. Later, an even more lucrative harvesting of sea cucumbers for Asian markets produced a boom locally and also drew in hundreds of immigrant laborers. Efforts to stop this and related resource destruction led to violent disputes, and drew in other sectors of the islands' population as well as populist politicians. Citizens blocked airports and tourists buses, attacked and blockaded offices of the Galapagos National Park Service and the Charles Darwin Research Station (CDRS) for several days, threatened violence, and in general proclaimed local opposition to many of the conservation efforts in this unique setting. Others groups joined them—teachers demanded salary bonuses, newly arrived immigrants feared restrictions, and owners of small shops and others argued that a burgeoning tourist trade had done nothing for the local economy.

Tourism had, to a certain extent, changed the population from one that was relatively homogeneous economically to one where socioeconomic differences clearly existed, but this gap did not resemble any of the sharp economic cleavages that characterized the mainland. Nevertheless, as disputes escalated, opportunistic/populist political actors began to "create" distinctions and social boundaries within the local population: they referred to some as the "oligarchy" (the science/park/tourist community) and the others as the "commoners" (fishermen, laborers, teachers, and all of the rest). Consequently, relations between these groups became more tense and social distance increased, as did threats or rumors of violence.

During and following these episodes of unrest and violence, a widely held impression emerged among people on and off the islands. The disruptive residents of the Galapagos Islands, they argued, were simply following charismatic political figures. Consequently, many of those who sought to manage the conflicts (or to help others do so) focused their attention on these political figures. This, in turn, strengthened the position of the political actors through increased attention and visibility, and shifted attention away from local needs and concerns. This perpetuated a cycle and did little to diminish or otherwise manage the conflict (Macdonald 1997:6).

Participation *As If* Common Property

The research conducted by PONSACS did not support the proposition that the unrest was limited to fisheries and/or manufactured by opportunistic political figures. From the standpoint of the residents, political figures largely provided them with a voice. People followed these "spokespersons" (not to be confused with leaders) in the absence of an alternative. Although the political figures expressed much genuine and generalized discontent, they did not accurately channel the specific, underlying concerns and sentiments of the population. Most residents, including many who did not support the highly publicized actions (strikes, stoppages, and demonstrations) were deeply concerned about existing patterns of decision making, from which they had been excluded. Partly out of frustration, residents funneled their resentment onto the outcome of decisions—i.e., the rules—rather than the process—i.e., rules-making—that produced them. The research suggested that the source of the dissent among the most vocal was, in fact, shared by nearly all of the archipelago's residents.

The PONSACS research report "Conflict in the Galapagos Islands: Analysis and Recommendations for Management" (Macdonald 1997) suggested that aspects of well-managed common property could provide a useful framework for interpreting the crisis in the Galapagos Islands, as well as tools for subsequent conflict management. The researchers could have suggested or recommended some form of "cooperative" or "co-management" plan. However, observations from other areas indicated, and local opinion strongly supported the notion, that such alternatives simply would lead, once again, to state control, with lip service provided to "local participation" and "co-management." Equally important, the common property framework could be extended beyond the analysis of a set of political and economic conflicts into broad ecosystem management. In doing so, it provided a social mechanism that could anticipate future problems and thus prevent the situation from deteriorating into a "tragedy of the commons" (Hardin 1968).

Common property, most broadly understood, exists where a well-defined community collectively exercises property rights over a resource. Individuals or groups who draw on the common-pool resource—users or appropriators—are also defined and regulated by the community. Many of the most successfully managed commons are situated in small, relatively isolated settings like the Galapagos Islands. Commons, like state and private ownership, have well-defined, widely understood rules of access to and appropriation of resources by a clearly defined community; the significant difference is that rules are often locally developed for common property. In areas of open access, by contrast, there is no clearly defined community or appropriators, and thus fewer clear rules to guide use (Ostrom 1990).

At the height of the conflict, resource rights and appropriation patterns in the Galapagos Islands reflected a local clash with state-run property regimes. This resulted in a de facto situation where failed efforts to exercise state ownership closely resembled "open access." Rather than simply dissecting the currently failed system and later recommending ways to resuscitate it, the researchers suggested re-thinking the situation *as if* it were managed as common property and building recommendations from there.

Much of the management dilemma rested on the residents' *sense* of rights to the resource. By contrast with those involved in common property management, the residents of the Galapagos had a feeling of marginality and, with it, resentment, as a result of government polices. Rules were perceived as alien, imposed, and inappropriate. There was, therefore, little local support for compliance and few in-centives for community self-monitoring. Though this was most no-ticeable in those areas where the most visible and highly publicized conflicts had taken place—marine resources—and with regard to cer-tain issues—immigration—research indicated that the negative sen-timents pervaded nearly all sectors and interest areas of the popula-tion.

The suggestion that the situation in Galapagos be understood as one of "common property management" sounded alarms for some government authorities and conservation groups. They argued that a national park was not "common property" and was, quite clearly, state property. Furthermore, many stated that even to consider it as common property simply invited the sorts of challenges to authority that had provoked and maintained the dispute in the first place. In November 1996, as government officials—the minister of tourism and the sub-secretary of fisheries—heard local ideas and recommen-dations for a "Special Law for the Galapagos" from residents, they expressed incredulity and anger simply at the mention of noncentralized policy making.

National and international authorities and institutions pointed to the fact that they have already developed and worked to imple-ment the rules that govern the lands. With regard to any new laws, they added that they had even "consulted" with all of the local resi-dents and resource appropriators. These agents and agencies, the re-search noted, could be expected to recommend solutions that either develop from the new laws and/or from stricter enforcement of legis-lation in general.

The researchers predicted that, if the government agencies persisted in their approach, those who draw on the resources—large- and small-scale fishermen, and large- and small-scale tour operators— and others who strain the fragile ecosystem—that is, all immigrants— would probably continue doing what they have been doing, legally or illegally. Newcomers would continue to immigrate, largely at will but, if necessary, with guile. Also, despite the residents' expressed desire to avoid more confrontation, they could again resort to violent protest if and when new restrictions are imposed.

How, then, the researchers asked themselves rhetorically, could one argue that local people were not the source of the problems, and thus not in need of strict controls, but instead should be regarded more as participants? The research suggested that local behavior was not simply a matter of obeying or disobeying the law, but was rather a response to the ways in which the laws were established, reestablished, annulled, or otherwise changed. Residents from all sectors expressed a broad and deep concern with their inability to inform and shape policies that most affected them. They deeply resented the fact that they were marginalized and saw as unjust the policies and practices that produced that alienation. Although only some expressed this through disobedience or support for those who disobeyed, all felt it.

In summary, research emphasized that, to a large extent, it was the manner in which rules had been made that frustrated and angered local people, not simply the rules themselves. These feelings, in turn, led the residents to act *as if* the land and marine resources were located in areas of open access despite clear state claims and related rules.

At the same time, national government agencies had been generally unable or unwilling to enforce their unpopular rules; inadequate facilities prohibited regular monitoring. This led to easy violation by local users. It also kept open an unregulated door for entrance by mainland appropriators. The research suggested that by altering this pattern and responding to deeper concerns, rather than simply beefing up enforcement, it might be possible to shift negative perceptions and subsequent actions toward new attitudes and more constructive resource management.

The model for a more positive role recommended by the researchers was drawn from successful efforts at common property management. Successful management often occurs in areas where there are

1. locally defined management rules,

2. locally developed institutions that are accepted and strong, and

3. higher levels of authority (within which local institutions are nested) that support local institutions and help to monitor and enforce compliance. (Ostrom 1990; McCay and Acheson 1987; Bromley et al., 1992)

Since such conditions were conspicuously absent in the Galapagos Islands, the analysis argued that, if they were introduced, they would fill a vacuum rather than radically restructure national or local political order. Thus the researchers recommended support for a general process that would draw all local trade and labor organizations (referred to as *gremios*) and government institutions into new "working relationships"; allow them to proceed toward local "rules-making"; and move toward a long-term institutionalization of the local groups/gremios onto a formally recognized civic body.

Some coordinated group, such as a council of gremios, could then provide direct input into any subsequent changes and modifications of the rules. The same body could also serve to inform and assist in the monitoring and other aspects of compliance.

The process would be slow and would require considerable give and take by the numerous interest groups. The alternatives, however, were a very strict enforcement program or a new set of rules. Enforcement would be costly and would risk infractions as it would most likely be regarded as punitive and would thus invite violation. New government-established rules also ran the risk of being viewed by many as yet another unilateral and uninformed mandate, to be ignored or protested.

The "Special Law"

The stimulus for local actions was the proposed "Special Law" for the Galapagos Islands. The archipelago's residents, in general, strongly and broadly supported the need for such legislation. This recognized need, however, had led several people to draft their own "law" that then became their political banner, and each subsequently hailed theirs as the best legislation. It appeared that who would write the Special Law was as important as what it would say. A deadlock developed.

Then, in July of 1996, the stimulus for such legislation increased. A special visit to Ecuador by officers of UNESCO, who had received earlier reports of problems, led to a statement that the archipelago, a UNESCO World Heritage Site, might fall into the category of "World Heritage Site in Danger of Extinction." The decision was to be made at UNESCO's early December 1996 meeting in Merida, Mexico. Consequently, on 31 October 1996, the Ecuadorian president's special assistant convened the first meeting of a special commission to draft a law in anticipation of the Merida meetings. The commission, working with a legal team, would then work to draw up and present the Special Law at the Mexico meeting.

Initial meetings were held in Quito, Ecuador, on November 7 and 8, 1996. Beginning on Saturday November 9, the commission traveled to three of the four populated islands of the Galapagos for five days. On the islands of San Cristobal and Isabela the meetings were conducted as a single large assembly to which all sectors were invited and in which each could speak. These meetings thus resembled the many public assemblies that had taken place in the islands during the previous few years; questions and answers ranged broadly and randomly, and interactions were frequently rancorous.

By contrast, on Santa Cruz, the most populated and economically active island, the visit was managed differently. Two days prior to the arrival of the commission, the mayor of Puerto Ayora called a preliminary meeting. He suggested that each of eighteen local associations or gremios be allocated a space of time, roughly half an hour, to make their presentation before the commission.[1] Following this mayor's meeting, some of those who attended the meeting, although applauding the alcalde's procedural gesture, nonetheless suggested that additional planning was necessary. These gremio leaders wanted to make sure that, although each gremio spoke of its specific interests, the presentations as a whole demonstrated a broad and unified position. On Tuesday, November 12, the commission met independently with each gremio from early morning till late evening. Each made its presentation in an orderly fashion and all were, in general, quite specific. Throughout the meeting, there was an independent four-person advisory/observation group that provided continuity as the various gremios made their presentations.

While outlining their specific needs, the gremios provided much purposive overlap of general concerns. This repetition openly frustrated and sometimes angered the fatigued members of the commission. The gremios, however, insisted that it was important to reinforce their earlier suggestions and to demonstrate their common concerns.

After the commission returned to the mainland, drafting of the legislation began. No new law resulted from this initiative, however. At the Merida meeting, a final decision on the status of the Galapagos was postponed. By contrast, at a local level the preparatory and actual meetings were particularly significant. These meetings, along with two subsequent ones, helped to create the opportunity structure through which local participation was made possible.

On Thursday, November 14, the alcalde reconvened the gremios to review their meeting with the commission. Though the discussion shifted back and forth between highly specific and very general needs, there was consensus on several points. They felt that the commission members had been arrogant and condescending and that they already decided what the law should contain. Local input, therefore, would have little impact on the design of the laws, so the meetings were simply pro forma.

Despite these perceptions and in addition to the written materials submitted by the gremios to the commission, the community agreed that their opinions and needs should be reiterated and formally submitted to the commission. In this statement, local concerns should be prioritized and top priority should be given to the issues of marine resources and immigration. They also decided to add that any subsequent or related legislation—basically the *reglamento* that would follow the laws—should include direct participation, not simple consultations, by the local stakeholders.

Meanwhile, mainland and international fisheries were also hard at work and enjoying the delay. On Tuesday, November 19, two Guayaquil newspapers published articles reporting on an angry meeting held by commercial and artisanal fishermen from the mainland port of Manta. The fishermen said that they would halt any and every efforts made by any civilian (i.e., anyone other than the navy) either to detain or even to observe their fishing activities in Galapagos Islands. In addition, they declared their opposition to INEFAN (Instituto Ecuatoriano Forestal y de Areas Naturales, or Ecuadorian Institute of Forests and Natural Areas), the national protected areas agency in charge of the Galapagos National Park, and its patrol vessel. Finally, and in response to some very critical news reporting, the

Manta fishermen declared Freddy Ehlers (a popular TV host and former presidential candidate) to be their "enemy" (Universo 1996).

This was a clear challenge to the Galapagos fishermen and the National Park. Both, in different ways, were working to end illegal industrial fishing and to expand the activities of the artisanal fishing/marine reserve within the archipelago.

The Santa Cruz fishing cooperative reacted to the article by calling yet another meeting of the island's gremios. They met as a group on Friday evening, and their concern obtained the broad support of the other gremios and selected representatives of several gremios to draft a response. On Saturday night they videotaped the formal signing session. At that ceremony, representatives of seventeen distinct gremios, representing the entire spectrum of interest groups on the islands, signed a joint statement in support of a broad conservation initiative for the Galapagos, not simply a defense of local interests or an attack against the Manta fishermen. They then sent the letter and the tape off to Freddy Ehlers. On Sunday evening, at the beginning of Ehlers' TV program, he read parts of the letter and declared support for conservation of the Galapagos. He also stressed that the statement from the islands was not the retort of a single interest group but, rather, one that reflected broad sectoral consensus on the island.

These meetings were significant and revealing in several ways. The gremios were civic organizations (existing or nascent), formally tied neither to government nor to political parties. Though several of the gremios were already formed and active, they had never mobilized in such a heterogeneous assemblage before. In addition, other individuals with shared interests but no formal ties coalesced into formal gremios in response to the opportunity provided by the meetings—that is, individual "interests" became "interest groups." The movement, for the first time, gained the fishermen strategic alliances with national and international environmental concerns. Previously, such groups stigmatized fishermen as the problem. All of this mobilization and linking took place because there was wide agreement regarding the interrelated, indeed symbiotic, nature of their interests—for example, at the meeting when someone raised the question of perceptions of self-interest on the part of the fishermen, several other gremios chimed in and declared that they were all affected by such actions and thus "self-interested."

There was also widely held concern over the lack of local participation. The expression of this was the formation of an ad hoc union of recognized civic bodies. This union was formally institutionalized later, so allowing the broad conjunction of interests to set the stage for more focused agreement on specific issues.

In summary, the importance of the meetings lay not in the events or the outcomes themselves but in the coordinated manner in which nearly the entire civic society of the island mobilized itself. Such meetings were qualitatively different from previous ones. Earlier mobilizations—ranging from protest work stoppages (*paros*) of the fishing cooperatives to counter marches by those who opposed the paros (e.g., the Comite por la Paz y Bienestar de Galapagos, or Committee for Peace and Wellbeing in the Galapagos)—had served to divide the population. Many of those who formed the Comite did so in reaction when the fishermen rose in protest. Consequently, in the eyes of the fishermen the Comite became the "elites," whereas for the Comite the fishermen became troublemakers. The November meetings brought the community together in a unified manner, produced joint documents, and won support from strategic allies. The same forces, initially mobilized for defense, could then be channeled toward more pro-active construction in a broad range of related contexts.

Subsequent initiatives involving staff of the Charles Darwin Research Station, the Galapagos National Park Service, and the leadership of the Cooperativa de Producción Pesquera de Galapagos de Santa Cruz (Santa Cruz Fishing Cooperative) foreshadowed the more focused work that such collaboration would produce in the future. Following the removal from the islands of inspectors from Dirección National de Pesca (National Fisheries Directorate), the cooperative requested technical assistance and support from the Galapagos National Park Service and the Charles Darwin Research Station. Both directors, each relatively new at his position and thus with no personal history of conflict, went directly to the cooperative and agreed to help. According to the fishermen, this was the first time any such initiative was attempted. On October 10 to 11, the three organizations held their first joint planning session. This work—practically and symbolically—created some of the working relations needed to consider joint rules-making for one of the area's most hotly debated and previously divisive set of interests—fishing and harvesting of marine resources.

Participatory Planning as Conflict Management

Building on the good will generated by the CDRS and Galapagos National Park directors, a planning workshop was organized from June 5 to 7, 1997, in the headquarters of the Galapagos National Park. The purpose was to initiate a process for rewriting the marine management plan, understood as a distinct but essential complement to any new Special Law. Though hosted by the park, the meeting was institutionally independent and run by a team of independent facilitators (Felipe Cruz, a local resident; Pippa Heylings, an experienced trainer in participatory planning; and this author). They invited the participants, conducted pre-meeting interviews, sought preliminary input, established the ground rules for participants, and directed the planning session.

Drawing on the earlier collective action sparked by the Manta fishermen, the participants of the workshop included all local institutions (gremios) that were related, directly and indirectly, to the management and use of the marine reserve. Each, ranging from the park director to the head of the fishers' cooperative, were guided by the facilitators and positioned as equals. Decisions were made by consensus for the first time on the islands. Representatives from other institutions in the Galapagos (e.g., the mayor's office) and on the mainland (e.g., the ministry of the environment) were invited to witness the process and ensure its legitimacy, but were not permitted to participate actively in this "appropriators" meeting.

The participants defined the general goal of the marine management plan, which was to protect and conserve the marine and coastal ecosystems and their biological diversity for the benefit of mankind, local populations, science and education. More important, however, they decided to form a working group (Grupo Nucleo) made up of representatives from the Ecuadorian Navy, the Tourism Association, the Guides' Association, the Fishers' Co-operatives of Santa Cruz, Isabela y San Cristobal, and the science, education, and conservation interests represented by the Galapagos National Park Service and the Charles Darwin Research Station. The Grupo Nucleo was charged with the task of overseeing the participatory planning for the marine reserve's revised management plan (Galapagos National Park Service 1997a).

For almost nine months they, accompanied and assisted by the local facilitators, worked to incorporate all interest groups of the Galapagos into the process, to draft parts of the marine management plan, to incorporate the marine reserve within the national system of protected areas, to create a permanent "Participatory Management Committee" for the marine reserve, and to ensure a role for the Grupo Nucleo in the government planning leading up to the Special Law. In doing so, the group's status was transformed from an ad hoc gathering to a widely accepted and quasi-official body.

After months of congressional debate, the Special Law was passed in February 1998 (see Ecuador 1997). Local participation in all future planning and decision making was directly incorporated into the law. Final ratification of the law, however, was conditioned on the still unfinished marine management plan. The Grupo Nucleo's work on the marine management plan, meanwhile, had been sidetracked by their direct and regular involvement in the drafting of the Special Law. Also, the initial task had become the most contentious issue in the preparation of the Special Law. Proper marine management, the islanders argued, required a forty-mile protectorate/buffer zone around the polygon that defined the periphery of the archipelago. Inside this zone the group fought to limit fishing rights only to locally controlled artisanal fishing. The proposal was strenuously opposed by powerful industrial-level mainland fishing interests. These groups had lobbied very strongly to prevent the forty-mile limit.

In a compromise solution, the Special Law was passed and the forty-mile limit was accepted on a provisional basis. The Grupo Nucleo, in coordination with the appropriate government agencies, had to develop and obtain approval of the revised marine management plan within one year. At present (mid-1998), work continues on the project, and is currently focusing the most contentious issue, that of zonation.

Progress to date, however, demonstrates that local participation strongly influenced the content of the Special Law and provided much of the pressure needed to pass it. The process has also served to initiate methods and mechanisms for joint conflict management mechanisms that can be invoked as needed to meet periodic and inevitable disputes and modifications of the laws. However, they now must maintain existing support, expand participation to groups that have never experienced it, obtain consensus on a number of contentious topics, and finish drafting the marine management plan. In brief, the islanders' initial enthusiasm with participation and delight with their accomplishments, now incorporated into law, will be tested by their ability to make participation routine and to manage jointly a fascinating but delicate balance of needs and resources.

CASE II, COLOMBIA: "CONSULTATION" WITHOUT PARTICIPATION

Background

In April 1995, the Colombian newspaper *El Nuevo Siglo* was the first to report that U'wa Indians were threatening to commit mass suicide if the oil company Occidental de Colombia (OXY) carried through with its plans for oil exploration on U'wa lands. The suicide threat was reported to have a seventeenth-century precedent, when an entire community threw itself off a cliff as missionaries and tax collectors were descending on their lands. The tale was soon recounted in other Colombian papers, as well as a September 1997 piece in the *Guardian* (London). The following month a *New York Times* article wrote that U'wa bones still glistened in the valley below a 1,400 foot cliff. U'wa Indians, each added, might again leap to their deaths from that cliff if the sacred border between the underworld and the upper world was broken when oil, referred to as the "blood of the earth," was extracted and the world order, as the U'wa knew it, was upset. National and international interest in and support for the U'wa situation grew exponentially as information flowed via e-mail and onto web sites. In light of this publicity, OXY and its international partner Shell halted all work in the area, the Samore Block, and sought to open discussions with the U'wa and other critics of the proposed work.

Reading such reports presents the OXY-U'wa dispute is a classic case of David and Goliath.[2] The most visible actors are a small isolated indigenous group (pop. 5,000), the U'wa (known more widely as Tunebo) pitted against two large international oil companies working through a "contract of association" with Ecopetrol, the Colombian National Oil Company. Occidental de Colombia, the "operator," is part of the U.S.-based Occidental Oil and Gas. OXY's partner was, until February 1998, Shell de Colombia, a subsidiary of the Royal Dutch Shell Oil and Gas (Holland and the U.K.), one of the world's largest publicly held companies and also one troubled by charges of environmental and human rights abuses.

Nevertheless, there are numerous other interests in the area. The Colombian Ministry of Mines and Energy and the national oil company, Ecopetrol (another partner in the contract), took a different position as they were looking to Colombia's future. They argued that, without increased oil production, Colombia would shift, by the year 2005, from the region's third largest exporter to a net importer of oil, and that this would produce national economic crisis. So they pushed OXY to fulfill the terms and work schedule of their agreement.

Other ministries and directorates, particularly the National Ombudsman and the General Directorate of Indigenous Affairs (DGAI, Dirección General de Asuntos Indígenas), argued in support of the U'wa's rights. The Colombian National Indian Organization (ONIC, Organización Nacional Indígena de Colombia), which had long argued that the DGAI was a superfluous example of paternalism, did not support DGAI's apparently pro-Indian stance, and undertook its own program in support of the U'wa.

Added to the soup of additional stakeholders are the various factions of the National Liberation Army (ELN), along with sectors of the Colombian Revolutionary Armed Forces (FARC). They are all well armed, control large sectors of the region, strongly oppose the presence of international oil companies, regularly blow up the existing Cano Limon pipeline, and kill oil workers, consequently encouraging increased Colombian Army presence. This mix, close to the U'wa's densely forested and mountainous terrain, places the Indians at considerable risk. Although most U'wa try to remain neutral, they are simultaneously recruited and questioned by the Colombian Army and the guerillas alike.

Consequently, the U'wa's situation—whether interpreted as a culture at risk or individual lives in jeopardy—has been elevated to a public arena. Within it many of the most active stakeholders worked to test Colombia's progressive 1991 constitution with regard to indigenous rights—particularly its requirement for informed consent, consultation, and territories. The case has thus become a platform for debating group rights and national economic priorities. It also serves to define, redefine, and test the roles of various government ministries, and it provides opportunities to expand the political space occupied by ONIC. The clear presence and influence of the ELN and the FARC, however, sidetracks this national debate: the oil companies argue that the guerillas' influence is inappropriately minimized, while the Indians respond that the companies' focus on the guerillas serves only to blur critical Indian rights such as consultation.

The U'wa Consultation: A Brief Summary

At the national level, the conflict centered largely on one question: were the U'wa "properly" consulted? The "right" to informed consent is included in the Colombian Constitution and is likewise guaranteed by Colombia's ratification of ILO Convention #169.[3] The U'wa case was the first to test this right. Hundreds of other communities, as well as a range of government agencies, await the outcome.

On February 3, 1995, the Ministry of the Environment, following its review of OXY's social and environmental impact analysis (part of which included a required process of community consultation) issued the formal license authorizing exploratory oil drilling in Samore Block. Following that, other government offices, particularly the DGAI and the Office of the Ombudsman (Defensoria del Pueblo), began receiving complaints from the U'wa people about the plans for further drilling on what the U'wa considered to be their traditional territory.

The Ombudsman, acting on behalf of the U'wa people, filed a legal motion with the High Court of Bogotá in favor of the U'wa people and against OXY and the Ministry of the Environment for having granted the environmental license. The Ombudsman cited the rights and duties of indigenous groups under Colombian law, and in the Constitution of Colombia in particular. The office argued that the U'wa people had not been properly consulted prior to the operations, a requirement in the legal steps toward obtaining the environmental license. The situation became even more complicated. The Supreme Court of Justice of Colombia ruled that the "prior consultation" that OXY said it had carried out was invalid. Shortly thereafter, the Council of State affirmed the opposite. OXY, it stated, had indeed complied with the requirement of prior consultation and did have a legal license to enter the territory.

Despite the Council of State's ruling, the Ministry of Mines and Energy and OXY indicated that they would seek talks with U'wa representatives with a view to re-opening the dialogue with the indigenous community. They also stated that they would discontinue prospecting operations until the conflict was resolved.

The Government of Colombia held a meeting on April 21, 1997, in the Office of the President. It was attended by representatives of the U'wa community and the Ministries of Mines and Energy, the Interior, and the Environment. Representatives from the ministries promised to pursue reconciliation with the U'wa community, to listen to their arguments on plans for the exploitation of oil in the Samore Block, and to take steps toward a new meeting. That meeting, which took place in Chuscal in U'wa territory on May 29 and 30, 1997, included three ministers as well as the U'wa leaders. It consisted largely of speeches, however, and thus did nothing to open any direct dialogue.

The focus of most government agencies and support groups has continued to rest on the process of community consultation. The array of events, interests, and actors, however, led largely to increasing levels of acrimonious public debate and produced only impasse among the principal stakeholders. Given the broad significance of the case—it affected the rights of indigenous people and influenced the national economy—and in light of the apparent stalemate, the Ministry of Foreign Relations sought outside help to review the case and make recommendations to advance toward some resolution of the conflict.

The OAS/Harvard Project[4]

In May 1997, the Colombian Ministry of Foreign Affairs requested that the OAS general secretariat enlist the participation of Harvard University to undertake an on-site investigation into the conflict. The general secretariat requested that its Unit for the Promotion of Democracy (UPD) create a joint team. This led to the OAS/Harvard Project on Colombia, which consisted of staff from the OAS's Unit for the Promotion of Democracy and from Harvard University's Program on Nonviolent Sanctions and Cultural Survival (PONSACS) at the Weatherhead Center for International Affairs.

The team's initial research suggested that, despite the apparent simplicity of the case, interests were far more complex, and clearly linked to a wide set of national and international interests. Nonetheless, the team focused its research on what, in its opinion, were the two critical themes: community consultation and indigenous rights to territories. Both are linked to Colombia's progressive, but often unclear and untested, 1991 Constitution. This chapter focuses on some of the problems, considerations, and implications of community consultation. This issue, one of the primary concerns to the indigenous groups and organizations, has also been the principal focus of most nonindigenous observers, particularly government officials and agencies.

Given the difficulty of establishing any sort of mutually acceptable agreement, or even the ability to create an open dialogue, the recommendations of the research groups, in part, were focused on issues and concerns that, they felt, were shared by the key parties. These shared concerns, reformulated as "shared problems," could serve to bring the parties together in some form of joint problem-solving process (Kelman 1996).

Initially, the team focused on the sharp cultural differences that separated the groups, and the mutually expressed need to understand each other. The logic was that, in contrast to some of the other issues, cultural differences lent themselves more toward mutual informing than to debate and could thus serve as a means to bring the deadlocked parties together in a discussion rather than a diatribe. The report's initial recommendation—unconditional and immediate cessation of all oil activities in the block—was understood as a precondition to any such talks.

However, ONIC's formal response to the OAS/Harvard report stated

> Among the causes of the conflict surrounding the Samore Block and the indigenous communities in general with the Colombia government, one can legitimately find the sorts of cultural differences noted in the OAS/Harvard report. However, in this as in many other cases the indigenous communities are confronting a case in which one has to recognize the fundamentally economic interests of the petroleum companies. One has to see that oil activities in Indian lands run up against the inalienable property rights of the indigenous communities. (ONIC 1997)

ONIC then argued that the case reflected Colombia's fundamental failure to recognize the multiethnic nature of the Colombian nation. Presenting the conflict solely in cultural terms, they stated, avoids the fundamental problem between the Indians and the Colombian Government. This concerned the extent and the formal existence of indigenous rights in opposition to economic interests. They went on to argue that "there is no doubt that petroleum interests have motivated the National Agrarian Reform Agency (INCORA) to hold back its work to increase the size of the U'wa's *resguardo*, and to formally convert the status of their reserve, items that are clearly stated and emphasized in Law 160 of 1993 and official government policy since the beginning of the 1990s." In brief, they shifted the focus away from the company to the Colombian Government and onto the issue of land rights. This coincided with the team's recommendation regarding the question of ambiguous land tenure, specifically that related to the U'wa's proposed "territory" (later referred to as the *resguardo unico*). The team recommended the formalization of the process to extend the U'wa protected zone.

Although the concept of indigenous territories separate and apart from the protected zone or reservation does exist and serves to affirm the right of indigenous peoples to own land, it is quite clear that the formalization of ownership of the protected zone would help them to feel more secure and clearer as to their rights. On the basis of a study to substantiate the U'wa's claim, carried out by a technical team from Bogotá's Javeriana University, the U'wa have requested an extension of their protected zone. The study has been handed over to INCORA and its validity appears to be above question. Nevertheless, several factors have created a perception that the U'wa request for an extension of the protected zone has been stalled as a means of exerting pressure on them. It is important that these perceptions be dispelled so that the question of the extension of the protected zone may be examined without prejudice to any oil exploration operations. (ONIC 1997)

As the U'wa leaders pointed out, however, simply drawing a line on a map would not resolve the problem. Among other issues, the U'wa were concerned that, before any activities got underway outside of their territory, there were a number of questions to be resolved. For example, how would an increased military presence needed to protect the facilities outside the territory indirectly affect attitudes and activities within the territory? Such concerns, they argued, required consultation and agreement. In brief, the case returned, over and over again, to questions of consultation and participation within that process.

Discussions with a member of the Council of State indicated that the decision to support the consultative process was based on their interpretation of the Colombian Constitution, *as it currently existed.* The team noted that sharper definition, clarification, refinement of that document, therefore, could lead to the sort of precision and detail need for the consultation process and, by extension, a basis for evaluating whether what was done was done correctly. The Ministry of Mines and Energy had already created a special research group to focus on indigenous issues, and took up this apparently simple need— clarification—as a task. At the same time, the Ministry of the Interior, working through its National Directorate of Indigenous Affairs

(DGAI), began to prepare its approach to the consultative process. Likewise, the Ministry of the Environment, the agency that had approved the initial consultation process, indicated that it too was reviewing and revising the process of consultation. There were also numerous comments and recommendations on the process being generated by Colombian NGOs. The e-mails were alive with criticism from international support groups. The OAS/Harvard Project concluded that the present conflict would not be resolved until the Colombian Government provided the U'wa with increased opportunities to participate in and influence decisions on the exploitation of petroleum in and around their territory.

In May 1997, the OAS/Harvard researchers were informed that the three ministries were meeting regularly to prepare a coordinated government redefinition of what, exactly, was required of a consultative process. However, on two separate occasions, May and September 1997, OAS/Harvard Project members met with the vice-minister of the interior, whose offices were coordinating the rewriting. During each visit government officials said that the document would soon be finalized, "that afternoon" in fact! Nevertheless, after each visit, the team was informed that the interministerial group had been unable to reach an agreement and, consequently, no refined, official consultative process was put in motion. As of this writing (mid-1998) no broadly accepted consultative process had been approved.

Given this impasse, the authors of the OAS/Harvard report "Observaciones y Recomendaciones sobre el Caso del Bloque Samore" (Macdonald, Anaya, and Soto 1997) sought first to emphasize that defining "consultation" was the role of the Colombian Government. The report noted that, in the media and among the U'wa people, there was a "perception of the oil companies as a form of government." The researchers noted that the U'wa often deal directly with representatives of OXY and expect the company to address their concerns. Although such dealings might be appropriate for some aspects of mandated consultation, neither OXY nor any other national or multinational company should be given the responsibility for determining or clarifying the nature of the consultative process, directly allocating the resources needed to implement that process, or clarifying territorial rights and rights to resources.

Emphasizing that conflict was the result, to a large extent, of unclear guidelines and that the competent government agency recognized this need but had been unable to produce the guidelines, the report recommended an executive decree or commission with the power of decision to coordinate and prepare the guidelines. In December 1997, Colombian President Ernesto Samper named Eduardo Diaz Uribe as his official representative for the case and as liaison with the OAS/Harvard Project. Diaz, rather than focus exclusively on the consultative process for the U'wa, argued that this was a national-level problem. Consequently, he focused on establishing a consultative process that would include indigenous organizations as well those ministries already involved in the process. The special representative's work ended with the mid-1998 change in government and, though the new government has stated its interest in continuing the OAS/Harvard Project, there is no indication of how they will deal with the need for a clearly defined consultative process.

CULTURAL ASPECTS OF THE CONSULTATION

The fact that the process of consultation is not clear is complicated by an absence of intercultural understanding. The consultations had been handled mainly by representatives of Occidental of Colombia and leaders and members of the U'wa community. A member of the U'wa community remarked that despite the indigenous peoples' attendance at the meetings sponsored by OXY and despite the signing of a formal agreement, he understood the meetings to be an opportunity only to listen, not to make decisions. He and other leaders of the ONIC pointed out that in order to take decisions, more information would need to be provided for further evaluation. In order to participate more effectively and reach an agreement, the U'wa would require more detailed information on both the economic and cultural aspects of the oil industry.

Likewise, when the U'wa people invited representatives of the Ministries of the Interior, the Environment, and Mines and Energy, as well as Occidental of Colombia, to participate in a dialogue on their territory, the community considered that it was an appropriate way to begin acquainting others with their culture. They added, however, that more time was needed to achieve genuine mutual understanding. As a result, both the U'wa and the ONIC considered that there was neither sufficient information nor time to make an informed decision. Therefore they felt that it would be premature to initiate negotiations or to conclude that an adequate dialogue had been held. For their part, the oil company officials who participated in the process of consultations felt that there had been a sufficient number of briefing meetings. Both these officials and the representatives of the Ministry of the Interior considered that the formal agreement signed by the U'wa represented tacit approval that the relevant legal obligations had been fulfilled. In brief, for both the Indians and the government, the issue of what constitutes a "proper" consultation remained, and continues to remain, unclear and thus unresolved.

CONCLUSION

What, drawing on these two ongoing conflicts linked by local understandings that resolution has been advanced by new laws and norms but, nonetheless, has been left dangling in the absence of specific applications, can be concluded or suggested concerning the value of such legislation? There seem to be at least two points. One relates to perceptions. The external realist might state that in such conflicts laws, by and large, are irrelevant and that, in the end, issues of political economy and power will not only hold sway but should be the proper focus for serious research. That "reality" may be true, but such expressions are not new. Moreover, they say or inform little about changing perceptions of norm building by local people. By contrast, the cases illustrate that, for those who generally see themselves as the weaker actors in disputes, the opportunity to draft, refine, and subsequently invoke legislation serves, directly or indirectly, to empower. It suggests to them that they *should* be included and that local participation *should* be part of the planning and implementation of resource management. As such, the ability to interpret "consultation" simply as informing becomes increasingly unacceptable and direct participation thus becomes progressively institutionalized.

In addition, despite the frustrations expressed by many of the parties, there have been advances in both cases. These have served to move laws toward greater clarity and, with it, have increased local participation and self-respect. Such advances are hard to quantify, and any effort to do so may be misdirected. For some of the local actors, simply advancing a process in which they play a role is as important as any result. In the future, norms and laws to codify those norms may be sufficiently well formed and tested, and issues of consultation will become established procedures rather than obstacles. In the meantime, it is impressive that, though stalemate in certain aspects of each case has not been broken, each is leading toward greater local participation in the development of laws that, in the end, will require and specify such participation.

The cases thus foreshadow a broader and legally mandated routinization of local participation—as opposed to a set of government actors whose defined or, more precisely, whose self-defined position is to "decide." This will not deny the role of government authorities, but it could streamline their work. For that to occur, however, local people must be in a position to require that government officials either negotiate or cede a bit of personal power in the face of emerging legal norms and related processes that define participation as a right rather than simply a benevolent "good thing."

NOTES

1. The commission was composed of the following individuals and government agencies: Ministerio del Medioambiente, Ministerio de Turismo, Ministerio de Relaciones Exteriores, Ministerio de Defensa, Nacional Subsecretaria de Pesca, Diputado Eduardo Veliz, Mayor Franklin Sevilla representing the alcaldes of Galapagos, and two representatives of international organizations.

2. This biblical analogy has become widespread in the U'wa-OXY conflict. It has also been used in similar asymmetrical disputes (see Smith 1997).

3. Convention No. 169 of the International Labor Organization, which was approved by Colombia under Law 21 of 1991, states that in cases like this one, the government is bound to hold consultations with the indigenous people (Article 15.2). The Convention specifies that the "consultations shall be carried out in good faith and in a manner appropriate to the circumstances, with a view to reaching an agreement or achieving consensus on the proposed measures" (Article 6.2). It further states that "interested peoples shall determine their own development priorities and shall participate in the formulation, implementation and assessment of national and regional development plans and programs which may affect them directly" (Article 7).

   As explained in the ILO document "Indigenous and Tribal Peoples: A Guide to the Implementation of ILO Convention 169" (Geneva 1996), these provisions require governments to consult with indigenous peoples from the start over decisions that may affect them directly. Furthermore, the consultation process must be one in which the indigenous people can participate and have a say in all decisions on projects involving their lands, including the early stages when the project is being drafted. According to the ILO document, this does not mean that they can veto development initiatives undertaken by the state; rather, the objective of consultations should be to seek common ground. When no agreement is possible, the government decides, but if its decision in contrary to the wishes of the indigenous community, it must present justification and provide, among other things, that the project will not violate the cultural integrity of the indigenous group but rather will benefit them.

4. Portions of text included in this paper are drawn directly from the OAS/Harvard report (Macdonald, Anaya, and Soto 1997).

7 WRITING AGAINST HEGEMONY: DEVELOPMENT ENCOUNTERS IN ZIMBABWE AND MALAWI

Anne Ferguson and Bill Derman

This chapter explores knowledge encounters and development practice in the context of four development programs in Southern Africa, two located in Zimbabwe and two in Malawi. Despite commonalities of history, culture, and development strategy, variations exist within and between these programs. Our aim is to draw attention to the existence of alternative, if not competing, development paradigms within nation-states. Escobar in his book, *Encountering Development* (1995), calls attention to the construction of a hegemonic discourse of development, arguing that the idea and practice of development silences other cultural worlds. He implicates anthropology in this construction, suggesting that it should liberate itself from the development encounter:

> [Development discourse] has created an extremely efficient apparatus for producing knowledge about, and the exercise of power over, the Third World. This apparatus came into existence roughly in the period 1945–1955 and has not since ceased to produce new arrangements of knowledge and power, new practices, theories, strategies, and so on. In sum, it has successfully deployed a regime of government over the Third World, a "space for subject peoples" that ensures certain control over it. (Escobar 1995:9)

Escobar holds that development constitutes a single hegemonic paradigm. The four case studies presented here raise questions about positing a master development narrative that has erased alternative paths. We remain skeptical of reducing all forms of development discourse, including sustainability, ecology, gender and development, the crisis in representation of the Third World, the construction of development economics, nutrition problems, and so forth to a single dominant discourse.

Norman Long's work (1992) presents an alternative, less totalizing perspective. He emphasizes the importance of agency, context, knowledge, and power that are embedded in the social processes of "development encounters." His is a very different reading, suggesting that development cannot be subsumed under a master narrative. Long observes that

> ...different social forms develop in the same or similar structural circumstances. Such differences reflect variations in the ways in which actors attempt to come to grips, cognitively and organizationally, with the situations they face. Therefore an understanding of differential patterns of behavior must be grounded in terms of "knowing, active subject[s]" (Knorr-Cetina) and not merely due to the differential impact of broad social forces (such as ecological or demographic pressure, or incorporation into world capitalism). (Long 1992:27)

The four case studies analyzed below draw attention to the interactions that occur between local and scientific knowledge in project contexts and between projects and the wider national and international development milieu in which they operate. We focus particularly on how scientific knowledge is constructed and used to achieve specific development objectives. This knowledge changes through time, and its bases may vary from project to project. It is socially constructed and deployed and is inextricably linked to power.

At the current time, the ideology underlying these four projects is sustainable development. Escobar implies that sustainable development, like other forms, has been subsumed under the dominant paradigm. Long, in contrast, suggests an empirical investigation, raising such questions as, Who is defining sustainable development? Whose science is being employed? How do different actors understand what constitutes both sustainability and development? and Who defines success?

The four case studies represent diverse development arenas, including resettlement, wildlife, agriculture, and fisheries. Two sites are in Zimbabwe's eastern Zambezi Valley, which has become a center for development activities involving international, national, and local organizations due, in part, to the perception that it is underpopulated, isolated, and lacks services, and, in part, to its potential for wildlife tourism. The two projects, the Mid-Zambezi Valley Rural Development Project (MZRDP) and the Communal Areas Management Programme for Indigenous Resource Management (CAMPFIRE), respond to different government and donor agendas within the same state and party structure, and they rely on contrasting models of development and participation. Thus, they present different opportunities for the intersection of local and scientifically derived understandings and development practices.

The two Malawi case studies focus particularly on the period of transition from authoritarian to democratic governance in the early 1990s. They demonstrate how political liberalization presents different opportunities for the intersection of local and scientific knowledge and development practice. In the case of the Bean/Cowpeas Collaborative Research Support Program (CRSP), local knowledge became increasingly irrelevant in the context of the increasing commoditization of beans, whereas it had been the centerpiece of earlier development efforts. In the case of the fisheries program, the opposite occurred. Local management and knowledge were emphasized whereas, previously, the state had attempted to regulate and control the fisheries with no local input. Political and economic liberalization thus has had different outcomes in these two cases.

ZIMBABWE

When Zimbabwe became independent in 1980 it had an excellent university, a relatively large number of scientists and researchers in most major fields, and many people with doctoral degrees who had returned after the war ended. The Zimbabwe African National Union (ZANU) won the first elections in 1980 with a platform based on national reconciliation and socialism. Central government working with the party was to set and initiate the nation's major development priorities. For the rural sectors, government dramatically increased assistance to communal area farmers. This included extension services, schools, rural growth points, and transport. Another major priority was the resettlement of farmers from poor and overcrowded communal lands to what had been European areas. Resettlement also was to take place in "frontier areas," such as in the Zambezi Valley. The government also continued to emphasize the importance of tourism based on hunting safaris and nonconsumptive tourism. Here again the Zambezi Valley figured in the government's plans, as it was a major destination point for hunters.

In this section, we explore how two different kinds of land-use development models, exemplified in two projects, were applied to the fragile environment of the Zambezi Valley. The projects are the Mid-Zambezi Valley Rural Development Project (MZRDP), a resettlement and agricultural project, and the Communal Areas Management Program for Indigenous Resources (CAMPFIRE), a community-based natural resource management program.[1] The MZRDP draws on scientific knowledge and models of the 1930s. It has been implemented through a blueprint approach in which the proposed beneficiaries have had little or no voice. CAMPFIRE, in contrast, is founded on participatory approaches, adaptive management strategies, and experimental science. The two programs differ in their understanding of valley residents, their uses of local and scientific knowledge, and their policies toward riverain cultivation. To explore these differences, we focus on the practice of riverain cultivation.

Historically, riverain cultivation has been the principal means of successful agricultural production and, hence, central to human settlement in the valley. Although riverain cultivation was made illegal in 1942 by the Natural Resources Act, the law was not widely enforced in the valley. A consideration of the illegal practice of riverain cultivation from the perspectives of long-term valley residents, more recent migrants and different project personnel illustrates the intersection of differently empowered knowledges in the context of development. We briefly describe the MZRDP and CAMPFIRE, focusing especially on how they have incorporated riverain cultivation, how it has been understood historically in Zimbabwe, and how different valley residents have responded to these projects.

The Mid-Zambezi Rural Development Project

The MZRDP was the first major postindependence development project in the Zambezi Valley. It was initiated in 1987 with funding from the African Development Bank, and it was staffed entirely by Zimbabweans. The MZRDP responded to the political priority of the new regime to resettle populations from more crowded rural areas to either commercial farm land or to frontier regions. The political rationale underlying the project was to be able to claim that 7,600 households (of which 3,000 were to be new settlers) were being resettled, thus demonstrating the government's ongoing commitment to resolving historic land grievances.[2]

The objectives of the MZRDP were to increase overall agricultural production, with particular emphasis on cotton; to protect the fragile environment; and to provide a resettlement zone for 3,000 farming families from other communal areas. Specifically, the MZRDP was to provide boreholes, schools, clinics, roads, and improved agriculture for all residents—both new and old. Planning documents stated that the valley was so underdeveloped and so many critical aspects of infrastructure were missing that any intervention would be better than none. A land-use study by FAO (Food and Agriculture Organization of the UN) sought to develop an overall plan for the valley anticipating the successful eradication of the tsetse fly by the EEC (European Economic Community) aerial and ground spraying program, and assuming the consequent opening of the valley to livestock with the correlative need for such planning. The consultants did not appreciate the historical legacy of colonial land use planning in Zimbabwe, and the subsequent MZRDP did not receive the requisite standard of design.[3]

Resettlement projects ordinarily fall within the purview of the Department of Rural and Urban Development (DERUDE), in the Ministry of Local Government and Rural and Urban Development (MLGRUD). This department was given primary responsibility for implementing the MZRDP. Most members of DERUDE were trained by the Department of Rural and Urban Planning at the University of Zimbabwe.

The Department of Agricultural Technical and Extension Services (AGRITEX) drew up the project plans in collaboration with DERUDE following the guidelines for an Accelerated Model Resettlement Scheme. This entailed allocating five-hectare arable plots to eligible household heads, setting aside lands for grazing, and resettling and reorganizing the local population into villages organized around boreholes. Using aerial photography, planners identified arable plots for the expected total of 7,600 households, both existing residents and new settlers. The valley's population consisted of long-term residents and more recently settled migrants, particularly from the province of Masvingo in southern Zimbabwe. The planners, however, seriously underestimated the number of resident families (long-term and more recent) living in the project area at only 3,600. By 1987 when the project started, there were already more than 7,600 households residing in the project area. As a result of this miscalculation, the government's objective of providing land for new settlers could not be achieved.

The MZRDP planning process exemplifies the way government and the project related to the proposed beneficiaries. Government planners believed that they possessed a successful model for rural development programs, and, thus, that it was unnecessary to consult with valley residents. This model and process were similar to that used by the Rhodesian colonial state and were so viewed by many valley residents.

The identification of arable, residential, and grazing areas was carried out by AGRITEX, using simple principles: vegetative complexes were used to identify arable areas, grazing areas were demarcated along the rivers, and residential sites were located near the new boreholes. These distinctions did not match those made by valley residents. In particular, the practice of riverain cultivation has long been central to human adaptation and agriculture in the valley. It allows people to have harvests when the rains are poor, a common occurrence in the valley, and when heavy rains damage or destroy a crop, the moist soil of these gardens permits a reliable dry season harvest. Nevertheless, the project disrupted this agro-ecological adaptation by prohibiting stream-bank cultivation, by designating arable areas away from rivers, and by allocating riverain land for grazing. This contemporary planning pattern has its roots in the intersection of conservation, racism, and colonial agricultural policy.[4]

The practice of stream-bank cultivation had long been considered by colonial officers to be one of the major factors promoting erosion, and laws were enacted during the colonial period to prohibit it.[5] The Water Act of 1927 to control use of Zimbabwe's wetlands was reinforced by the Stream Bank Protection Regulation under the 1942 Natural Resources Act, which prohibits cultivation within 100 feet (now thirty meters, but often interpreted as 100 meters) of the normal flow of a stream or wetland. The policies on stream banks and wetlands grew out of studies conducted on the high plateau that were applied nationwide, regardless of ecological variation and river slope.

Colonial policies reflected the view that African knowledge and practices were inimical to progress. The MZRDP planners' attempt to ban riverain cultivation essentially reproduces this view. The MZRDP planners made no attempt to draw on local opinions and knowledge in the design or implementation of the project, although these have had a decided impact on its operation. When the MZRDP was initiated, residents were told that their lands would be demarcated, and that they would get schools, boreholes, clinics, tractors, and electricity. They were not told that the project would decide where they were to live and farm. Indeed, the first action of the project occurred when peggers entered two areas in the valley and began demarcating arable areas. When residents inquired what they were doing, they were told not to ask questions or else they would be arrested. That night all the pegs were pulled out of the ground and placed at district council offices. This act forced representatives of the district councils and project staff to explain the project to valley residents. The most objectionable part of the MZRDP for valley residents has been the effort to ban riverain cultivation, which, despite the colonial laws, had continued in the valley.[6] The prevention of riverain cultivation and the conversion of these most highly valued lands to grazing areas are described by valley residents as "throwing away land." Although everyone tries to obtain access to riverain land, it is usually the long-term residents, often from the most influential families, who own or have use rights to large tracts of riverain land. More recent migrants have acquired only small riverain gardens, and, thus, have had much less of a stake in this issue.

The major cash crop in the valley is cotton cultivated mostly in the uplands, away from the alluvial riverain soils. Although many migrants were able to keep land that was located away from the rivers, those with fields along the rivers were relocated. In addition, wealthier migrants who owned cattle were not as opposed to the project's setting aside riverain areas for grazing as were those without cattle. But those migrants who own relatively large herds of cattle (herds over ten) are few and did not, until very recently, hold local leadership positions such as *sabhukus* (headmen), chairmen of village development committees (VIDCOS), or ward councilors. Even though residents did not and do not speak with one voice, project and AGRITEX personnel, who overwhelmingly come from outside the valley, tend to listen to the wealthier, cotton-growing, cattle-owning families.

On several occasions, farmers and researchers have argued with DERUDE officials, resettlement officers, Natural Resources Board officers and AGRITEX planners against the opinion that stream-bank cultivation causes erosion. In general, officials, planners, and technicians argue that unless valley residents cease this practice, river banks will erode, the rivers will widen, choke with sand, and ultimately stop flowing. When questioned by researchers as to how the erosion process works in the relatively flat valley, the answers the project personnel gave were appropriate to steeply sloped river beds and not to those that characterized most of the valley.

Valley residents exhibited far more nuance in their explanations of why riverain cultivation did not usually cause erosion. They pointed to how their crops and cultivation practices held the soil in place. They described their practices of shifting their fields and the rationale underlying these moves. They identified and recognized erosion as a natural process that could be affected by human action. Although these processes were understood, they were not necessarily acted upon by younger farmers, many of whom were expanding cotton cultivation in riverain fields. Moreover, these younger farmers apply pesticide to their streambed gardens, despite the cautions on pesticide bottles not to use these chemicals near water or fish. Such practices presumably lend weight to project staff's preconceptions about poor farming practices.

The MZRDP's commitment to a blueprint planning approach has made real dialogue among residents, technicians, planners, and other development personnel nearly impossible. The structure of the resettlement program and its shortage of resources (including trained people) make it difficult for project personnel not only to learn from local residents but also to incorporate the results of research that would be relevant to the project. The outcome to date in the Zambezi Valley has been a pattern of serious resistance by valley residents to different aspects of the MZRDP, but especially to the notion of ceasing riverain cultivation.

The Communal Area Management Program for Indigenous Resources (CAMPFIRE)

At the same time that DERUDE was undertaking the Mid-Zambezi Rural Development Project, the Department of National Parks and Wild Life Management (DNPWLM) in the Ministry of Environment and Tourism, in conjunction with various national and international NGOs, was implementing another program, CAMPFIRE, also located in the eastern valley. CAMPFIRE began in the early 1980s with a focus upon the equitable distribution of wildlife revenues. It has since expanded its emphasis to include community-based conservation and development, including land-use planning. In the words of Simon Metcalfe, one of the founders of CAMPFIRE,

> The old protectionist approach [toward wildlife] had been instituted at the turn of the century and reflected the country's colonial legacy. A strategy of linking protected areas [national parks and safari areas] with sustained utilization of wildlife on communal and commercial land ultimately replaced this protectionism. (1994:161)

Initiators of CAMPFIRE responded to different political histories and mandates, and they drew on a different corpus of scientific literature than did the MZRDP planners. CAMPFIRE also relied on a bottom-up approach, which empowered local knowledge, practices, and institutions.

Although CAMPFIRE activities exist in twenty-two districts, the most significant revenue-generating projects are in the Zambezi Valley where communal areas are adjacent to national parks and safari areas. These areas are best known for their wildlife populations but also are characterized by systems of riverain cultivation. Unlike the high veld and the MZRDP, the ban on riverain cultivation has not been enforced in CAMPFIRE areas of the Zambezi River Valley.

In the valley, CAMPFIRE was first established in Nyaminyami (part of Omay Communal Land) followed by the small ward of Kanyurira in Guruve District. To facilitate CAMPFIRE's program, district councils that obtained appropriate authority (see below) were lobbied by DNPWLM, ZimTrust, World Wide Fund for Nature (WWF), Center for Applied Social Sciences at the University of Zimbabwe (CASS) and others to distribute revenues from wildlife to participating communities.[7] The legal context and framework that made this possible were the Parks and Wildlife Act of 1975. This permitted the authority for wildlife resources to be devolved from national government to district councils, but not directly to communities. Subsequently, the Ministry of Local Government and the DNPWLM have permitted authority to be further devolved to the ward level, although this is not yet recognized in legislation.

Although CAMPFIRE principles initially reflected a concern for rights of access to wildlife resources, the program has raised broad issues of representation, participation, and communal area governance. The devolution of rights of access from the central government to rural district councils, and if CAMPFIRE advocates have their way, to wards, has plunged CAMPFIRE into the heart of debates about land use and development.

Riverain cultivation has not been directly included in any of these debates as yet, but the support by CAMPFIRE organizations for communities' rights to determine their own land use means that, unless national policy changes are implemented, confrontations will soon emerge. A locus of potential conflict lies in the Omay Communal Area in the Zambezi Valley, where a land-use planning program is underway that will replicate many of the MZRDP's features.

The contrast between the MZRDP and CAMPFIRE's approach to riverain cultivation can be seen through an examination of Kanyurira Ward, which lies just to the west of the MZRDP. As noted above, the CAMPFIRE program began as a means to return wildlife revenues (primarily from hunting) to local communities. It evolved rapidly, however, from the principle of distributing wildlife revenues to communities themselves to arguing that wildlife resources should be subject to local and not national ownership and management. Indeed, the founders of CAMPFIRE believed that the best means to maintain Zimbabwe's natural resources and biological diversity were to encourage local responsibility and benefit.

In Kanyurira Ward, a national NGO (ZimTrust) and faculty from CASS initiated discussions with local communities. They were supported by DNPWLM, which was interested in changing the nature of its relationship with communities. This relationship previously had been characterized by scientific investigation of wildlife resources and policing of poaching activities. The residents of Kanyurira Ward were primarily concerned about wildlife predation—upon both fields and people. After much discussion, they opted to accept the CAMPFIRE program, and they requested assistance in obtaining protection from the game. The WWF provided technical expertise for the construction of a solar-powered electric game fence to surround their village and fields.

In the discussions that took place, Kanyurira residents were free to say that they wanted to continue cultivating their riverain fields. They were supported in this decision by ecologists, social scientists, and institutional specialists. The local community also decided on the location of the fence and the gates, as well as how they would be maintained. It established rates of pay for residents who would work for CAMPFIRE in addition to deciding how to allocate and spend the wildlife revenues.

The lessons that can be drawn from Kanyurira are open to debate. On the one hand, Kanyurira is an unusual ward. Because it consists of only one village, it has an unusual degree of homogeneity. On the other hand, it represents, on a relatively small scale, all of the critical issues involved in engaging scientists, planners, technicians, and community members in development planning and implementation. For example, the initial distribution of wildlife revenues went to the heads of each household. Two problems emerged from this practice, which were noted by both observers and community members. First, as most heads of household were men, in some cases women did not benefit from the head's decision on how to spend the money. Second, the potential revenues attracted new people to the community. The first problem has been resolved by paying benefits to all adults, rather than to household heads. In this manner, women and men obtain equal access to wildlife revenues although they are all subject to community decision making about how the revenues should be spent. The second issue has led the community to compile a list of all current members. New membership in the community is not restricted, but access to wildlife proceeds will not be given until a new household remains in good standing for five years.

Because of its success, this CAMPFIRE program has been the subject of numerous studies. Kanyurira's internal decision-making processes have been altered by its participation in the program and by this intense scrutiny. How the community copes with such intense interest remains to be seen, and represents another aspect of its ongoing participation in CAMPFIRE. For example, despite external advice,[8] community members decided to purchase a tractor for community use. Their aim was to discourage the purchase of cattle, which could threaten the wildlife program. Kanyurira has decided, at least for the moment, that wildlife is more profitable and compatible with how they want to live than is cattle keeping.

The issue of stream-bank cultivation has not arisen here as the ecologists, biologists, and soil scientists who have worked in Kanyurira, as well as the local residents, do not see that it causes erosion.

In summary, these two case studies of projects that exist side by side in the Zambezi Valley illustrate how very different approaches to development can and do coexist in the same government framework. These different approaches encouraged different types of interactions between project planners and valley residents. Valley residents themselves are acutely aware of the contradictions between these two ap-

proaches to development. Thus, when efforts were made to intro-
duce CAMPFIRE to the MZRDP area by telling residents that they
"owned" the animals, they questioned these assertions, noting that if
they could not determine where they should live or cultivate their
crops, how could they "own" the wildlife? Project and government
personnel have no answers to these questions, and, thus, the development of CAMPFIRE activities within the MZRDP area remain on
hold and are unlikely to proceed.

In the MZRDP, the blueprint style provided little room for local
knowledge or participation of any sort, and it resulted in forms of
local resistance to development familiar in the social science literature. Much of this resistance has centered around the ban on riverain
cultivation. The top-down style adopted by the project planners was
reflected in their unquestioning adoption of the science-based knowledge system regarding the effects of riverain cultivation. These understandings derived from research carried out in the highlands during the colonial era, and they were imbued with the elitism and racism
of the times. As local people were accorded little voice and as project
planners and implementers themselves were strangers to the area,
these views have remained unchallenged, although they are much
resisted.

In contrast, the participatory approach adopted by CAMPFIRE
led to an open-ended process of discussion and change at the local
level stimulated by interactions between local people, on the one hand,
and scientists and project planners, on the other. In this context, residents' views of riverain cultivation were given serious consideration
and, as a consequence, new studies are being undertaken that question the colonial-based knowledge system supporting the uniform
ban on riverain cultivation. Much of this work is being undertaken
by NGOs rather than state-affiliated research departments, pointing
to the significant role that NGOs are now playing in setting research
and development agendas. In this way, also, local peoples have gained
a voice not only in determining the shape of the project in which
they are involved, but also in setting scientific research priorities that
may have far-reaching implications for valley development.

MALAWI

The National Bean Improvement Program

The third case study comes from Malawi, and involves the National Bean Improvement Program and its associated Bean/Cowpea Collaborative Research Support Project (CRSP). Over a fourteen-year period, the project has brought together researchers from the National Bean Improvement Program at Bunda College of Agriculture, on the one hand, and Michigan State University (MSU) and the University of California, Davis, on the other. The case study illustrates how interactions among scientists and between them and farmers have evolved over time in relation to changes in scientific knowledge and methodologies, the salience given to legumes in national development strategies, broad processes of political and economic change in Malawi, and the evolving foci and discourse of development at the national and international levels.

The situation described is, on the surface at least, counterintuitive. In the case of the Malawian National Bean Improvement Program, recent processes of political and economic liberalization, coupled with the promotion of development strategies emphasizing sustainability and participation, have led to less, not more, dialogue between scientists and farmers and among scientists themselves. Economic liberalization, diversification of crop production, and the re-structuring of international and national development organizations have resulted in a tighter integration of the crop into a commodity-based research structure, a process that has reduced opportunities for dialogue among scientists, and between them and farmers.

The following discussion of the changing interactions between farmers and scientists and among scientists themselves is divided into two phases: 1981 to 1988 and 1989 to 1995, periods that correspond to major reorientations of the program's research and development agenda, and that partially overlap with changes in Malawi's political economy.

1981 to 1988: The Early Stages of the Research Process

The Political and Economic Context

Up through the 1980s, the then Life President Dr. Hastings Kamuzu Banda and his Malawi Congress Party kept tight reins on research, especially social science research, that had the potential to reveal the conditions of poverty in which most Malawians lived. Studies of nutritional status and infant mortality, as well as almost any form of political inquiry, were severely restricted.

Much of the agricultural research in the 1980s focused on maize, the basic food staple and an export crop of regional significance, and on tobacco, Malawi's major foreign exchange earner. Beans, a major source of protein in the diet and an important cash generator for many families, received little attention or funding. They were regarded as a subsistence crop of relatively minor importance compared with maize or with other legumes such as groundnuts. In fact, when the National Bean Improvement Program was established in 1969, it was headquartered at the College of Agriculture rather than at one of the Ministry of Agriculture research stations, and it remained there until 1993 when the program was moved to Chitedze Research Station.

The perceived marginal status of beans in the economy and in the Ministry of Agriculture's crop portfolio, coupled with the repressive political climate, had implications for the kinds of research that could be conducted. First, the location of the National Bean Improvement Program at the agricultural college provided some shelter. Social scientists working at the college were not as visible, nor was their work as likely to be scrutinized as those (few) located at Ministry of Agriculture research stations. Second, the focus on a secondary crop such as beans, which was relatively unencumbered with extension messages, had implications for the kinds and quality of information that could be gathered from farmers. Farmers proved more willing to talk freely about their bean production practices than they were to talk about maize, a high-profile crop laden with extension advice and occupying a central place in national research and extension agendas.[9]

In 1981, a collaborative research project was initiated between the National Bean Improvement Program at Bunda College, and Michigan State University under the auspices of the Bean/Cowpea Collaborative Research Support Program (CRSP), funded by USAID.[10] CRSP goals were imbued with the development thinking of the time, which identified the "poorest of the poor," particularly women, as a target population, and which addressed basic human needs. In this scenario, common beans were depicted as a protein- and vitamin-rich crop, produced principally for household consumption, which, with the assistance of production increases brought about through plant breeding, would contribute to the nutritional well-being of farm families and poor urban consumers.

The research goals of the project during the 1981 to 1988 period complemented those of the National Bean Improvement Program. The aim was to understand the role of beans in the different farming systems in Malawi and to develop improved cultivars for these production systems. Scientists were particularly interested in identifying the factors that accounted for farmers' practice of growing numerous local varieties of beans on their small farms. Hence, an initial goal was to identify the full range of forces that accounted for this intravarietal diversity. Once the role of diversity in the different farming systems was better understood, researchers were able to develop a plant improvement strategy that would simultaneously increase national production, maintain diversity, and meet some of the smallholder farmers' other needs.

The original CRSP research team was multidisciplinary, consisting of an agronomist in the Department of Crop Production at Bunda College, a bean breeder from Michigan State University, and a psychologist with expertise in women-in-development, also from MSU. Two Ghanaian postdoctoral students, an agronomist and a sociologist, were hired to assist in the research while Malawians from the college were sent for graduate training in the United States.

The knowledge encounters that occurred among these scientists and between them and Malawian farmers at this point reflected the scientific research methodologies used at the time, as well as the prevailing thinking regarding the process of agricultural technology development.

Relationships Among Scientists

Many of the interactions that occurred among scientists were guided by the farming systems methodologies in use in the early 1980s. In the case of CRSP, although the research team was multidisciplinary, each member had his or her own research agenda related to project objectives. Social science expertise was regarded as particularly useful at certain stages of the investigation—the beginning, or diagnostic stage, and at the end when monitoring impact of the released varieties was required. In the farming systems research of the times, the role of women in agricultural production was particularly salient (Feldstein, Sims, and Poats 1989; Poats, Schmink, and Spring 1988). This became the principal focus of the CRSP social science research.

To understand the distribution of diversity in beans across the country and to identify the factors that accounted for it, project agronomists relied largely on germ plasm collecting trips in the three regions of Malawi. They also grew out and characterized the materials they collected at research sites set up for these purposes in different agro-ecological zones. The bean samples were described according to standard methodologies of the time, involving estimations of outcrossing and of phenotypic variability in features such as days to flower, pod fill and maturity, disease resistance, yield, and the like (Martin and Adams 1987a,b).

The sociologist and psychologist focused especially on documenting the labor input of women in bean production in northern Malawi, relying on interviews conducted over the span of three cropping seasons (Barnes-McConnell 1989). Outside of the short spaces of time when the U.S. researchers visited Malawi, relatively little interaction took place between the agronomists stationed at the college and the sociologist who lived in the northern region.

Scientist–Farmer Interactions

The agronomists came into contact with farmers in the course of their germ plasm collection trips when they sought permission, usually from male household heads, to collect bean samples from fields. The sociologist's interactions with farmers, especially women farmers, were more direct and intensive than those of the biological scientists, but they focused on measuring labor input and not primarily on farmers' local knowledge of bean varieties.

These methodologies and the resultant kinds of interactions that took place among scientists and between them and farmers were considered to be state-of-the-art research at the time. They influenced the study findings themselves and the breeding strategy that emerged from the investigations (Ferguson 1994). Agronomists defined a *landrace* as the totality of beans grown on an individual farm (Ayeh 1988; Martin and Adams 1987a, b). They attributed the bean diversity present on these farms to three processes: (1) naturally occurring out-crossing; (2) adaptation of the materials to their environments; and (3) mechanical, nonselective mixing, which occasionally took place between farms or in markets. Farmers were not regarded as playing a central role in the process of bean varietal selection.[11]

Although the sociological studies involved discussions and interviews with farmers, because these focused on time and labor input studies of farm women's work, they produced little to contradict the interpretation of landraces or the role of farmer selection in the maintenance of diversity put forward by the biological scientists. Indeed, because the sociological and biological studies, although different in orientation, were focused on the level of the farm, little information emerged about the integration of farms into wider market networks or concerning the effects of this integration on farmer selection practices and bean diversity (Ferguson and Mkandawire 1993). The profile that emerged from these studies was one of beans as a heterogeneous subsistence crop grown principally by women for household consumption.

The plant improvement strategy that was developed based on this early research reflected these views. It was premised on breeding and releasing packages of different improved bean varieties mixed together to replace the varieties found on Malawian farms. Although it correctly identified many of the advantages that diversity conferred to smallholders, it did not take into account the role that farmers themselves played through selection in shaping this diversity, and, if implemented, the strategy would have reduced their planting options.

1989 to Present

The Political and Economic Context

By 1988, Malawian scientists sent for graduate training were returning home to take over the direction of the National Bean Improvement Program. At approximately the same time, the Center for International Tropical Agriculture (CIAT)/SADCC Bean Program stationed its regional plant breeder at the agricultural college in Malawi. In addition, new U.S. researchers replaced many of those originally associated with the CRSP project. In 1989, a plant geneticist at the University of California, Davis, became the U.S. principal investigator while an anthropologist (Ferguson) at MSU retained the U.S. social science position.

These changes mirrored others occurring in the agricultural and social sciences. Plant genetics and breeding were undergoing a transformation as the result of new biotechnologies that allowed scientists to characterize and manipulate genetic diversity at the molecular level. In the social sciences, farming systems approaches were giving way to participatory research methodologies described in early work by Chambers, Pacey, and Thrupp (1989).

In Malawi, by the late 1980s, structural adjustment programs (SAPs) were having a profound effect on the economy, as they were elsewhere in the region. Key elements of SAPs included liberalization of marketing and trade, increases in and diversification of export crop production, the removal of subsidies on maize and fertilizers, and the gradual elimination of restrictions on smallholder burley tobacco production, a major export crop (Harrigan 1991). Over the long run, as will be discussed, these changes increased the attention given to beans and other legumes by Ministry of Agriculture officials. Finally, funding cuts in and the downsizing of Ministry of Agriculture programs were accompanied by an increase in the number of national and international NGOs with agricultural programs (Glagow et al. 1997).

In the early 1990s, the Malawian Government came under growing pressure to democratize from citizens themselves and from the international donor community (Chirwa 1994; Kees van Donge 1995). With the end of the Cold War, these organizations redefined their priorities, placing emphasis on "democratization" as essential for the success of SAPs. Between March 1992, when the Catholic bishops issued a scathing episcopal letter criticizing Banda's government for decades of repression, and June 1994, when President Banda and his Malawi Congress Party were defeated in the country's first multiparty election, Malawi underwent profound political change.

Taken as a whole, these transformations had numerous, cumulative effects on the National Bean Improvement Program and its associated projects. Most immediately, the nature of knowledge interactions among scientists and between them and farmers changed. At the same time, as the role of beans and other legumes in the national economy was given more salience, the relationships among policy makers in the Ministry of Agriculture, college-based researchers, and donor organizations funding bean research were reconfigured, with significant implications for knowledge encounters.

Relationships Among Scientists

Relationships among scientists were significantly altered as a result of changes in personnel and their disciplinary foci. A Malawian rural sociologist at Bunda College joined the research team, adding a needed local social science dimension. Although biological research remained centered on diversity issues, the new focus was on characterizing host-pathogen co-adaptation using newly evolving molecular techniques. In essence, in this second phase of the project, much of the research carried out by U.S. biological researchers moved from the field to the laboratory.

While this occurred, the newly returned Malawian scientists remained field and greenhouse oriented as neither the Ministry of Agriculture nor the college had the funds or facilities to support the new research techniques. A division of labor thus arose between the "upstream" or fundamental research carried out at the U.S. university and the applied, field-based studies conducted in Malawi. Malawian scientists were thus increasingly relegated to a second tier of scientific status, as they lacked training in these emerging areas (see Juma 1989 for a similar discussion in another African context). The new division of labor also significantly reduced interactions among these scientists, as researchers increasingly shuttled plant materials back and forth between the United States and Malawi rather than traveling to research sites themselves. Thus, each group had a declining appreciation of the context in which the other worked, a change that had potential implications for varietal development. (In the 1997–2001 extension of the project, to address this issue, Polymerase Chain Reaction (PCR) laboratories are being established at Bunda College and Sokoine University in Tanzania with CRSP funding.)

A similar division of labor did not take place among the project social sciences. Indeed, the newly emerging participatory methodologies, coupled with the changing political climate, encouraged an interactive, field-centered approach bringing Malawian biological scientists, Malawian and U.S. social scientists, and farmers together around common research problems.

Scientist–Farmer Interactions

One of the key unresolved issues, which received attention from 1987 onward, was the role that farmers played in maintaining and shaping the diversity present in the bean crop. Information was gathered using a variety of anthropological and sociological techniques that brought scientists directly into contact with farmers. These included open-ended interviews and focus groups and rapid rural appraisal techniques as well as large-scale surveys. These studies demonstrated that farmers played a central rather than a peripheral role in bean varietal selection. They also revealed that significant gender- and resource-based differences existed among them in their selection practices (Ferguson 1993, 1994; Ferguson and Sprecher 1987). The results led to a reconceptualization of the concept of landraces as it had been defined previously in the project and to a revised plant improvement strategy that recognized the farmers' role in selection and offered them significantly more varietal choice (Ferguson and Sprecher 1990; Ferguson 1991).

Efforts also were made at this stage to institutionalize farmer-researcher contacts and information sharing. This was accomplished by offering short courses on participatory research techniques to scientists and technicians, by bringing farmers on to experimental fields to evaluate early generation materials in research trials, and by instituting farmer-managed on-farm trials for the evaluation of varieties nearing release.[12] These activities showed that the division between farmers' knowledge, on the one hand, and scientific knowledge, on the other, is problematic. Biological researchers, in particular, became increasingly aware of farmers' strategies of experimentation and innovation.

In sum, similar to the early stages of the project, the voice that farmers had in the research process and the kinds of interactions that took place between them and scientists were filtered through the various research methodologies and scientific interests currently in use. By the 1990s, however, these had changed significantly from the methodologies and interests of a decade earlier. As noted above, as molecular techniques developed, U.S. biological scientists retreated from the field to the laboratory, resulting in an emerging division of labor between them and their Malawian counterparts.

In the social sciences, in contrast, participatory strategies gave impetus to efforts to engage farmers directly in the research process. They also fostered closer cooperation among Malawian scientists in different disciplines at the college, as both biological and social scientists took part in these new research activities. This process resulted in the de-construction of the category "smallholder farmer" as scientists became increasingly aware of the differences among these farmers based on resource endowments, gender, market integration, and so on, and as they tried to tailor their research agendas and varietal development to accommodate these differences (Ferguson 1993).

After 1992, the increasingly liberal political climate of Malawi gave added stimulus to these efforts, making it possible to carry out research that was not directly supervised by state officials and that addressed previously off-limit topics such as malnutrition. Although these democratization initiatives created a more positive research environment for the bean program, processes associated with economic liberalization and SAPs have not been so kind.

Beginning in the late 1980s, the place of legumes in the national agricultural research agenda underwent a gradual process of change. Soya beans, common beans, groundnuts, and, to a lesser extent, pigeon peas and cowpeas took on added importance in government and NGO efforts to diversify smallholder production and to increase farm incomes. Beans underwent a metamorphosis in planners' eyes, from the status of a food crop produced primarily by women for household consumption to a potentially lucrative male cash crop, even though beans have long been an important cash crop as well as a food crop (Ferguson 1987). Declines in smallholder use of fertilizers as a result of the removal of subsidies also functioned to increase the profile and profitability of legumes. Recent studies also have increased the environmental profile of legumes as they indicate that working residues of these crops into fields represents a promising, low-cost, sustainable way to improve soil characteristics and fertility (Kumwenda et al. 1995; Snapp 1995).

In 1994, the heightened value of beans in the national agricultural research agenda, coupled with pressure from powerful donors, resulted in the transfer of the National Bean Improvement Program from the college to one of the Ministry of Agriculture research stations. The British Overseas Development Agency agreed to support the financially faltering regional CIAT program and to provide funds for bean research in Malawi if the National Bean Improvement Program was moved to Chitedze Research Station to bring it more in line with other commodity research efforts. The ministry agreed, despite the fact that a full array of biological and social scientists trained in bean research existed only at the college and it lacked funding to hire the necessary ministry staff for the relocated program.[13]

Although scientists at the college had attempted to develop a bean improvement strategy that recognized smallholders' diverse cash and food needs, the new bean program at the research station, in line with their view of the crop more exclusively as a commodity, placed emphasis principally on increasing yield through breeding for disease resistance and low soil phosphorus.

The composition of the new National Bean Improvement Program staff reflected this narrowing of interests. In contrast to the college program, which consisted of a multidisciplinary team of Ph.D.-level personnel in plant breeding, pathology, physiology, seed technology, agricultural economics, sociology, and food science, it consisted of an expatriate CIAT bean breeder supported by the British Overseas Development Authority (ODA), a Malawian plant breeder, and a part-time B.S.-level pathologist. As the Ministry of Agriculture has few social scientists on its staff, an expatriate social scientist was also hired on a two-year ODA contract. His research role is tangential to the plant breeding improvement program itself. Interviews with the CIAT/ODA plant breeder and the head of the National Bean Improvement Program in 1995 indicated little perceived need for sustained farmer input, and a role for the expatriate social scientist reminiscent of that described above for the early 1980s.[14]

In summary, this longitudinal case study calls attention to how knowledge encounters are partially constituted by interactions that take place between the research context and the wider political economy. In the case of beans in Malawi, recent processes of economic liberalization are furthering the commercialization of the bean crop and promoting its integration into a commodity-based research structure where relatively little dialogue occurs among agricultural and social scientists or between them and farmers. In the second Malawian case study, which follows, similar macrolevel processes of development and change have resulted in quite different knowledge encounter outcomes.

Fisheries Development on Lake Malawi/Nyasa[15]

As the dominant water body, Lake Malawi has always held an important place in development thinking and practice in the country. Until the 1990s, most studies focused on its fish populations. Little was known about fishers and little differentiation was recognized among them. They figured in fisheries planners' agendas only tangentially, as entities to be regulated and controlled to prevent them from depleting the fish stocks and from threatening the lake's biodiversity. Fishers and fishing communities fully entered the planning arena only as the effects of economic and political liberalization became more apparent in the early 1990s, and then principally as a consequence of the failure of development—that is, after the Fisheries Department recognized its policies of surveillance, regulation, and outreach were failing. This section considers relations among scientists and between them and fishing people in two different periods of Malawi's history: from independence in 1964 to 1991, and from 1992 through 1995.

The 1964 to 1991 Period

Following independence in 1964, fishing policy and regulation were designed and implemented by the Fisheries Department (FD). This department, although receiving some government funding, came to rely heavily on external donor support. It also depended heavily on expatriate fish biologists, economists, and other scientists who dominated the scientific and development agenda. Indeed, relatively few Malawians received advanced graduate training in relevant disciplines during this period. The model developed for interdisciplinary work on Lake Chilwa was not adopted for Lake Malawi. One of the earliest studies undertaken of a lake in Malawi was the Lake Chilwa Research Project.[16]

The development agenda within the FD was influenced, in part, by research in evolutionary biology and speciation that revealed that Lake Malawi contained perhaps the greatest cichlid diversity in the world. Thus, even before independence, the effects of overfishing on the conservation of fish stocks and diversity were an issue for FD personnel. Coupled with this concern with conservation was a modernist orientation that assumed that larger-scale fishing operations would "develop" the fishing industry for the benefit of the country while at the same time prove easier to regulate than small-scale fishing operations. One of the early postindependence projects (1972) underwritten by the United Nations Development Program (UNDP) formulated this notion and established the classification of fishers and the fisheries that remains the dominant framework used in Malawi today. The UNDP recognized three categories of fishers: commercial, semicommercial, and subsistence or artisanal. In so doing it reinforced existing views of most African fishers as noncommercial and subsistence oriented.[17] It also introduced the notion that these different kinds of fishers exploited different fisheries stocks and thus co-existed on the lake rather than competed with one other.

Small-scale fishers entered more fully into the FD research agenda via the Traditional Fisheries Assessment Project initially funded by FAO and then by ODA. This project, which began in 1976, was intended to provide a continuous stream of statistical information on the catches and species variation in different sections of the lake. More recently, this information-gathering system was criticized by the FAO Chambo Fisheries Project (1988–1992), which proposed a new gear-based computerized data system termed, without irony, the Malawi Traditional Fisheries System. Both data-gathering techniques were designed without any input from fishers, and the results produced from these surveys are not communicated back to them.

Because of the scale of the lake and the paucity of national funds and trained personnel, even with donor assistance, the FD was unable to maintain many of its basic functions during the mid to late 1980s. This crisis only deepened with the general fiscal crisis of the state and the reductions in donor funding in the early 1990s that were instituted as a means to end Banda's authoritarian regime. For example, although the Fisheries Act of the Laws of Malawi provides the framework for regulating gear and licensing and for imposing minimum allowable catch sizes and closed seasons for particular fish species, the FD lacked the funds, staff, and boats needed to enforce these regulations among artisanal semicommercial or commercial fishers. Indeed, to raise funds for its operations, the FD engaged in fishing itself, at times circumventing its own regulations. The extension arm of the FD faced similar constraints. When we first began our research in 1989, FD personnel and fishers all agreed that the few extension messages that existed were outdated, and that, because of lack of personnel, funds, and means of transport, FD extension staff had virtually no presence in fishing villages.

During the 1964 to 1991 period, knowledge was envisioned as flowing only in one direction: from FD researchers and extension agents to fishers and fishing communities. Neither the FD nor its donors envisioned a dialogue among FD personnel, scientists, and fishers. In this regard, fisheries research and extension had remained immune from farming systems research methodologies and the emerging participatory research strategies of the time as well as from the growing literature on the management of common property resources.[18] Although it would be tempting to blame this state of affairs on the authoritarian regime of President Banda, the situation is more complicated. The FD was not politically blocked from engaging in farming systems style research (which was, indeed, being carried out by the International Center for Living Aquatic Resource Management in Malawi). Rather, modernist views of development, coupled with a conservation focus that provided no place for input from fishers or social scientists, together with low levels of funding and staffing all played a role in shaping research agendas and modes of operation of the time.

The 1992 to 1995 Period

The Chambo Fisheries Project (1987–1992) marks a turning point in the FD's relationship with fishing communities. The project documented a major shift in the species composition of Lake Malombe, a lake connected to Lake Malawi by the upper Shire River. Its research findings chronicled the crash of chambo stocks in Lake Malombe and suggested that these stocks were seriously depleted in the southeast arm of Lake Malawi as well.

For the first time, a socioeconomist was engaged on a major fish study. She and her co-researchers began serving as a vehicle through which fishers' voices could be heard in the Chambo Project as well as in FD planning and policy making. These alternative voices led to strong differences of opinion within the project and the department itself concerning priorities. These differences could be summarized in the question of who should come first, the chambo or the people who depended on the fisheries for their livelihood. The fisheries biologists' focus on fish stocks led them to seek solutions to the crisis that would have seriously harmed fishing communities.

The Chambo Project, in close consultation with the FD, decided that the only way to cope with the collapse of the Malombe chambo fishery was to reduce fishing pressure through changing the behavior of fishers and fishing communities. At first, the FD proposed a total ban on specific kinds of equipment. As it had been unable to enforce its regulations in the past, however, the department also recognized the need to examine a wider range of alternatives. In a study designed to consider some of these options, Bell and Donda (1993) gathered detailed information from fishers about their understandings of the Malombe crisis and the actions they were willing to undertake to address it.

In light of these findings, the FD revised its plans, opting to take fishers' understandings of the crisis into account in devising a new management strategy. It was assisted in this decision by the Malawi and German Fisheries and Aquaculture Development Project (MAGFAD). MAGFAD agreed to fund community development officers, to implement a program to form village-level beach committees to help monitor and regulate fishing effort, and to establish a fund to make loans available to fishers to purchase nets with larger mesh sizes.

In sum, the collapse of the chambo fishery on Lake Malombe was an important step in redefining the relationship between scientists and planners within the FD and between them and fishing people. It has resulted in the formation of a Participatory Fisheries Management Program, which the FD describes as

> …an awareness raising campaign to enable the fishing communities around Lake Malombe and the Upper Shire River to understand the long term implications of over fishing. The programme concentrates on extension and education through the fora of newly formed community level institutions and by supporting fishermen to adopt sustainable harvesting techniques through the provision of limited financial support. (FD Planning, Monitoring and Evaluation Unit 1994:2)

Although this statement suggests a strong privileging of the knowledge base of scientists and planners, it marks initial efforts to open a discussion with fishers.

This new initiative has garnered support from numerous donors, including the World Bank, Deutsche Gesellschaft für Technische Zusammenarbeit GmbH (GTZ), ODA, and UNDP/FAO. Its aim is to establish beach village committees that will have a voice in setting regulations as well as a role in enforcement activities. At this time, it is too early to assess the success of this initiative.[19] It is clear, though, that the creation of these intermediary institutions was not possible under the former one-party state. It is only in the new political climate that they become imaginable.

The FAO Chambo Project findings also raised questions about a number of other FD assumptions. By suggesting that artisanal, semicommercial, and commercial fishers in many cases competed for the same fish stocks, it dealt a blow to the notion that these sectors were independent from one another. The results also suggested that the developmental hopes pinned to expansion of the commercial and semicommercial fishing operations in the southeast and southwest arms of the lake were misplaced, as most of the stocks there were likely to be at or nearing optimal harvesting. This raised serious questions about the World Bank Malawi Fisheries Development Project funded in 1992, with the goals of setting the fisheries development agenda until well into the next century (Ferguson, Derman, and Mkandawire 1991). One of the aims of this project was to revitalize the Malawi Development Company (MALDECO), Malawi's only commercial fishing company, which was owned in large part by President Banda. Although this project was subsequently canceled, this did not occur until after the MALDECO facilities and fleet had been significantly upgraded.

Although the Chambo Project initiated a continuing process of re-evaluation in the FD, social change even within the context of a single department does not take a single direction, nor do all the actors necessarily agree on the same strategy. At the same time as the FD has embarked on this experiment in co-management, it has also undertaken two other projects that demonstrate strong continuities with past styles.[20] The first was the United Kingdom/Southern Africa Development Committee Pelagic Fish Resource Assessment Project (known as UK/SADC Lake Project) and the second is the Global Environmental Facilities Project (GEF) to conserve Lake Malawi's biological diversity.

The UK/SADC Lake Project was the first regional study involving Malawi, Mozambique, and Tanzania. This investigation, like most others, involved no social scientists but engaged water chemists, limnologists, fish biologists, acoustical survey experts, and so on, utilizing a new research vessel and superior laboratory facilities. Its purpose was to discover the extent of pelagic resources in Lake Malawi and, if any new fisheries were found, to recommend ways to exploit them. For example, the species that they expected to find, *Engraulicypris sardella* (*usipa*), was not present in the open waters but *Diplotaxodon, Rhamphochromis,* and *Bathyclarias* were found to be fairly abundant, if in unknown numbers. The ODA fisheries economist assigned to the FD argues that, if these stocks prove commercially exploitable, the "artisanal" sector should be given preferential access if possible.[21]

The second major project that shows strong continuity with past development styles is the GEF project for the conservation of the Lake Malawi's biological diversity.[22] This project, funded by the World Bank through the United Nations Environment Program, reflects a continuation of concerns raised in the 1930s about the ecological health of Lake Malawi. It will carry out basic biological research, teach Malawians about the value of biological diversity in their lake, and improve tourist facilities at Lake Malawi National Park. Ironically, part of what the GEF proposes to do is to study the impact of the commercial trawl fishery on biodiversity. As noted above, the commercial trawl fishery—MALDECO—just underwent expansion and renovation with funds from the World Bank Fisheries Development Project! Despite the growing emphasis placed on participation, there appears to be little place for fishers' voices and knowledge in the GEF, at least as the project is currently described. As far as can be determined, no efforts are being made to study and build on what fishing people themselves understand about the value of diversity of fish species. Rather, current plans are to hire a South African theater troupe to devise messages to educate local people about diversity.

Fishers' knowledge, in both its distribution and its variation, remains unknown and underutilized by the FD. In a consultancy carried out for the Fisheries Research and Management Support Project, Quan identified fishers' knowledge as one of the five priority areas for future research. He states:

> There is no research which seeks to compile, understand or corroborate fishermen's indigenous knowledge of water bodies, fish species, fishing techniques and operations etc. although some insights on fishermen's knowledge and views are scattered throughout the literature. (1993:19)

The balance between seeking this understanding, creating the mechanisms to hear different voices, and rapidly implementing management controls will not be easily negotiated, particularly in a setting where local institutions have been suppressed and where local knowledge has been devalued for more than a generation. The pressure to use fishing communities to act as policing agents for the FD will be strong. In a recent assessment of directions for the FD, Bland and Donda conclude:

> Effective resource management must involve the fishing communities, the current open-access nature of small-scale fisheries in Malawi must change to a limited access regime and this change must occur in parallel with the development of alternative income earning opportunities for lakeshore communities. Therefore, new approaches to fisheries resource management by encouraging greater community or user participation are being developed alongside the promotion of alternative economic alternatives. (1995:11)

Their perspective redefines fisheries management as the management of people rather than fish. It tries to balance the enforcement of laws and regulations with the real situation of those who depend on the fisheries for their livelihood. How these different knowledge bases and interests interact will be determined by the FD's capacity to adopt a management style that creatively melds together scientific findings and understandings with fishers' knowledge and ideas concerning fish management.

The attainment of these objectives will not be easy, as the FD is not the only player on the lake. The interests of fishers and the FD have often had to take a back seat to other national development priorities. For example, an immediate challenge is posed by the development of the tourist industry, which is rapidly alienating lake-front property from fishing communities (see Ferguson, Derman, and Mkandawire 1993). Clearly, the FD must also successfully represent and defend fishers' interests in the broader national context.[23]

An important point in the evolution of the FD came in 1996, when the FD's major donor organization ODA withdrew its support. The establishment of the Fisheries Planning, Monitoring and Evaluation Unit was funded by ODA. The ODA fisheries economist has been at the core of reassessing the objectives of the department. It is unclear whether the FD will continue in its new mode or how the new economic and political context will shape its strategies.

With the demise of the one-party state and the fragile transition to democracy in Malawi, the terms of debate and action have changed. On the one hand, for some citizens, democracy has meant the removal of state constraints on natural resource use. On the other hand, the government increasingly has sought to give communities some role in managing their resources. The FD is caught up in and reflects this state of transition. Although it fosters community participation and involvement in the management of the fisheries, it still attempts to set the terms and arenas of this participation. Thus, an uneasy tension exists within the department. It promotes community engagement and participation in enforcement activities while at the same time it is less willing to give fishers an expanded voice in setting the research and management agendas.

CONCLUSIONS

Four development interventions have been examined with particular emphasis upon the following intertwined dimensions: (1) the changing use and practice of science, including the social sciences; (2) the relationship of the interventions to the wider political economy including government policies; (3) the form and nature of the proposed beneficiaries' participation; and (4) the kind of development envisaged by the scientists, planners, and governments involved. The studies demonstrate how development intervention changed over time in response to changes in science, new perspectives about what constitutes development, alternative views on implementing development projects, and transformations in the wider political economy. Different models of science, development, and participation existed simultaneously within a relatively small region of southern Africa. Of the four development sites, only one, the Mid-Zambezi Rural Development Project, was relatively unaffected by the changes just cited and remains an example of older styles of development thinking co-existing with other models.

In general, a dramatic shift has occurred in thinking among governments, donors, and researchers about how rural people should be incorporated into development processes and projects in southern Africa. Rural peoples are now regarded as knowledgeable agents in three of the four projects. However, this shift, from encountering rural residents as passive recipients of scientific and developmental knowledge and practice to incorporating them as knowledgeable and active subjects, will vary by context. As our cases demonstrate, change proceeds in different directions and responds to new systems of knowledge and power, thus making conclusions about successful transitions problematic. For example, processes that lead to the incorporation of women farmers into bean-growing strategies may be reversed, as the Malawi CRSP case study suggests. In the case of Lake Malawi, it is quite possible that providing greater voice and participation to small-scale fishers in the management of the fisheries will be beyond the capacity and interest of the FD. CAMPFIRE, which has been so successful in its participatory and multilayered approach, could unravel from any number of different directions. This includes the possibility that higher levels of government will attempt to capture resources now going to local communities; or that the NGO coordinating CAMPFIRE activities, the Campfire Association, could become disconnected from its constituencies; or that local communities could opt for agricultural and livestock options rather than wildlife ones. These possibilities are, of course, not mutually exclusive, but point to the program's contingency and the importance of agency.

In terms of more general development objectives, the four programs examined all have *sustainable development* as their goal. Sustainable development is, in our view, a process, and perhaps a new vision of learning. Certainly there is little agreement concerning its definition among the central players in the process. The case studies also suggest that scientific and local knowledge systems have permeable boundaries, with information and practices interpreted and appropriated by different social actors (Long and Long 1992). In all cases, it is clear that the interaction among diverse bodies of knowledge takes place in a politicized arena—one in which some actors and knowledge bases are more empowered and/or have greater legitimacy than do others.

Nonetheless, these studies suggest the new kinds of science and development that may emerge. For example, the vision of science and development being advocated by CAMPFIRE could be called *civic science* as the term has been used by Lee (1993). Civic science remains open to learning from multiple sources, not just from science. It recognizes that politics is inherent to all decisions about science. Civic science, in Lee's view, attempts to inject into politics the idea that decisions must make sense in biologically significant time frames. To this perspective, we would add Long's emphasis upon human agency. He contends that individuals and social groups are

> within the limits of their information and resources and uncertainties they face, 'knowledgeable' and 'capable'; that is they devise ways of solving 'problematic situations,' and thus actively engage in constructing their own social worlds, even if this means being 'active accomplices' to their own subordination. Hence the life-worlds of individuals are not preordained for them by the logic of capital or by the intervention of the state, as is sometimes implied in theories of development. (1992:33)

Thus, three of the cases presented here are examples of partially decentralized political and scientific activity and changes in policy. Even if small, these changes reflect alterations in understandings and actions brought about by the melding of different knowledge bases. Whereas Escobar argues that development operates in a hegemonic fashion, others like Long point to its contingent character. We find that emphasizing contingency in the context of the wider political economy and competing paradigms of knowledge is a fruitful perspective in comprehending development encounters.

NOTES

1. For a more detailed description of the Mid-Zambezi Valley Rural Development Project, see Derman (1997a,b). There is a large literature on the CAMPFIRE program. See Child (1995), Metcalfe (1994), and Murphree (1993, 1997).

2. For the complex land question in Zimbabwe, see Bratton (1994), Moyo (1995), and Roth (1994).

3. See the Food and Agriculture Organization of the United Nations (1990) and the African Development Fund (1986).

4. For a detailed consideration of the continuities between colonial and postcolonial planning, see Derman (1997b); Drinkwater (1991, 1992), and Scoones (1996).

5. Government planners relied upon the results of the controversial scientific findings of agricultural research during the 1930s and 1940s, which blamed only African cultivators for land degradation without examining the consequences of land alienation, and the policies of permanent cultivation using hybrid maize and tobacco promoted by the Department of Agriculture itself.

6. Stream-bank or riverain cultivation in this area is not a single practice. It encompasses both rainy and dry season cultivation, and it involves the cultivation of current river beds and former river beds as well as the use of stream banks. Rainy season areas of cultivation are referred to as *fields*; the dry season areas are termed *gardens*, especially when they are small in size. Rainy season crops include maize with smaller areas of sorghum, squash and pumpkins, and, increasingly, cotton. In the dry season, farmers cultivate maize, sweet potatoes, and a range of vegetables for sale and household use. Depending on the depth of ground water, most gardens are now hand-irrigated during the long dry season.

7. The intellectual underpinnings have been best expressed by Murphree (1993). He enunciates a set of principles that emphasize the importance of maintaining units of proprietorship at a scale as small as possible; allowing those who receive direct benefits from managed natural resources to do the actual management and increasing the benefits that flow to those who improve the quality of that management. Communities adjacent to or living with wildlife are referred to as *producer communities*. They are the ones, according to CAMPFIRE advocates, who should receive most of the benefits because this enhances management and lessens the very real costs of living with wildlife.

8. This advice was provided by World Wide Fund for Nature—Zimbabwe and individuals from nongovernmental organizations working with CAMPFIRE. They argued on the basis of experiences throughout Zimba-

bwe and in the eastern Zambezi Valley with the Lower Guruve Development Association that tractors were always a drain on resources and never succeeded in generating sufficient revenues to cover their operating costs over the longer term. The villagers rejected their arguments and purchased the tractor.

9. In the mid-1980s, it was difficult to interview farmers without the presence of a Ministry of Agriculture extension agent. As this agent had no messages to convey regarding beans, farmers could speak more freely about varietal selection and production practices than they could about maize, a crop with strong extension messages that the majority of farmers ignored.

10. In contrast to USAID's short-term technical assistance projects, CRSP's represent a long-term agency commitment to agricultural research, usually focusing on food crops, domesticated animals, or production constraints neglected by national agricultural research organizations.

11. For example, in discussing the heterogeneity of a landrace, Martin and Adams (1987b:201) noted, "Overall, though, Malawian farmers simply may not care if their landrace is uniform for size; they appear to apply very little selection for other traits either."

12. Some of these techniques have proven more successful than others in the context of a university-based research program. Rapid appraisal techniques, focus groups, and farmer-managed on-farm trials have been easier to institute than bringing farmers onto the research plots to evaluate materials. The latter requires sustained labor and time input on the part of researchers and technicians. As teaching loads are demanding and funding for technicians to staff these efforts limited, it has proven difficult to institute a full-fledged participatory breeding program.

13. In 1992, the CIAT/SADCC Bean Program lost its CIDA funding. To retain a presence in the region, CIAT linked up with ODA, which was willing to provide funding for the regional CIAT plant breeder stationed at Bunda College. The CIAT breeder, supported by ODA, lobbied for the relocation of the National Bean Improvement Program, arguing that other commodity-based programs were located at national agricultural research stations and more rapid breeding progress could be achieved in this context with full-time personnel compared with the college environment where faculty members had teaching in addition to research responsibilities. ODA agreed to provide initial limited funding for the new National Bean Improvement Program if its headquarters were to be at the research station. As a large portion of the new research funds goes to support the CIAT breeder's salary and regional travel, and as the Ministry of Agriculture, similar to other government agencies, has been under pressure to decrease its staff, the new national program is inadequately staffed. The funds, how-

ever, go directly to the ministry rather than to the college, as is the case with the CRSP project.

14. The bean program at the college, supported by funding from the CRSP project, continues to carry out multidisciplinary research. Its relationship with the new National Bean Improvement Program remains ill-defined.

15. The lake is known as "Malawi" in Malawi, "Nyasa" in Tanzania, and "Niassa" in Mozambique. For brevity's sake we simply refer to it as "Lake Malawi."

16. This project was multidisciplinary in nature, involving biological and social sciences. In addition to the UNDP project, a long-term project (1975–1986) with Rhodes University of South Africa was carried out to study Lake Malawi's ornamental or aquarium fish. It focused principally on the study of cichlids in what is now Lake Malawi National Park. Similar studies have been conducted by U.S. scientists Kenneth McKaye and Jay Stauffer, who did pioneering work on cichlid territoriality, speciation, and taxonomy. Although hundreds of publications have resulted from these studies, very few of them have involved Malawian scientists. In general, the FD has felt that it has not had the resources to monitor either the researchers or the aquarium trade. This is significant because of the large business in tropical fish that emanates from the lake and that is currently controlled by one individual.

17. In more recent categorizations, subsistence fishers have been subsumed under the artisanal or traditional category, and a third group of semicommercial fishers has been recognized. For a discussion of the bias that is introduced into Malawi's recent fisheries development efforts through the use of this categorization see Ferguson, Derman, and Mkandawire (1991).

18. Two consultancies have recently been completed that summarize past results and make recommendations for future strategies. These are G.W. Coulter's report "Fisheries Research Strategies" (1993) and "Socio-Economic Research Strategies" by J. Quan (1993). Both Coulter and Quan were consultants hired by the ODA/Fisheries Research and Management Support Project.

19. For example, the FD and donors incorrectly assume that beaches and fishing communities are undifferentiated entities. We found in our research, however, that there is a marked divergence of interest between crew members and craft owners although they are both regarded as fishers. For an elaboration of this perspective see Ferguson, Derman, and Mkandawire (1993).

20. We will not discuss the World Bank Fisheries Development Project, which we have already have analyzed (Ferguson, Derman, and Mkandawire 1991). The project itself keeps on shifting, attempting to incorporate new research results and changing priorities within Malawi. The two constants are the purchase of a new trawler for MALDECO, the largest fishing company on Lake Malawi, and the construction of a new headquarters for the FD.

21. His comments can be found in the Official Minutes of the Fisheries Department Research Strategy Meeting, 1993 (p. 12).

22. The project is described in Thurairaja (1993), although it has changed somewhat since then. Its funding has also been reduced.

23. An example of a successful effort to block a potentially destructive project was the alliance of the FD, national parks, the World Bank, and the WWF to prevent the construction of a huge hotel and casino at the heart of Lake Malawi National Park (Derman and Ferguson 1995).

8 Developing International Health Science Research: Measuring or Marginalizing Quality?

James A. Trostle

Those who take the various subjects of knowledge from city to city, and offer them for sale retail to whoever wants them, commend everything that they have for sale; but it may be, my dear Hippocrates, that some of these men also are ignorant of the beneficial or harmful effects on the soul of what they have for sale, and so too are those who buy from them, unless one of them happens to be a physician of the soul.

(Socrates, to Hippocrates son of Apollodorus, in Plato's *Protagoras*, section 313D (Plato 1956:44)).

INTRODUCTION

The scientific method and the craft of doing scientific research have spread worldwide, both as forms of inquiry and as forms of communication. Despite this worldwide dominion, notions of success and quality, and even strategies to undertake research, develop differently in different contexts. Local technical knowledge and local institutional incentives are therefore highly relevant to the practice of biomedical research, even though such research is thought—by most of its practitioners—to be transnational, value free, and culturally neutral. What would happen if, like a physician of the soul, we were to ask about the beneficial and harmful effects of a subject of knowledge called international biomedical research? This would seem to be a prototypical form of knowledge taken from city to city and offered for sale.

Examining biomedical research in non-Western settings offers an opportunity to highlight the presence and importance of the different notions, practices, and incentives relevant to biomedical research. The process of supporting international biomedical research, especially applied research, has its own forms of development knowledge, processes for creating and transmitting that knowledge, and rhetoric about expertise and quality. Agrawal (1995), among others, has argued forcefully against dichotomizing knowledge into those forms labeled indigenous or local ("ethno"astronomy, or "ethno"botany) and those variously labeled as scientific, orthodox, or international. This chapter presents international biomedical research as a borderland where culture and experience influence scientific knowledge.

Those who study the social aspects of Western science should pay more attention to which scientific projects are allowed to emerge, in addition to how scientific knowledge is produced and how knowledge is made convincing. This emphasis is important to studies of knowledge creation and diffusion because recent work on knowledge creation in science has tended to focus on producing and disseminating scientific results. A recent paper on the sociology of scientific knowledge (SSK) in the *Annual Review of Sociology* put it this way: "The 'rhetorical turn' in SSK has now yielded a large body of empirical work on the techniques of scientific exposition—the textual and informal means by which scientists labor to persuade others, to extend experience from private to public domains, to assure others of their disinterestedness, to assert the significance of their claims, to argue that their body of knowledge is indeed 'scientific'" (Shapin 1995:305). In this chapter, I extend this insight to original applications for scientific funding that allow claims to be given a chance to emerge in the first place. Decisions about what constitutes convincing scientific evidence are made not only when results are produced and distributed, but also at the very first stages of searching for financial and technical support to allow study to proceed.

BIOMEDICAL RESEARCH PRACTICES AS CULTURAL CONSTRUCTS

To facilitate crosscultural comparisons of different scientific traditions, anthropologists have defined science as "a body of knowledge distinguishable from other knowledge by specific methods of validation" (Nader 1996:1); or as including "(1) the formulation of one's knowledge of the world in abstract and conceptual form; and (2) empirical verification and intersubjective validation of that knowledge" (Obeyesekere 1992:161). Seen in this way, biomedical research practices are scientific because of the methods of empirical verification they use, not because of the form in which findings are presented. Some components of intersubjective validation commonly associated with biomedical research include publication of results, peer review of manuscripts, a certain distanced voice in writing, and reference to related research.

Each of these has cultural influences. For example, judging quality of manuscripts on the size or currency of their literature review invokes cultural tradition rather than objective standards (see, e.g., Kelly 1993). In similar fashion, publication in peer-reviewed journals is an important component of dissemination and validation of scientific research, yet the Association of American Universities and the Association of Research Libraries have written that, "For the faculty of a university or college, the act of publication constitutes what many have termed a 'gift exchange' among the community of devotees bound by a common interest; the giving of such gifts is intended to win the regard of other members of the community" (Zemsky 1998:2–3). North American reliance on publication quantity to measure scientific worth seems increasingly open to question, if only because its usefulness as an indicator diminishes given reduced ability by libraries to purchase journals in quantity.

Thus, because of the important role publications play in gift exchange, North American libraries are, for the first time, confronting a challenge present for decades—though at a very different scale—to libraries in developing countries: how to pay for publications? But if publication through supposedly cheaper and more accessible sources such as the World Wide Web is the next objective, does that not put developing country scientists and libraries even further behind? After all, publication on the web is only cheap for those who have computers, software, modems, reliable electricity, and knowledge about how to maintain them. Donors and technical consultants often, despite their best intentions, reproduce many of the weaknesses and foibles of "overdeveloped" models of scientific production and performance. Using foreign yet putatively objective standards of assessment, they label—sometimes unwittingly—work from different scientific traditions as "low quality." This process can marginalize innovation in the guise of measuring its worth. This chapter explores some of the ways local innovation was presented to, and dealt with by, a large international health research project.

DEVELOPMENT KNOWLEDGE AT THE ADDR PROJECT

I am interested in the topic of science development because of my former work in a large international applied health research project called the Applied Diarrheal Disease Research Project (ADDR).[1] ADDR supported research on diarrheal diseases and respiratory infections, the leading preventable causes of infant mortality in most impoverished environments. It funded research proposals written by scientists in developing countries and provided technical assistance by sending foreign experts to work with local scientists; organized local workshops on proposal development, data analysis, or writing; and sponsored topical conferences and literature reviews. The project had two primary goals: to help produce high-quality applied research results, and to build local research capacity to evaluate and contribute to solving local or international priority health issues. As written in an early project report, ADDR "is an example of an attempt to systematically stimulate the growth of indigenous scientific capabilities in developing countries. There is extensive literature and experience dealing with the processes of technological transfer, but relatively little analytical attention has been given to the transfer, or indigenous growth, of scientific research capacity, except in the area of food production" (ADDR 1988:1).

ADDR and other similar projects (the BOSTID project [Greene 1991]; INCLEN [Higginbotham 1992]; and WHO/TDR [Vlassoff and Manderson 1994]) developed at about the same time.[2] All these projects were designed with the assumption that it was both possible and necessary to increase indigenous capacity to undertake scientific research. Nonetheless, this capacity-strengthening approach (see Trostle et al. 1997) can be distinguished from a participatory research strategy like that advocated by Robert Chambers (1997) or Norman Uphoff (1992). In the capacity-strengthening approach, local resources are identified according to external standards, and "built" or "strengthened" using external resources. The participatory approach identifies local resources through a combination of local and external resources, and (often, but not always) uses those local resources in new configurations to strengthen local capacity. In part, the difference here between these techniques of knowledge acquisition can be reduced to a classic opposition between distancing and participatory strategies (Tambiah 1990).

Between its start in September 1985 and its official end in May 1996, ADDR had spent about $17 million from USAID on financial and technical assistance to 158 health research projects in seventeen countries. These funds supported about 360 principal or co-investigators who worked full- or part-time on these studies, and an additional 1,000 other scientific and technical personnel who collected and analyzed data for periods from one up to three years. The funds also paid salaries of approximately four full-time equivalent scientists and managers and three administrative staff at HIID in Cambridge; two professionals who worked for one or two years as resident advisers; another two scientists who worked part-time for the project in subcontracting U.S. universities; and more than 100 U.S. and foreign consultants who were employed by ADDR for periods ranging from a few days to a few months. These consultants usually worked directly with funded scientists outside the United States, either in workshop settings or at their home institutions.

Though one of ADDR's goals was to produce high-quality research, not all the work it sponsored broke new scientific ground and, in fact, some was pedestrian. Rather than being designed only to be published in scientific journals, some was done primarily to influence local decision makers, or to enable scientists to learn and practice new research techniques. As reported in the project's final annual report, more than half of the funded research studies published at least one scientific paper, and another 40 percent were completed but not yet published (ADDR 1996:vii).

But some of the project's research did contain innovative science. ADDR-funded scientists developed new public health interventions, tested new methods, and produced new and important descriptive data drawing attention to health problems. Between 1988 and 1996, in addition to making grants and providing technical support, ADDR staff themselves inquired about the impediments to following a career in health research in developing countries, the structural constraints that prevented local capacity from being built or sustained, and the constraints that prevented donors from developing more effective programs (see, for example, Henry 1994; Trostle 1992; Trostle and Simon 1992; Trostle et al. 1997). For these reasons, the project provides interesting case material for a discussion about knowledge in development sites.

The following discussion is divided into sections stressing the conditions of research and the content and methods of research undertaken by ADDR scientists.

Conditions of Research

Funding biomedical researchers in developing countries could be called development work among local elites. But the formation, growth, and sustainability of professional elites varies in different cultures. Even the classic definition of a *profession* (an independent, self-regulating, privately organized group, operating under some accepted code of conduct) needs adjustment. In some contexts, particularly where there are legitimate alternatives to professionally based services (Janzen 1978), or where there is an oversupply, professions have lower status and are relatively dependent on the state. This is particularly true of clinicians. The international evidence still supports theorists from the early 1970s who saw professions as a mean to control occupations, possible only where an occupational group has sufficient power to be able to impose its own definition of proper producer-consumer relations, and where consumers are a large, heterogeneous source of demand (e.g., Johnson 1972; Klein 1973).

Levels of professional control also vary internationally: in some countries specialists have career tracks that range all across the public sector; in others they enter or leave public service as regime changes occur, implying little independence. In yet other countries, professionals hold titles equivalent to those of managers, implying less self-regulation and private organization (Cohen 1993:14). There are differences across countries in the extent to which regime changes influence levels of professional control: in some (e.g., Afghanistan, Argentina, and Uganda) regime changes bring dramatic differences; in others (e.g., Costa Rica, Korea, and Thailand), regime changes bring relatively few differences. ADDR tended to work in countries where political stability was relatively high, and political changes were not likely to create dramatic differences in professional power. Only one country where ADDR worked, Zaire, saw regime changes so dramatic that scientific research became impossible to continue.

The ADDR project supported professional development through what was called *research-capacity building* or *research-capacity strengthening*, phrases now much bandied about in development agencies such as USAID, UNDP, the World Bank, and UNESCO.[3] It is important to remember that this present interest in building or strengthening local capacity to undertake research is only the latest in a long string of outside efforts to improve the quality and scope of scientific research in developing countries. We can crudely summarize a century of technical assistance by saying that colonial research efforts at the turn of the last century were more concerned with gathering accurate information than with building local capacity. Colonial powers in the last century invested in the research reports of their own local administrators. Beginning in the 1920s, government funds were spent on tropical laboratories staffed by expatriates, and these labs dominated international health research through World War II and well into the 1960s. Foundations such as Rockefeller and Ford provided extensive support to such centers, and also invested in local universities (Stifel et al. 1982). From the mid-1930s, and then increasingly in the post-War independence era, many scientists were sent for research training overseas to receive advanced degrees and then (at least in theory) to return home (Mabogunje 1982). Many of these scientists did not return home. To counter this "brain drain," during the 1970s and 1980s more funds were invested in research support following training and return home, through proposal-based grants and program support. In the late 1980s and 1990s donors began to experiment with support to networks of scientists in addition to their project-based support.

These phases of donor support reflect (and help cause) different types and rates of development of indigenous professions. After all, no matter how well trained a scientist may be, the ability to develop a local identity as a professional is predicated on the presence of others with similar training and goals, and requires access to tools of the trade. As more people receive research training, a collective professional identity can be established and maintained. As the production of physicians outstrips local demand, as in some Latin American countries, professional identity becomes more diffuse and professions less powerful.

Trained scientists, capable of producing immediate useful results for their countries if they receive financial support, clamor for support. Yet they work in environments of great political instability, and they may not be working in the same university or country in a year's time. Even if they do work in the same university, promotions to administrative positions cause them to use the skills they learn in research to design or manage programs or make political decisions (Frenk 1992).

Let us pay closer attention to the social effects of these ideas. To put the argument in terms of the "development" model put forward by James Ferguson (1994[1990]:xiv–xv), the development discourse about health professionals in developing countries constructs them as a particular kind of object, that is, as professionals "just like us" only with less of everything that we have (lower income, fewer library books, unreliable electricity, fewer consulting opportunities, less reliable accountants, fewer frequent flier miles, fewer opportunities to publish). It then creates a structure of knowledge around this object, consisting of studies of the difficulties of access to journals in Africa, or the relatively low quality of local medical journals in India, or the problems of maintaining active contact with peers on return home following training overseas. Interventions based on this knowledge are then organized, ranging from sending journals to organizing writing workshops or producing research manuals, to funding research studies of scientists who have recently returned home. They have less: we give them more.

But as with other development efforts, many of these projects fail: well-stocked laboratories are destroyed following a government coup; well-trained scientists leave their home countries to find work with international agencies, or they graduate to doing policy instead of research; computers and e-mail connections fail for lack of electricity or spare parts or maintenance; programs are poorly designed and unresponsive to local needs and abilities. So far, so good (or bad)—there are parallels between "development" in agriculture in Lesotho and "development" in scientific research capacity building efforts. But here things get more complex, for J. Ferguson suggests that despite the failures of these interventions they have regular effects, including "the expansion and entrenchment of bureaucratic state power, side by side with the projection of a representation of economic and social life which denies 'politics' and, to the extent that it was successful, suspends its effects" (1994[1990]:xiv–xv).

It might be argued that health research on applied issues is likely to suffer less from this generic issue of the depoliticization of social life because of the potential for closer connections between applied research and politically charged local issues. From Ferguson's perspective, however, whether scientific research is applied or basic makes little difference: interventions to support professional development in foreign countries (and at home) promote, and prevent, particular types of structural change. The power of the state is enhanced when scientists become more dependent on government (or even international) assistance following successful donor efforts. Professional power is expanded when local universities develop community fieldsites, or equip expensive laboratories, or solidify consulting relationships with government or private agencies. The relationships between local universities and local communities may become more distant, or more instrumental. (Of course, they may also become closer and more egalitarian, though this is rare when investments are directed to universities and not also to communities.) Development institutions and contractors themselves expand their power: for example, more than one-third of foreign assistance to Africa in the late 1980s was spent on 100,000 expatriate professional advisers of various types (Cohen 1993:5). Decades of support in Africa for training local professionals to replace expatriates in the public sector has thus had only limited success. Such efforts are further weakened when local professionals join the development institutions themselves, through what has been called "donor poaching."

In summary, efforts to change the conditions of research in developing countries have focused on training more scientists and providing them with more local resources. Until recently, less attention has been paid to helping build local linkages, or creating more stable institutions.[4] Little attention has been paid to the possibility that donors suffer the curse of Midas, a legendary king of Phrygia. According to Greek legend, Midas requested, and was granted, the ability to turn any object to gold by touching it. He discovered that this was a curse when he touched his food, and, in some versions of the tale, his favorite daughter. The next section of this chapter asks about the content of research more than the conditions of research. It asks what models of science are being disseminated through health research capacity building efforts, how responsive these models are to local culture, and what might be done to recognize and foster the growth of local alternative research paradigms. It asks whether donor support to local researchers could be said to suffer from Midas's touch.

CONTENT OF RESEARCH

What Research Strategies Are Scientific?

I open this discussion with a discussion of a specific research proposal reviewed by the ADDR project, chosen not because it represents the mainstream but rather because it challenges the definitions of science and research followed by the ADDR staff and external reviewers. The work described in this proposal was not the dominant research topic or evaluation outcome, but the project did review other projects like it from other sites.

ADDR received a proposal from a Latin American research team in mid-1992 for a study entitled "Popular Knowledge about Diarrhea and Unconventional Epidemiologic Surveillance." The study was to involve participatory research among twenty-two neighborhoods in a poor urban zone to learn about knowledge, attitudes, and practices (KAP) related to diarrheal diseases. Then an unconventional epidemiologic surveillance system was to be designed and tested in two of these neighborhoods, drawing at least partly on the KAP study. It was labeled "unconventional" because it was to use graphics and simple data descriptions to help marginalized periurban communities understand their burden of disease, and to help them focus on practical and relevant prevention activities. (More conventional epidemiologic surveillance methods take data from rather than bring data to communities. If they are used at all, such data are used by government agencies to allocate resources or describe local variations in disease burden.) The proposal contained eighty pages of text and tables, more than twice the length of most submissions to ADDR. After two rounds of revisions, the proposal was rejected.

Two external reviews were solicited from biomedical experts after the first full revised submission was received. One reviewer opened his review with the following paragraph:

This was one of the hardest proposals I've had to review, for it was an extremely closely argued discourse on the nature of praxis, e.g. a development of the concept of knowing work in the doing, not beforehand; and of course the authors are hoping for funding without knowing what the investigation will bring or how they will define all the variables they will use to characterize the groups' attitudes, practices, and beliefs about diarrheal disease; moreover, the study was also written in sentences like this one, that go on forever, that are convoluted, and should be split up. This was a brutal proposal to read....

This reviewer continued on a later page:

The philosophical terms necessary for understanding what the authors wish to do are well stated and form a coherent whole. However, variables dealing with diarrhea and the variables they are looking at are not defined. They state that the reason for this was that these variables will be defined during the process. That is to say that the process of examining the differences in oppositions between traditional and nontraditional systems will lead to the definition of new variables and concepts. This is something of a leap of faith.

The reviewer recommended in the end that the proposal be given "extremely serious consideration for funding." But the excerpts given above illustrate the tenor of this support: excitement about the project was coupled with skepticism about the authors' ability to carry it out; a coherent philosophy was contrasted with undefined variables; leaps of faith were unwelcome in a scientific proposal; and, although the proposal was written in Spanish, the concise language and simple declarative sentences of scientific English were nonetheless desirable.

The second reviewer showed less enthusiasm. He wrote that

The concept was interesting and the authors obviously have much theoretical experience. The details of selection, sampling size and sampling framework, format of the questionnaire, structured or unstructured [sic], individuals responsible for the questions, digitization, analysis of any of the quantitative aspects was not given.... Hard definitions of any of the criteria are not in the proposal. Many of the associated activities that have been included as factors affecting diarrhea are either not mentioned or not detailed in the proposal.... Clearly some assistance in developing the protocol was required for quantitative issues. This should be done by an individual versed in the variables and behaviors that affect diarrheal disease. The above was especially important since the protocol was highly theoretical. The group will need assistance if they are to perform more applied research and interventions.

This reviewer recommended splitting the proposal into two parts, one descriptive and one operational. He sought clarity of design, exact specification of variables and definitions, and more detail about the nature of the intervention. He was less willing to accept the ambiguities of a proposal based on praxis, and less eager to experiment with this idea than the first reviewer was.

Both of these reviewers acknowledged the theoretical competence of the proposal authors, but both criticized their lack of compliance with accepted norms of science. The proposal came out of a long Latin American tradition of scientific engagement with communities (Franco et al. 1991; Morgan 1998), but in the end the inability (or unwillingness) of the authors to describe this engagement concretely, in terms familiar to the North American scientists, led to its rejection. From the perspective of the donor, the proposal did not meet prevailing scientific standards. But its rejection on these terms eliminated consideration of an innovative approach to community intervention design. A majority of ADDR staff did not label this an alternative model of science, and did not apply different criteria to assess it.

This case from Latin America clearly demonstrates one of the claims that contemporary SSK analysts make about science: it is uniquely able to promulgate its own definitions of what work corresponds to its claims and what work does not. That this proposal fell outside these reviewers' definitions of science can be seen in Reviewer One's use of the metaphor of a "leap of faith," probably the image most antithetical to standard science.

One particular irony in this example is the recent movement within United States' medical schools toward so-called community service learning, where research projects and classes are structured around exchanges with community members and agencies. A national initiative called Community-Campus Partnerships for Health is three years old and growing rapidly, proposing projects quite similar to the earlier Latin American one described here. But there is little recognition of the Latin American university precedent for these activities.

Local Variants of International Knowledge

ADDR project staff also confronted divergent scientific traditions and customs after, rather than before, specific proposals were funded. Work in Indonesia, for example, brought at least three instructive surprises to ADDR project staff. In the first instance, ADDR staff were chagrined to learn that an Indonesian researcher who had obtained forty outside grants in his career faced strong criticism from his colleagues for his success. The prestige that project staff accorded to his external financing was at variance with his colleagues' concern for group solidarity and threats that such differential performance provided. In similar fashion, local authority structures sometimes took project staff by surprise. An application for human subject (ethical) review from an Indonesian group specified that individual informed consent from research participants would not be required, because the governor of the province had already given his consent for the study to take place.

Explorations of barriers to international publishing by Indonesian scientists have shown that local career incentives were organized to support dissemination inside Indonesia more than outside (Hull 1994; Trostle 1993). A system of points accumulated toward promotions and salary increases valued local distribution of reports in Indonesian almost as highly as international dissemination of articles in English. Though seen from the perspective of the donor as a system of disincentives to international publication, the system did work to maintain local networks of information exchange and to ensure that research results by Indonesian scientists would circulate in Indonesia. These are some of the advantages of local over foreign publication: such publication better reaches national technocrats or the larger society, and more effectively strengthens new fields of scientific research (Useem et al.1979). Researchers have argued that local publication reflects an intentional choice to communicate applied findings more than it reflects an inability to publish internationally (Sanz et al. 1995).

Similar surprises emerged from ADDR work in Thailand. One notable example concerned peer review, a scientific convention in manuscript reviews with a strong and specific cultural origin in the West. (See the twenty-six papers published in the *Journal of the American Medical Association* (JAMA 1994) from the Second international Congress on Peer Review in Biomedical Publication, and abstracts from the 1997 Third International Congress on Biomedical Peer Review and Global Communications (conference abstracts at http://www.ama-assn.org/public/peer/session.htm).) A dean of a Thai graduate school reported that his colleagues preferred to return reviews of manuscripts to journals only when they had positive comments to make. When they were critical they sometimes did not return them at all. This reluctance to make overt criticism of colleagues was revealed as oppositional to the Western values of frank presentation and open exchange revealed in peer review. (I acknowledge this gloss on the complexities of contemporary culture, focusing on differences between local and Western rather than on differences within a local culture. But I do this to accentuate some aspects of scientific research that are relatively culture laden rather than culture free.)

In fact, we should not assume that Western biomedical science is unambiguously committed to neutral review. There is, for example, a documented concern in the medical literature with so-called publication bias. Publication bias springs from the tendency for statistically significant research results to be submitted and published while inconclusive findings remain unpublished. This systematically distorts any publication-based attempt to summarize research outcomes across studies, as in a technique called *meta-analysis*, because the published literature will overestimate both the size and frequency of treatment effects (see, e.g., Light and Pillemer 1984).

Local Differences in Purposes of Research

I have argued that these adjustments or variations on scientific research processes stem from broader cultural and political ideals about the purpose and appropriate forms of communication. What notions circulate about the breadth of audiences served by science, and what mix of nation-building, institution-building, and individual career-building prevails? What proportion of scientists view their work as including advocacy as well as disinterested dissemination? What combination of client relationships is established with government, the private sector, or a broader public? Stepan (1981:112–113), for example, argues that the growth of the Oswaldo Cruz Foundation in Brazil rests on its service to multiple clients by providing practical solutions to applied problems. These solutions helped balance the uncertain outcomes of the foundation's basic science, some of which led to dead ends while others led to important discoveries.

In similar fashion, these refashionings of scientific research are also strongly influenced by cultural values about the nature and appearance of professional success. They take particular expression within national boundaries, but their expression is also based on the organization of the state, of local universities, and of professional groups within nations. To some extent, the decision to publish internationally versus locally depends on how one defines a peer reference group. Though scientists try to publish both for international standing and for national recognition, there is an inherent conflict in the means of counting these efforts. Citation counts as a measure of scientific prestige reflect (and reward) only the work published in international venues (Gaillard 1991:104–105). Moreover, access by industrialized country scientists to research from developing countries is strongly circumscribed by the difficulty of finding it: only about 2 percent of the journals in the Science Citation Index come from developing countries, and "over 80% of all scientific research published in indexed journals is in English" (Zielinski 1995:1481).

ADDR and other research donors project a particular representation of science, admittedly more plastic than that of the bench scientist, but still carefully constructed with rules about how to review the literature, when to describe findings and when to discuss them, the value of anonymous peer review, and the difference between being a scientist and being an advocate. Nonetheless, as a development project ADDR was forced to move between two very different standards of evaluation. On one hand, ADDR was designed to develop scientific quality. On the other, it was designed to develop scientists and scientific institutions. That this dual aim can be achieved is suggested by Stepan for the Oswaldo Cruz Foundation in Brazil early this century: the success of scientific institutions can be measured through numbers of publications or prizes, but also through the permanence of institutions through time, their ability to recruit staff and maintain public support, and their ability to "serve local needs or understand local problems" (1981:9). In the ADDR project, however, staff, consultants, reviewers, and grantees were never encouraged to ask whose standards of quality would apply. Nor was the conflict between international quality and local relevance ever resolved.

Effects of Recipients on Donors

It is misleading to suggest, as I have so far, that the relationship between donors and grant recipients involves only donor effects upon recipients. Grant makers and grant recipients form networks of mutual dependence. Donors (or at least project staff in donor agencies) need their recipients to be successful just as much as recipients themselves need to succeed. Donors respond to the initiatives of their grant recipients, and sometimes even adapt their evaluation criteria to recognize and reward unexpected outcomes and local initiatives.

By the end of the ADDR project, staff placed more emphasis on the application of results than they did at the beginning. This was at least partly a response to investigator-initiated actions in their local communities. Local scientists learned from local communities and from local decision makers that creating change in response to research data sometimes required skills and resources beyond those they had at their disposal. They in turn taught this to ADDR project staff, who consequently began to pay more attention to supporting the dissemination and application of research findings. But research dissemination and application, and the role of research in policy making and decision making, was newer and less well understood by all than issues in research design, implementation, and analysis. Although the project began sponsoring didactic workshops on research design and analysis in its second year, it was only in year nine that it began to hold workshops on the relationship between research and policy.

The project staff had fewer problems recognizing and rewarding local innovations undertaken by specific researchers. Though the project staff did so on a much smaller scale, they funded and supported dissemination activities that included puppet shows, community theater, discussion groups, and formal scientific meetings. Here the local scientists were more readily recognized as authorities about what should be undertaken, and qualms about differences in dissemination strategies were less often articulated with reference to scientific quality. It is intriguing that local variations in dissemination and application were relatively acceptable, while local variations in articulation of objectives and forms of data collection were not. These latter types of variations were more likely to generate critical reactions among reviewers and project staff. They came at a point in the review process—when money would be spent—where conformity with accepted definitions of science was most important. Once funds had been spent, project staff had far less ability to enforce specific ideas about how research should be disseminated.

CONCLUSION

Donors have considered the objects of development assistance for research (health scientists in less developed countries) too often as (merely) impoverished cousins. Donors themselves could be more self-reflective, paying more attention to the strangeness of their managerial customs and to the implications their brief residence in these other families has on the validity of their perceptions. Health scientists in developing countries often possess different systems of organization and incentive, more permeable boundaries between disciplines, and frequent transitions between academic and political life, not to mention challenging new theories and research findings. Yet these differences are too often defined as irrelevant given present assumptions of what is good science, and how good science should be organized and produced (Banerji 1986; Goonatilake 1984).

ADDR staff tried to take some (though not all) of this local knowledge into account in the proposal development process: the project asked what made a good question and who should care about a given set of research results. It pushed researchers to move from hypothesis testing to formative research or hypothesis generation. It assisted local scientists to develop research questions and focused on local issues of potential applied significance. It used workshops and local conferences to form and sustain local networks, sent grantees to consult with other ADDR grant recipients, and employed grantees on short-term contracts in the central office. In addition to these project initiatives, grant recipients themselves sometimes contradicted, expanded, or transformed donor assumptions in the course of undertaking their research.

Even with this relative openness to and fostering of local participation, the ADDR project's rules and standards prevented some of the more innovative and "foreign" groups from participating. More attention needs to be paid to this process, and to its detrimental effects. These effects can be seen in at least two arenas: first, in the substantive content of the research itself (what questions are worth asking); and second, in the rhetorical and applied objectives of the research (who is the perceived audience for the answers, and what methods are best used to reach them).

In the end, even in a development project designed to assist researchers to undertake better research, donor influence is problematic and controversial. As an ADDR staff member, I sought to investigate local cultures of science, improve obvious problems, and respond to the urgent pleas of potential grant recipients. But, like the rest of my colleagues on the project, I also succeeded in replicating the foibles and frailties of the U.S. research enterprise. We have contended that the proposal writing and publication part of this enterprise suffers from "overdevelopment" in the United States just as much as it suffers from "underdevelopment" in Haiti or Malawi (Trostle and Simon 1992). To the extent that projects such as ADDR focus on publication and grantsmanship as measures of success, they run the risk of recreating some of the more counterproductive and unsustainable elements of Western scientific research. I described early in this chapter the challenges even U.S. libraries face in keeping up with many expensive journal subscriptions: these expenses are clearly unthinkable for libraries in developing countries. Other counterproductive outcomes of support for Western-style research include "salami publishing" (Susser and Yankauer 1993), where research is divided into the largest number of publishable slices; promulgating the notion that quantity of research and publication is more important than quality or elegance; creating soft-money institutions that depend on research grants for their continued existence; and attaching value to citing extensive current reference lists, requiring huge sums for library resources and computer reference searching.

Unfortunately, within the larger context of international research today, economic measures of utility have greatest value, and coordinated multicenter studies of specific global policy issues are a common method. The international research funding environment is not particularly hospitable to constructing local solutions for local priorities, or to innovation and experimentation with local research designs. Larger-scale projects with more ambitious goals are being supported more readily than small ones. Indeed, we need more of those physicians of the soul Socrates recommended, to assess the beneficial and harmful effects of the knowledge and knowledge production methods now offered for sale.

Notes

1. ADDR received eleven years of project support from the U.S. Agency for International Development (USAID). It formally ended in May, 1996, but was replaced by a new project called Applied Research in Child Health (ARCH), also awarded to Harvard University.

2. BOSTID: The Board on Science and Technology for International Development; INCLEN: The International Clinical Epidemiological Network; SS&M: Social Science & Medicine; WHO/TDR: UNDP/World Bank/WHO Special Programme for Research & Training in Tropical Diseases.

3. See, for example, Berg (1993), Jaycox (1993), and copies of recent *Human Development Reports* from the *United Nations Development Program and World Development Reports* from the World Bank.

4. But see the 1997 *World Development Report* and chapters in Grindle (1997).

9 RETHINKING THE ROLE OF ELITES IN RURAL DEVELOPMENT: A CASE STUDY FROM CAMEROON

Paul Nchoji Nkwi

INTRODUCTION

People's participation in communal activities has long been a feature of the social organization of Kom, one of the grassland kingdoms of Western Cameroon. But this participation took a new turn in the mid-1980s with the founding of the Njinikom Area Development Association (NADA), an organization devoted to rural upliftment and development in one of the three administrative areas into which the kingdom is divided. In this chapter I sketch the background, both national and local, to the establishment of NADA, and focus on the role of the modem elite, many of whom are based in Cameroon's towns and cities, in the stimulation and management of grassroots rural development.

I should make it clear at the outset that I am an interested party in this account, since I am both a member of Kom society and a university professor based in Yaounde. I have also been one of the leaders of the Njinikom Area Development Association: I was founding president of the association in 1984, and was reelected as its president in 1993, having been ejected from office between 1990 and 1993 under circumstances that are detailed below. Given my past and present offices, I will obviously write as a protagonist for the association, drawing attention to its ideals and successes to date. At the same time, however, the positions I have held give me close insight into the nature of the problems and challenges that the association has faced, and will continue to face in future.

CAMEROON DEVELOPMENT POLICY

It is a commonplace observation that development in Africa was a top-down undertaking during the colonial period. It is also the case that in the postcolonial period there has been increasing lip service paid to, if not actual respect for, the principle of bottom-up development—development that is focused on the grassroots level, and that organizes financial and technical resources around ordinary people, the main social players in the field.

Cameroon may be taken as an example in this regard. Since independence, Cameroon's development has been guided by a series of five-year development plans. Five such plans have been drawn up since 1960. French interests were instrumental in designing the first two plans, which treated Cameroon (the larger, eastern part of which had been a UN mandate territory under France) as if it were a part of the metropole rather than an autonomous political entity requiring specific attention. Cameroon's first economic plan was "the explicit work of the French private concerns, namely the *Société Générale d'Etudes et de Planification* (SOGEP) and the *Société pour l'Etude du Développement Economique et Sociale* (SEDES)" (Joseph 1978:139; cf. also Hugon 1968:251). The second plan (1965–1970) was known as the "Peasant Plan," but, like the first, it was a top-down exercise that resulted in failure. The third development plan (1971–1976) was more ambiguous, in that, although France once again played a major part in shaping its outline, there was a considerable change in the accompanying rhetoric. Cameroon's first president, Ahmadou Ahidjo, said of the third plan (the "Production and Productivity Plan") that it

is not merely the work of experts, the product of the cogitation of a few initiates ...but the work of the whole Cameroon population. The population of Cameroon has co-operated in establishing democratically the nation's aspirations and the means whereby these might be achieved. (Joseph 1978:149)

Indeed this plan was not drawn up in Paris, to be implemented by French business concerns; its creation witnessed a proliferation of commissions and committees down to the local level in Cameroon, and the wide participation of people in drawing it up. The fourth and fifth plans (1976–1986) also gave the people a nominal opportunity to express their aspirations through discussion at village, district, and provincial levels, and this discussion was ostensibly incorporated into the plans by the Ministry of Planning and Regional De-velopment. But in all these instances, there was a significant gap be-tween the stated commitment to high principles of consultation and the actual practice of development on the ground. As far as imple-mentation was concerned, the execution of the plans depended on the goodwill of the bureaucrats who, as is often the case, presumed that they knew well enough the desires of the people (Uphoff 1991:468).

In fact, however, the government officials knew little or nothing about the needs of the local people. Those local communities that had their own sons and daughters in government were usually the greatest beneficiaries because these officials wrote the needs of their own local communities into the plans. Implementation depended on how long these administrators could maintain their government po-sitions.

President Ahidjo's public rhetoric was at odds with these kinds of practices. He articulated a doctrine of "balanced regional develop-ment," which

> upholds the idea that equal attention should be paid to the different sectors of activity in the economy; to the regions, town, and countryside; and to men, women, adults, and lin-guistic diversity, it has been felt that it would be unfair to con-centrate development efforts in only one part or area of the country. Because missionary and colonial penetration in in-land and northern areas of Cameroon was slow, difficult and often unsuccessful, many regions and rural areas have remained comparatively impoverished. Consequently, balanced devel-opment is an attempt by the government to redress regional inequalities by providing education, infrastructure, and the public amenities necessary for bridging the country and the town. (cited in Ndongko 1986:101)

Ahidjo's statement was intended as a guideline for administra-tors, but the outcome of widespread favoritism and nepotism was that many regions of Cameroon stagnated during the first two de-cades of his rule. The Anglophone provinces (northwest and south-west) were the most neglected. Ahidjo's policy was not built on a sys-tematic needs assessment, but rather on his personal vision. It was meant to be an exercise in the redistribution of national wealth by the building of basic social and economic infrastructure in every region. In principle it was a wonderful policy, but in practice it was a failure. The policy did not succeed in satisfying the different ethnic and cultural constituencies (Bayart 1986; Eyinga 1978), even though the president stretched the policy to mean a balanced representation of all regions in the cabinet and in governmental positions. Its appointees were meant to be responsible for ensuring that their regions got the required development projects defined in the development plans. More often than not, however, they did little to promote development in their regions, and everything to ensure their political survival within an oppressive system that adored "hand-clappers" and abhorred constructive social thinkers, critics, and social actors in rural development.

Development plans were executed on the basis of political pressure, lobbying, clientelism, and the good will of the few. Appointments to positions were also political rewards for services rendered to the regime. Receivers of such rewards remained loyal to the regime rather than to their people whom they were supposed to represent. Richard Joseph stated that Ahidjo was "able to keep the bureaucratic class in check through restrained and intelligent repression coupled with the liberal provision of material inducements. The art of keeping in power at all cost and by all means seems to have been perfected by this regime" (1978:186).

During the Ahidjo years (1960–1982), technocrats and party faithfuls worked for political stability and economic consolidation of the regime. Ahidjo's dictatorial methods submerged the egos of many who were content to do what they were told, regardless of right or wrong. By 1975 the country became increasingly prosperous; there was a relative absence of internal conflicts as the turbulent factions had been brought under control, and Ahidjo spent the next seven years devoting himself to development issues (Le Vine 1986:35). When he resigned in 1982, he left a vibrant economy with huge foreign reserves and a dormant civil service. Ahidjo's handpicked successor, Paul Biya, acknowledged Cameroon's buoyant economy in a speech to the nation four years later in 1986.

Biya had served quietly under Ahidjo from 1962 to 1982, and remained a largely unknown quantity during the Ahidjo years. It is only in the thirteen years of his rule (1982–1995), that Cameroonians have come to know him as a weak and unreliable leader who has gathered around himself technocrats with kleptocratic tendencies and little concern for the common people.

The period from 1987 to 1995 has been characterized by severe economic crisis accompanied by social and political unrest, structural adjustment programs (SAPs), and deteriorating standards of living. The fall of prices of primary products in the world market has further exacerbated the situation. The national budget, which was based on the foreign earnings of these products, has undergone serious cuts. Previously subsidized social programs have come under a cost recovery program that has led to major cutbacks. As elsewhere in Africa, cost recoveries imposed by structural adjustment programs have made rural populations the ultimate losers and victims. Health services are now inaccessible to a majority of rural people. Foreign reserves built up by the Ahidjo government have been squandered by a kleptocratic regime almost within a decade. It is said in Cameroon that "the goat eats where it is tethered" (Bayart 1993:235); certainly, the goats have overgrazed the lucrative paddocks of the Ahidjo years and there is now very little left for them to eat.

Biya prepared the sixth plan (1986–1991) as the economic crisis was setting in; foreign reserves were diminishing; foreign debt was on the rise; and corruption was at its height. Such a plan could not be executed under such poor economic conditions. The regime, whose reputation for corruption is no secret to Cameroonians, has operated no long-term plans. Government operates on a day-to-day basis, with contingencies seeming to guide governmental action.

Furthermore, Ahidjo's pretense of balanced regional development seems to have been abandoned totally, in favor of a more kleptocratic and nepotic machinery (Bayart 1993). It is said that the president's province, his ethnic group, and his close friends and clients have been favored. The building and improvement of the social infrastructure in other regions have been openly carried out on the basis of political support and reward. During this period, institutional corruption has increased the level of opulence of the few, the "nouveaux riches" (Bayart 1993), while the vast majority of village communities have been abandoned to themselves. Ahidjo's agricultural policy, which sought to encourage small-scale production, is today the economic savior of thousands of households.

There is no doubt that institutionalized corruption has been the result of the absence of democratic institutional structures. Most Cameroon leaders are still resisting genuine democratic reforms vital for good governance. Excessive military expenditures against a background of scarce resources constitutes another serious drain on economic growth. Cameroon, like other African countries, continues to import large consignments of military hardware at the expense of health, education, nutrition, basic social services, and investment in rural areas. New taxes have been imposed in the starvation salaries of civil servants; farmers have for a long time not received the true value of their farm products. As a consequence, the development of the rural areas has been neglected or abandoned to the missionaries and local elite organizations (NGOs) whose activities have attracted minimal and inadequate funds.

It was in reaction to this state of affairs that a group of civil servants from the Kom ethnic group met in Yaounde, the capital, and established an organization to assist local communities to mitigate the effects of government neglect. For the past decade, the state has become irrelevant in a number of critical domains. Ihonvbere rightly asserts that, "Given the violent, coercive and exploitative nature of the state, the masses turn to ethnic, religious and philanthropic organisations for hope, leadership, self-expression and support. The state becomes irrelevant in their consciousness and existential conditions" (1994:43).

The Njinikom Area Development Association (NADA) was established in 1984 to provide the hope and leadership vital for the survival of local villages within the area of Kom. NADA's main purpose was to provide the services the state and local council were unable to provide. The rest of this chapter attempts to cast this initiative within a historical context, describing its innovations, achievements, and failures, and reflecting on the lessons that can be learned.

FORERUNNERS OF THE NJINIKOM DEVELOPMENT ASSOCIATION

Njinikom area is one of the three regions that comprise the Kom kingdom; the others are Abasakom and Ngvin-Kijem. The Kom polity was founded in the late eighteenth century, and its rulers embarked on an expansionist policy by creating and maintaining war lodges (*manjong*) and promoting warfare as a viable channel of wealth accumulation. The rulers of Kom also established a national regulatory society (*kwifoyn*), as well as village governing bodies (*mukum*) throughout the kingdom. Between 1864 and 1904, the seventh ruler used these war lodges, composed of young men of fighting age, to acquire territory and to secure the present boundaries of the state.

He rewarded members of the war lodges with booty and captives taken in war. In peace time, their members carried out communal work, such as keeping roads clear, building bridges, providing labor to the household, clearing the royal farms, watching over borders, and reporting unfriendly or suspicious moves or visits. The traditional governing institution, kwifoyn, was based at the royal palace while the mukum performed similar functions in the villages. The membership of these institutions (manjong, kwifoyn, and mukum) had a 60 percent representation of young men who performed most of the communal activities and fought in wars. The idea of serving the community was thus already ingrained in Kom's political culture at the time of German penetration. The palace was also built and maintained by the villages. In the villages, households relied on one another in the performance of certain activities (house construction, marriages, death celebrations, births, hunting, and farming).

People's participation in communal activities was therefore very much part of the culture. The colonial encounter, however, led to a recognition of the value of people's participation, and one has to admit that the notion of participation has also evolved through development theory and practice. When the Germans finally reached Kom in 1889, fifteen years after Cameroon was declared a German *schutzgebiet*, the ruler used his war lodges (manjong), kwifoyn, and mukum to resist their punitive expeditions. Between 1904 and 1905 the Germans tried to impose their rule and met with strong resistance. Although a peace treaty was signed, the ruler *(foyn)* refused to supply labor to the Germans for the building of a fortress sixty kilometers away. Doing so would have been a sign of capitulation and payment of tribute. When the Germans finally left Cameroon in 1915, Kom still adamantly refused to supply labor (Nkwi 1976).

The British took over Southern Cameroon in 1916. They quickly recognized the value of traditional institutions and incorporated them into the administrative apparatus. The regulatory institutions, kwifoyn, manjong, and mukum largely made up of the kingdom's young men, became instruments of governance for the colonial administration. Orders went from colonial administrators to the Native Authority (comprised of ruler and village heads) and were passed down to the people by these local institutions. They collected taxes, dug and maintained roads, and were instrumental in the introduction of new agricultural techniques. The Native Authority, made up of local leaders with little or no formal education, ruled the Kom nation in collaboration with the British from 1916 to 1958 (Nkwi 1976).

During this same period missionaries were entrusted with the responsibility of building schools and training future servants of the colonial administration. They effectively used the principle of community participation for the building of schools, hospitals, clinics, health centers, bridges, and roads. They raised funds from their home parishes and, with the labor supplied by Christians, were able to build these institutions and improve the quality of life of the people. They worked very closely with the local communities, whose involvement in projects was, however, limited to labor contributions and did not extend to design and planning.

Toward the end of British imperialism, agitation for self-rule gathered momentum as the educated minority (such as teachers and clerks) began to build pressure groups. They were eager to participate in the management of local affairs. The Kom Improvement Association (KIA) emerged in the early 1950s. Its main purpose was to bring educated people together and to articulate their demands for full participation in the political process and local development activities. In a petition, Sama Ndi, one of the leading KIA members, accused the British administration of using "unqualified messengers and interpreters instead of utilising men of intelligence and local talent" (UN T/PET.419, 22 November 1949). This position was reaffirmed by a collective petition addressed to the UN visiting mission to Kom, when the KIA had this to say on self-government:

> The worse neglect of all is the absence of training for self-government whereby the people might hope to do things for themselves. Instead, by the damnable Native Administrative System, there is the role of things remaining where they were. This is done by excluding the literate and enlightened from administration councils. Most council members are there by right of birth, no matter whether they can serve the people or not, whether the people supposed to be represented like it or not. When will these illiterate old men being trained for self-government rule? In their graves? Of course, it does not matter with the government; the longer they are unable to rule the better for the British government (UN T/PET. 4/L.35, 8 March 1950, p. 3)

In the late 1950s and the 1960s, the KIA became caught up in regional and national politics, and ceased to be an active grassroots organization. It ran out of steam as most of its leaders took up new government positions (as district officers, directors, and civil servants). One of its leaders became a leading member of the Kamerun National Democratic Party (KNDP) and a proponent of the Southern Cameroon cause (Johnson 1970). He later became prime minister of West Cameroon (1965–1968). While enjoying their newfound political positions, the KIA group designed and implemented limited development programs as they perceived them: they provided some of the necessary resources but rarely consulted local communities. When their political fortunes turned into misfortunes, they left behind an unfinished agenda (uncompleted roads, schools, and health centers), and since ordinary people had not been involved from the beginning, sustainability became a serious issue.

In 1968, the Kom Development Union (KDU) was born out of this frustrating experience. Its leadership, a remnant of the KIA, believed in a more resourceful takeover from where the KIA had left off. They were, however, overoptimistic. The KIA had operated under an open British democratic system that permitted free expression and debate. But given the unification of Cameroon under an autocratic ruler, the KDU was unable to have any significant impact on local development in Kom in the sixteen years that followed until 1984.

In quality and substance, the KDU leadership was the same as that of the defunct KIA. It was made up of a clique of school teachers, policemen, clerks, messengers, and warders who had little international exposure and had been traumatized by the oppressive rule of the Ahidjo years. Its most articulate member, Ngom Jua, had the misfortune of having been made minister of West Cameroon by Ahidjo in 1968.

The KDU was unable to deal with the new political events and a government that rewarded political support and commitment with government involvement in community projects. The expansion and exploration of new avenues required a new quality of leadership that the KDU could not provide. Over the years its leadership turned into a group of "hand-clappers" to a dictatorial regime that refused to tolerate criticism of its management of public affairs. Their efforts remained unproductive, although attempts at raising funds for projects produced some meager resources. The Kom kingdom remained without any significant government action to develop the area or maintain existing structures.

Little assistance was forthcoming from the Njinikom Rural Council (later called the Fundong Rural Council). Established in 1968 to manage local affairs and provide leadership to the traditional chiefs, the council went from financial solvency to bankruptcy and economic stagnation. By 1987 this council could no longer maintain the existing infrastructure, pay the salaries of its workers, and handle the bills for public water supply. By 1989 the council owed the Cameroon Water Corporation (SNEC) millions of francs (CFA). Public water points were all disconnected. The KDU was again unable to assist the bankrupt council to serve a people abandoned by the state and the politicians.

During the sixteen years of KDU's existence, however, the university systems in Cameroon and abroad produced intellectuals with new visions and challenges, eager to bring about change and innovation. The emergence of the Njinikom Area Development Association (NADA) in 1984 changed the entire political and development landscape of the Kom kingdom. Highly educated and fully aware of the philosophy of "putting people first," the leadership of the new association began to break new ground, bringing local communities to the forefront of development. Within a year similar associations were created in the other regions of the Kom kingdom. Most of these new development associations were created under the 1975 law governing cultural development, which permitted ethnically based groups to exist as long as they did not hamper nation-building efforts.

THE NEW INITIATIVE: THE NJINIKOM AREA DEVELOPMENT ASSOCIATION

Njinikom area is one of the three sectors that comprise the Kom kingdom, an ethnic group located in the mountainous western district of the northwest province of Cameroon (see Figure 1). The three main divisions of the kingdom are Njinikom, Ngvin-Kijem, and Abasakom. The Njinikom area has a population of over 40,000 covering 12 villages, with over 7,500 households.

Historically, Njinikom area was the first region to be exposed to European influence. Missionaries began operating there in 1920. Within a couple of years they built schools that attracted pupils from all over the present northwest province. Most of the Kom elite were trained here, but a majority of them were from Njinikom area. By 1980, Njinikom area had produced university teachers, lawyers, medical doctors, intellectuals, and hundreds of university graduates. Even the first Kom political and religious leaders were educated here. Comparatively, Njinikom area had far more educated people than any other part of Kom (Nkwi 1976), and these people were progressive and forward-looking. With such a critical mass, the area was therefore in a position to generate new ideas and see them through.

The founders of the Njinikom Area Development Association (NADA) were resource persons from government, research, and uni-

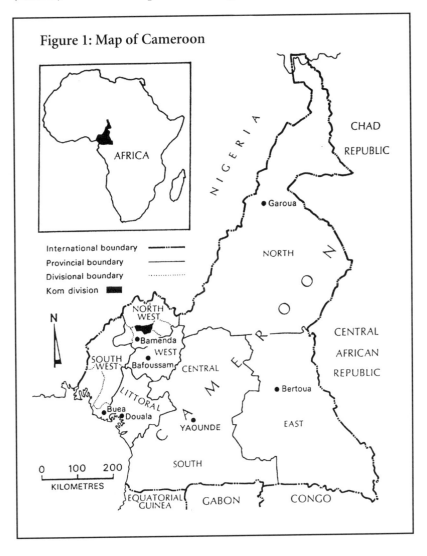

Figure 1: Map of Cameroon

AFRICA

International boundary
Provincial boundary
Divisional boundary
Kom division

CHAD
REPUBLIC

NIGERIA

● Garoua

NORTH

NORTH WEST

● Bamenda

WEST

SOUTH WEST
Bafoussam
CENTRAL

● Bertoua

CENTRAL

AFRICAN

REPUBLIC

LITTORAL

Buea
● Douala
YAOUNDE

EAST

N

0   100   200
KILOMETRES

SOUTH

EQUATORIAL
GUINEA
GABON
CONGO

versity institutions who knew that "putting people first" was an essential prerequisite for sustainable development. It was their convic-
tion that real participation of people could only be "determined in
consultation with some of the intended beneficiaries" (Uphoff
1991:486). It could also be said that NADA was a covert opposition
group to a one-party state that had marginalized the local populations and taken away their right to determine their destiny. In June
1984, the group produced a white paper stating that "unless a people
takes its development into their own hands, nobody will do so for
them" (NADA 1984:1). Reviewing the failures of previous efforts by
the KIA and KDU, the NADA designed a people's participatory program, and called on the people not to fold their arms and wait for
state intervention in development. All civil servants, businessmen,
local politicians, and adult residents, both men and women, were also
called on to rally together and develop their communities by making
financial contributions to development projects. Participation, it was
decided, would be built on personal financial contributions and provision of labor by the elite and the rural people.

In the by-laws of the association adopted in 1984, the rules and
regulations included an obligatory annual contribution of 6,000 frs
($24) for all urban elite, and a contribution of 500 frs ($2) and 250
frs ($1) for all village male and female adults respectively. These con-
tributions were collected by the branches in the urban centers and by
chapters in the villages, in consultation with the urban elite who provided the technical support. Villages were required to determine their
priorities and submit these to the executive board for appropriate
funding. The rural population represented 80 percent of the NADA
membership but contributed less than 30 percent of the total annual
budget. This fundraising process was so successful that NADA's strategy was adopted by newly established NGOs in the Abasakom and
Ngvin-Kijem areas. Jealous of NADA's autonomy and success, some
members of the KDU tried to have the association outlawed by the
administration. Reluctant to do so because of NADA's impact on the
local population, the administration tacitly permitted it to operate
and actually legalized its existence some years later.

NADA's first congress in 1984 was attended by hundreds of people
representing the different villages and the elite, living and working
outside Njinikom area. This was the first major conference ever held
in Kom to deal with issues of development. A tidy sum (equivalent to
U.S. $10,000) was raised, to the great surprise of the administration

and KDU leadership. KDU had never, during the sixteen years of its existence, raised more than U.S. $2,000 at a single sitting. People's response to this new initiative and its impact on their perception of development was reflected in the financial contributions made.

It was now necessary to maintain the momentum of this process. Clichés and metaphors, such as "home is always home," "a mother's child is only in the womb," "a hunter always returns with game," and "people first" emerged in this context after the initial experience.

"Home Is Always Home"

The urban-educated elite active in the association were people from very humble backgrounds. Their parents came from a generation that had never known formal education. They were born and bred in the rural villages. For these people (including myself) "home" was not just a geographical location but a meaningful cultural niche, representing the past, the present, and the future. "Home" for my generation is still where the umbilical cords of children born in the cities are buried; "home" is where we ourselves will eventually be buried. Formal education gave us the opportunity to work in the public and private sectors outside our villages, but we are very much part of our village environment. Conscious that we will one day retire from public life and return to our villages, improving living conditions there now rather than later is a motivating factor. Furthermore, our desire to retire to the village strengthened our ambition for a viable development organization. Our financial contributions for village projects is a sign of commitment to development. Of the $10,000 contributed in 1984, $8,000 was contributed by members of the urban elite.

"A Mother's Child Is Only in the Womb"

Although the idea of a viable development organization was born outside the village context, the elite were fully aware that their efforts would be futile if the participation of local people was not guaranteed at all levels. Measures were taken to educate the villages on the new development strategy and philosophy. After the first meeting in 1984, a NADA delegation visited all the villages, distributing project funds, educating village leaders about participation, and discussing the role to be played by each village. Henceforth, development projects would be designed by the people and undertaken by them. Therefore the improvement of their quality of life was to a great extent in their own hands. The association was responsible for the mobilization of resources required to achieve this task. The concept of ownership of the process of development was imbued in the people. Active participation was also an exercise of ownership that was vital for the sustainability of projects. The successful completion of 70 percent of the twenty-seven NADA projects undertaken can be largely attributed to this sense of ownership and full participation in their execution. The 30 percent of the projects that remain uncompleted have been so largely due to mismanagement and lack of funds.

Today, the bulk of the financial support comes from the hundreds of Njinikom sons and daughters living and working in the towns and cities of Cameroon. For years the urban branches of the association have acted as mechanisms for resource mobilization. The Christmas season was chosen as the most appropriate time for the "hunter to return home with the game"—the funds collected from urban members.

The Organizational Structure

The Njinikom Area Development Association owes its achievements and success to the way it is organized. When its members met for the first time in 1984, they adopted an organizational structure that permitted popular participation in fundraising, project formulation, and implementation. Villages and urban centers were organized into chapters and branches. Every year an annual congress is held bringing together the representatives of chapters and branches for fundraising evaluation and the financing of rural development projects. Congress elects its executive board every three years; the board supervises the work of the various technical committees. The congress is attended by village heads, community leaders and local administrators, and often by representatives of government departments, especially extension services and external urban elite groups. Its primary purpose is to chart the program for the year, raise funds, and allocate them to the different projects. For the past ten years the congress has been held on schedule except in 1992. In order to empower different interest groups and facilitate the working of the association, three wings were established in 1986, namely, the Women's wing, the Youth wing, and the Student wing. But the most vibrant organs have been the urban branches, which not only provide entry points into urban systems for migrants (Ihonvbere 1994:53), but also ensure the provision of services to their members (in cases of ill-health, accidents, transport of corpses to villages for burial, sources of information, and social security).

The executive board ensures the internal cohesion of all functional units. Its members represent all the different interest groups (women, youth, traditional leaders, villages, and the urban elite). Its key actors, the president and treasurer, have always been chosen from among the urban elite on whom the association relies for the mobilization of funds from the donor community in Yaounde, the capital. Over the years, they have also lobbied for funds from the various ministerial departments in the capital.

Elected for a three-year term, the executive board of fifteen is responsible for monitoring the work of the various committees, branches, chapters, and wings of the association. In the composition of the board, care is always taken to have all villages or groups of villages represented. But the actual work of the association is carried out by the committees—Projects, Finance, Social and Sports, Education and Environment, and Socio-Cultural.

Projects Committee

A majority of members of the Projects Committee are local opinion leaders, most of whom live in the villages. The committee assists the villages in identifying priority projects; it supervises and evaluates costs and makes recommendations to the executive board. During the last eleven years, twenty-seven village projects have been designed and implemented by and for the villages under the supervision of this committee. These projects include the creation and running of a community primary school (now taken over by the state), the building and maintenance of roads and culverts, the creation of a social center for teenage mothers, the establishment of a scholarship scheme for secondary and university students, the promotion of environmental hygiene, provision of clean water to most villages, and the support of health infrastructure (hospital, health centers, orphanage). People have always provided labor and local materials (stones, wood) for the execution of these projects. Their role has been vital in the implementation process.

Finance Committee

Composed mainly of retired civil servants with financial management skills and experience, this committee's responsibility is to devise strategies for raising and managing funds, and also to audit the accounts of the association. It also reviews and determines the contributions of members, and lobbies for additional contributions in cash and in kind from well-to-do members of the community who may desire to enhance their social status and influence.

Over the last ten years, the organization has raised 51,430 000 frs CFA (about $205,720), and received more than $60,000 from different donor agencies as well as about $10,000 from the Ministry of Planning and Regional Development. The bulk of the local contributions has come from the external elite ($140,600), while the local people have contributed about $65,000. These sums may sound small, but in real terms the twenty-seven executed projects, plus communal labor, cost more than a million U.S. dollars according to the financial evaluation of the projects committee (cf. NADA Review 1996, and Financial Records 1987–1994).

The elite who contribute most of the money are from the urban middle class. In the early 1990s, their average earnings per month were about $800, but after drastic salary cuts in 1993, they now earn less than $200 per month. These cuts notwithstanding, their commitment to the improvement of the quality of life in their home villages has remained undiminished. Their greatest reward is honor, prestige and the possibility of political capital in the newly-democratized civil society of Cameroon.

Social and Sports Committee

The economic crisis that hit the nation in the 1980s brought about unemployment, crime, and drug abuse in the 1990s. Young people who have lost employment in the cities have returned home with little or nothing to survive on. Even coffee production, which used to provide at least some income for most rural households in Kom, has lost its economic power in the world market. Food crops have suddenly gained more importance, creating land scarcity in a land tenure system that is centrally controlled. Most youths are turning their attention to agriculture and running into serious land distribution problems. Motivated by these factors, the association established a social and sports committee to pay more attention to the plight of youth. The committee organizes different sport activities (football, tennis, athletics, mountain races, and indoor games). It focuses on better ways of keeping young people busy and away from crime and drugs. Under its leadership, the Njinikom area produced a second division football team in 1986.

Early dropouts of teenage mothers from schools have been given special attention in recent years. A Women's Social Centre (WSC) has been created to provide training in domestic science (sewing, knitting, cooking, and child care), health care, and family planning for teenage mothers and unemployed young women. Today, the center caters to over forty-five teenage mothers and early dropouts.

Education and Environment

One priority identified by this committee has been the need to assist students in secondary schools and universities whose parents cannot afford tuition fees. A scholarship scheme was therefore established to serve this purpose. From 1984 to 1990 over sixty scholarships were awarded. More than 500 students have competed for them. Although environmental hygiene was given more attention in the first three years, environmental education emerged as a priority when the Ijim Forest mountain project was put into place in 1991–92 by BirdLife International, with funds from the British Overseas Development Agency (ODA).

Socio-Cultural Committee

Development efforts operate in cultural contexts. The search for ethnic and cultural identity remains a driving force in efforts to improve the quality of life in rural communities. Most of the current urban elite grew up in the rural areas, but have been caught up for years in the web of modernization at the expense of their culture. Returning to their roots becomes a matter of urgency in a context of cultural decolonization. Attempts to revive culture have been enhanced by the organization of an annual festival and the allocation of funds for language training. In order to promote linguistic and cultural identity, funds were also allocated to the Kom language program. Text books (primers) are produced for the teaching of Kom in the primary schools. Every year the committee organizes a cultural festival during which the different villages compete in portraying the Kom culture. The festival often attracts the urban elite who come home to see how an earlier way of life is being relived by the old and the young.

These activities enhanced the image of the association at a time when political repression is interfaced with political clientelism. The state's long-standing withdrawal from its traditional duties to civil society harmed its image during the democratization process of the early 1990s. The fact that the state suddenly became interested in the activities of the association, and evinced a desire to be of assistance, created suspicion and resistance.

NADA Runs into a Political Storm

There is little doubt that the Njinikom Area Development Association has succeeded in several areas where local and national politicians have failed. It was, and still is, the organization that commands most respect from the local people of the district. It has given the people a sense of pride in their capacity to achieve. Its leadership commands more respect and popularity than any political leader in the area because the association has given the people a sense of ownership of their projects. Between 1984 and 1988, the presidency of NADA became a coveted position in the Njinikom area. It was seen as a political platform for greater things. In 1989, a cabinet minister whose popularity had sagged to its lowest ebb attempted to install his candidate as president and some of his henchmen on the executive board. As founding president, I was summarily removed from the leadership, in large measure, I believe, because of what the association had achieved since its inception. The association's achievements brought me a measure of popularity in Kom, and this was distasteful to the leadership clique in what was then a one-party state. I was succeeded by a member of the Njinikom elite who was known, from the beginning, to have been opposed to the establishment of the organization in the first place. From 1989 to 1993, the organization steadily lost grassroots support and confidence, and its resources began to dwindle. Moreover, when the country returned to a more democratic system of governance in 1990, key members of the association's leadership remained faithful to the former ruling party, of which the cabinet minister was a blind follower.

This exposed a weakness in the association of which I had not been fully aware before. One must remember that Cameroon has been a one-party state since 1966. When NADA was established in 1984, its leaders were all members of the only party allowed in Cameroon—the Cameroon National Union (CNU), which later became the Cameroon Democratic Movement (CPDM) in 1985—but most, I supposed, were simply nominal members. At that time no one with even a modest public profile could afford to criticize or be seen to oppose the party for fear of victimization. With the launching of the democratic process in 1990, however, I found that 80 percent of NADA leadership declared their support for the ruling party, while a majority of the ordinary members joined the strongest opposition party, the Social Democratic Front (SDF). Because of its past performance, the ruling CPDM was seen as a party that had ruined the Cameroon economy through fraud and official corruption. It had lost the confidence of the people not only because of its social and economic neglect of the rural areas but also for squandering farmers' reserve cash built up over the years through a now-defunct marketing board.

In 1993, elections were conducted to select a new executive board for NADA. The opposition party won most of the elective posts, and the ruling party lost its control of NADA leadership. The cabinet minister witnessed the greatest showdown of his political career. After having publicly donated 500,000 frs, almost one-fifth of the entire contribution for that year, he found that the voters jeered and turned down his candidacy for any elective post. Having been removed from office three years earlier, I found myself overwhelmingly brought back by a popular vote.

There were, of course, important lessons to be learnt from this episode. One of the reasons why members of the association wanted a change of leadership was the rumors of mismanagement of funds by some members of the previous executive. Some entrenched members of the executive board, respectable community leaders, were suspected of financial malpractice. The treasurer (1984–1993), a CPDM staunch supporter, had not rendered a full financial account of the association since his eviction as treasurer in 1993. In a sense, then, their membership of the Cameroon Democratic Movement party was only a pretext by which to justify their being rooted out of the NADA leadership.

In a letter addressed to me as president of the association, the cabinet minister expressed dismay at the fact that most members of his party had been thrown off the executive board. In my reply to the minister I stated that "the real reason for their dismissal was the mismanagement of funds and their allegiance to a government that was notorious for corruption, fraud and violation of basic human rights. The development-oriented objectives of the association would be pursued irrespective of party affiliation. It was important to respect the will of the people within the framework of Cameroon's democratisation process."

Furious that his party had virtually lost its local constituency, the cabinet minister decided to disrupt the 1994 annual congress of the association. One week before the annual congress, he spent a week persuading villagers, especially members of his party and the local administration, not to attend the congress. Word spreads very fast in face-to-face societies. His campaign had a devastating impact on the people. They could not accept that, in the new democratic dispensation, a senior member of the government was not interested in the development of the area. It was clear that the state was prepared to frustrate local initiatives that did not serve its interests. Guided by their own wisdom, people attended in huge numbers and made the congress a tremendous success.

Immediately after the congress, NADA made a tactical move by reopening water points closed down three years previously while the same cabinet minister had been in charge of Natural Resources, Mines and Water. The political implications were enormous, and his party had to move fast to salvage the party's image in the constituency. The national media (TV, radio, and written press) gave wide publicity to the achievements of the 1994 congress, driving the ruling party to provide 6,000,000 frs CFA for the restoration and supply of water to the community. The damage was, however, done. It had become evident that grassroots movements can make their own way through the gaps created by state negligence, by establishing an autonomous space of mass expression outside state control and by seeking new forms of legitimacy outside of state structures and politics (Bayart 1986:1). The future of NADA is, however, precarious and uncertain, given the possible manipulation of such an active grassroots organization by politicians within or outside the association.

DISCUSSION

It has often been argued that the impetus for development comes from above, from social groups outside rural villages. The structural theories of development assert that active groups are outside these villages, which are seen as passive or at best as reacting to outside stimuli. The present case study sees the urban elite as both an outside stimulus and an integral part of the internal cultural milieu. These theories fail to consider the fact that the educated elite have remained very much part of their local communities, despite their mobility up the social ladder. Even though their lifestyle fluctuates between town and countryside, they are still very much part of their roots. They are aware of their responsibility to act as agents of change; they can make people want what they need (Pitt 1976:17). They have provided the flexibility needed for traditions to adapt to the exigencies of time and space. As actors and agents of change, they are also brokers of the modernization process and have used local knowledge to construct a development paradigm. The local epistemological system is central to development and local knowledge is an ingredient of development from below.

The conventional theorists who advocate exogenously induced development approaches see foreign investment, aid, and the massive transfer of capital to Africa as a unique way of curing underdevelopment on the continent. Radical theorists see this as another form of gradually siphoning the wealth of Africa to the developed countries. Again, even accelerating economic growth rates are offset by population increases, so that per capita income continues to diminish. Designing projects and programs around people's needs, priorities, and capacities is putting them first in the development process. As social actors and ultimate beneficiaries, rural people "are the core and backbone of any development process." Acknowledging this central role of people "is the key issue of the development paradigm" (Cernea 1985:31). Although the path has been far from smooth, both the urban elite and the village community in Njinikom area have brought this principle to life.

The idea of sustainable development is used more often today as the hallmark of all development assistance. Sustainability implies the full participation of people in the formulation and implementation of projects. Without this active involvement and sense of ownership, induced development from outside will inevitably collapse when the initiators have withdrawn. Cernea rightly observes that many rural development programs "collapse for want of grassroots organisation able to foster collective actions" (1985:27). In the past, the transfer of knowledge and skills has not always been effective, because the people's participation was negligible and sustainability was never an ingredient of the process. Development is not a matter of the transfer of new technologies but "is about people and their institutions" (Cernea 1985:28). Only local people can adapt new technologies to their social organization and social structure, and cause socioeconomic and cultural change. The local people are in a better position to relate family size/population issues to resource availability, if they are given the chance to do so.

Furthermore, in the bulk of literature on development "there is an assumption that there is a continuous evolution that goes on from a traditional state towards a modernisation goal and follows steps that are similar to those presumed to have been followed by Western industrialised nations" (Lerner 1964). Western development agencies regard this process as desirable and beneficial, while former Marxists' regimes saw it as exploitative. Although there are certainly "variants in definitions and interpretations of what constitutes tradition or modernisation, the process of social change is regarded as inevitable" (Pitt 1976:10–11). This process can be left to drift or be managed from within by social actors and players themselves. Most educated elite of Africa live in both worlds and are usually catalysts in the process. They are not only eager to bring greater improvement in the quality of life by alleviating poverty, but they are also conscious of the need to maintain their cultural identity within a fast-modernizing Africa. This chapter has attempted to demonstrate how the concept of development from below has been understood and carried out by an educated elite whose perception and development initiatives have mobilized people at the grassroots for a meaningful participation in development.

Today, the concepts of "people's participation" and "putting people first" are often presented as if they are new ideas and concepts. There has been a failure to understand that the concepts date back to local African institutions and traditions. The principle of community involvement or commitment was very much part of the culture of the people in Kom, even in colonial times. Missionaries and the colonial state maximized this potential, but the postindependent managers of civil society neglected it. The nation-state gave people the impression that it would provide the resources and do things itself. But with the collapse of the economy in Cameroon and the state's withdrawal from community development, especially in certain critical social programs, the principle of people's participation is now being re-invented. Although there have been many problems along the way, this re-invention has been successfully carried out by the Njinikom Area Development Association.

Bibliography

Adamolekun, Ladipo. 1991. Promoting African Decentralization. *Public Administration and Development* 11:285–291.

African Development Fund. 1986. Appraisal Report: Mid Zambezi Valley Rural Development Project, Zimbabwe. July. Agriculture and Rural Development Department. Agricultural and Rural Development Authority.

————. 1982. Mid-Zambezi Valley Development Study. Hawkins Associations, Harare.

Agrawal, Arun. 1995. Dismantling the Divide between Indigenous and Scientific Knowledge. *Development and Change* 26:413–439.

Ahluwalia, Meenakshi. 1997. Representing Communities: The Case of a Community-Based Watershed Management Project in Rajasthan, India. *IDA Bulletin* 28(4):23–35.

Alexandre, Pierre. 1970a. Chiefs Commandants and Clerks: Their Relationship from Conquest to Decolonisation in French West Africa. In *West African Chiefs: Their Changing Status under Colonial Rule and Independence.* Michael Crowder and Obaro Ikime, eds. pp. 2–13. New York: Africana Publishing Company.

————. 1970b [1959]. The Problems of Chieftaincies in French Speaking Africa. In *West African Chiefs: Their Changing Status under Colonial Rule and Independence.* Michael Crowder and Obaro Ikime, eds. pp. 24–78. First published as "La problème des chefferies en Afrique noire française," in Notes et Etudes Documentaires, No. 2508, 10 February 1959.

Anaya, S. James. 1996. *Indigenous Peoples in International Law.* New York: Oxford University Press.

Applied Diarrheal Disease Research Project (ADDR). 1988. Mid-Project Report, September 30, 1985 – March 30, 1988. Cambridge, Mass.: The ADDR Project, Harvard Institute for International Development.

————. 1996. ADDR Project Annual Report 1995. Cambridge, Mass.: The ADDR Project, Harvard Institute for International Development.

Ayeh, Eric. 1988. Evidence of Yield Stability in Selected Landraces of Bean (*Phaseolus vulgaris* L.). *Experimental Agriculture* 24:1–7.

Baland, Jean-Marie, and Jean-Philippe Platteau. 1996. *Halting Degradation of Natural Resources: Is There a Role for Rural Communities?* Oxford: Clarendon Press.

Banerji, Debabar. 1986. *Social Sciences and Health Service Development in India: Sociology of Formation of an Alternative Paradigm.* New Delhi: Lok Paksh.

Barclay, F., M. Rodriguez, F. Santos, and M. Valcarcel. 1991. Amazonia 1940–1990, el extravio de una ilusion. Lima: Terra Nova and Centro de Investigaciones Sociológicas, Económicas, Políticas y Antropológicas (CISEPA) from the Pontificia Universidad Católica del Perú (PUCP).

Barnes-McConnell, Patricia. 1989. Culture and Agriculture in Northern Malawi: Social Contributions to the Maintenance of Genetic Diversity in Beans. Michigan State University, East Lansing, Mich: Bean/Cowpea CRSP Management Office.

Bassett, Thomas J. and Donald E. Crummey, eds. 1993. *Land in African Agrarian Systems.* Madison: University of Wisconsin Press.

Bayart, F. 1986. Civil Society in Africa. In *Political Domination in Africa: Reflections in Limits of Power.* African Studies Series 50. P. Chabal, ed. pp. 109–125. Cambridge: Cambridge University Press.

———. 1993. *L'Etat en Afrique: La Politique du Ventre.* Paris: Fayard.

Bell, R.H.V., and S.J. Donda. 1993. Community Fisheries Management Programme: Lake Malombe and the Upper Shire River. Mangochi, Malawi: Government of Malawi, Department of Fisheries.

Benavides, M., and M. Pariona. 1995. La Cooperativa forestal Yanesha y el sistema de manejo forestal comunitario en la Selva Central Peruana. En *Empresas Forestales Comunitarias en las Americas: Estudios de Caso.* Land Tenure Center/Institute for Environmental Studies. Madison: University of Wisconsin Press.

Berg, Eliot J. 1993. Rethinking Technical Cooperation: Reforms for Capacity Building in Africa. Washington, D.C.: United Nations Development Program/Development Alternatives, Inc.

BKF (Government of Burkina Faso). 1985. Decret No. 85-404/CNR/PRES portant application de la Réorganisation Agraire et Foncière au Burkina Faso.

———. 1991. Textes Portant Reorganisation Agraire et Foncière. Zatu No. AN VIII-0039 Bis/FP/Pres du 4 Juin 1991, Kiti No. AN VIII-0328 Ter/FP/PLAN-Coop du 4 Juin 1991, Ouagadougou June 1991.

————. 1993a. Schema Directeur pour l'Aménagement des Formations Naturelles Autour de Ouagadougou. Resume, UNDP/FAO/MET/Direction de l'Environnement, Ouagadougou, July 1993.

————. 1993b. Aménagement des Forêts Naturelles pour la Sauvegarde de l'Environnement et la Production de Bois: Plan d'Amanegement et de Gestion de la Forêt Classée du Nazinon. UNDP/FAO/MET (FO:BKF/89/011), Ouagadougou, January 1993.

————. 1993c. Aménagement des Forêts Naturelles pour la Sauvegarde de l'Environnement et la Production de Bois: Status de l'Union Pré-Cooperative des Groupements de Gestion Forestière. UNDP/FAO/MET (FO:BKF/89/011), Ouagadougou, August 1993.

————. 1993d. Loi No. 007/93/ADP Portant régime electoral des conseillers de village, de secteur communal, de département de province. Government of Burkina Faso.

————. 1994. Première session du comité de suivi du projet TCP/BKF/2352 a d'élaboration des textes legislatifs sur la forêt, la faune et la pêche. Compte-rendu par Albert Compaore, 28 June 1994, Ouagadougou.

Bland, S.J.R., and S.J. Donda. 1994. Management Initiatives for the Fisheries of Malawi. Paper presented at the American Association for the Advancement of Science Annual Meetings, San Francisco.

————. 1995. Common Property and Poverty: Fisheries Co-Management in Malawi. Fisheries Bulletin No. 30. Lilongwe: Fisheries Department.

Botswana *Gazette* News Paper, 1st September, 1993, Gaborone.

Botswana Government. 1992. Unpublished Figures. Central Statistics Office.

————. 1993. Dialogue Between Government and Basarwa. Regional Conference on Development Programmes for Africa's San/Basarwa Populations, 11–13 September, Gaborone.

Bratton, Michael. 1994. Land Redistribution, 1980–1990. In *Zimbabwe's Agricultural Revolution.* Mandivamba Rukuni and Carl Eicher, eds. Harare: University of Zimbabwe Press.

Brokensha, D., D. M. Warren, and O. Werner, eds. 1980. *Indigenous Knowledge Systems and Development.* Washington, D.C.: University Press of America.

Bromley, Daniel W, et al.,eds. 1992. *Making the Commons Work: Theory, Practice, and Policy.* San Francisco: Institute for Contemporary Studies.

Buell, Raymond Leslie. 1928. *The Native Problem in Africa.* Volumes I and II. New York: MacMillan.

Cernea, M. 1982. Indigenous Anthropologists and Development-Oriented Research. In *The Social-Cultural Dimension in Development: The Contributions of Sociologists and Social Anthropologists to the Work of Development Agencies.* Workshop Proceedings, pp. 28–38. Germany: GTZ.

Cernea, Michael, ed. 1985. *Putting People First: Sociological Variables in Rural Development.* New York: Oxford University Press.

Chambers, Robert. 1997. *Whose Reality Counts? Putting the First Last.* London: Intermediate Technology Publications.

Chambers, Robert, Arnold Pacey, and Lori Ann Thrupp. 1989. *Farmer First. Farmer Innovation and Agricultural Research.* London: Intermediate Technology Publications.

Chapin, Mac. 1994. Recapturing the Old Ways: Traditional Knowledge and Western Science Among the Kuna Indians of Panama. In *Cultural Expressions and Grassroots Development.* C. H. Kleymeyer, ed. Boulder, Colo., and London: Lynne Rienner.

Chauveau, Jean-Pierre. 1994. Participation paysanne et populisme bureaucratique. Essai d'histoire et de sociologie de la culture de développement. In *Les Associations Paysannes en Afrique: Organisation et dynamiques.* Jean-Pierre Jacob and Philippe Lavigne Delville, eds. pp. 25–60. Marseille: APAD, and Paris: Karthala.

Child, Graham. 1995. *Wildlife and People: The Zimbabwean Success.* Harare and New York: The Wisdom Foundation.

Chirif, A., ed. 1983. *Saqueo Amazonico.* Iquitos: CETA.

Chirif, A., P. Garcia, and R. Smith. 1991. El Indigena y su Territorio. Lima: OXFAM/COICA.

Chirwa, W.C. 1994. We Want Change: Cleaning House in Malawi. *Southern Africa Report,* 9(4):26.

Clark, Andrew F., and Lucie Colvin Phillips. 1994. *Historical Dictionary of Senegal.* Metuchen, N.J.: The Scarecrow Press.

Cohen, John M. 1993. Building sustainable public sector managerial, professional, and technical capacity: A framework for analyswas and intervention. HIID Development Discussion Paper No. 473, October.

Cohen, John M., and Norman Uphoff. 1977. Rural Development Participation: Concepts and Measures for Project Design, Implementation and Evaluation. Ithaca: Rural Development Committee, Cornell University.

Cohen, Stephen S., John W. Dyckman, Erica Schoenberger, and Charles R. Downs. 1981. Decentralization: A Framework for Policy Analysis. Report of the Project on Managing Decentralization, University of California, Berkeley.

COICA, OXFAM America. 1996. *Amazonia: Economía Indígena y Mercado.* Quito: OXFAM.

Conyers, Diana. 1984. Decentralization and Development: A Review of the Literature. *Public Administration and Development* 4:187–197.

Coulibaly, Cheibane. 1994. Mali: Les Ruraux et la Gouvernance Démocratique. Institut Malien de Recherches Appliquées au Développement, Bamako, April 1994.

Coulter, G. W. 1993. Report on Fisheries Research Strategies. Consultant's report to the ODA/Fisheries Research and Management Support Project, Malawi. Lilongwe.

Cowan, L. Gray. 1958. *Local Government in West Africa.* New York: Columbia University Press.

Crowder, Michael, and Obaro Ikime, eds. 1970. *West African Chiefs: Their Changing Status Under Colonial Rule and Independence.* New York: Africana Publishing Company.

Cruise-O'Brien, Donald. 1975. *Saints and Politicians: Essays in the Organization of a Senegalese Peasant Society.* London: Cambridge University Press.

Davis, Shelton H. 1978. Vitimas do milagre, o desenvolvimento e os Indios do Brasil. Rio de Janeiro: Zahar Editores.

Derman, B. 1997a. Nature, Development and Culture in the Zambezi Valley. In *Life and Death Matters: Human Rights and the Environment at the End of the Millennium.* Barbara Rose Johnston, ed. pp. 63–80. Walnut Creek: Altamira Press.

———. 1997b. How Green Was My Valley! Land Use and Economic Development in the Zambezi Valley, Zimbabwe. In *Research in Economic Anthropology.* Barry Isaac, ed. Volume 19. Greenwich, Conn.: Greenwood.

Derman, B. and A.E. Ferguson. 1995. Human Rights, Environment and Development: The Dispossession of Fishing Communities on Lake Malawi. *Human Ecology* 23(2):125–142.

Deschamps, Hubert. 1963. Et Maintenant, Lord Lugard? *Africa: Journal of the International African Institute,* 22(4):293–306, October 1963.

Diallo, Mahamadou A. 1994. Problematique de la Decentralisation au Niger. Preparatory Document for the Praia Conference, CILSS, République du Niger, Financed by the Netherlands and USAID-Niger, May 1994.

Downs, R.E., and S.P. Reyna, eds. 1988. *Land and Society in Contemporary Africa.* Hanover, N.H.: University Press of New England.

Drinkwater, Michael. 1991. *The State and Agrarian Change in Zimbabwe's Communal Areas.* London: Macmillan.

————. 1992. Cows Eat Grass Don't They? Evaluating Conflict over Pastoral Management in Zimbabwe. In *Bush Base, Forest Farm: Culture, Environment and Development*. Elisabeth Croll and David Parkin, eds. pp. 169–186. London and New York: Routledge.

Earl, Timothy, ed. 1991. *Chiefdoms: Power, Economy and Ideology*. New York: Cambridge University Press.

Ecuador: Congreso Nacional. 1997. Ley de Regimen Especial para la Conservación y Desarrollo Sustentable de Galapagos. Quito (18 November 1997).

Eicher, Carl K., and John M. Saatz, eds. 1984. *Agricultural Development in the Third World*. 2nd edition. Baltimore: Johns Hopkins University Press.

Elbow, Kent M. 1996. Legislative Reform, Tenure, and Natural Resource Management in Niger: The New Rural Code. The Land Tenure Center, Madison, Wisc., for CILLS and USAID, May 1996.

Escobar, Arturo. 1995. *Encountering Development. The Making and Unmaking of the Third World*. Princeton, N.J.: Princeton University Press.

Eyinga, A. 1978. From African Socialism to Planned Liberalism. In *Gaullist Africa: Cameroon Under Ahmadou Ahidjo*. Richard Joseph, ed. pp. 129–141. Enugu, Nigeria: FDP.

Fairhead, James. 1993. Representing knowledge: the "new farmer" in research fashions. In *Practising Development: Social Science Perspectives*. Johan Pottier, ed. pp. 187–204. London and New York: Routledge.

Fairhead, James, and Melissa Leach. 1996. *Misreading the African Landscape: Society and Ecology in a Forest-Savanna Mosaic*. Cambridge: Cambridge University Press.

Feldstein, Hilary Sims, and Susan V. Poats. 1989. *Working Together. Gender Analysis in Agriculture*. Volumes 1 and 2. West Hartford, Conn.: Kumarian Press.

Ferguson, Anne E. 1991. So the Grandparents May Survive: Farmer Participation in Bean Improvement in Malawi. In Progress in Improvement in Common Bean in Eastern and Southern Africa. Workshop Proceedings of the Ninth Sokoine University/Bean/Cowpea CRSP and Second SADCC/CIAT Bean Research Workshop held at Sokoine University of Agriculture, Morogoro, Tanzania, 17–22 September, 1990. *Bean Research*, Volume 5, 379-392.

————. 1993. Differences Among Women Farmers: Implications for African Agricultural Research Programs. In Proceedings of a Workshop on Social Science Research and the CRSPs, June 9–11, 1992. Carnahan Conference Center, University of Kentucky. Lincoln, Neb: University of Nebraska, INSORMIL Publications No. 93-3, pp. 47–62.

———. 1994. Gendered Science: A Critique of Agricultural Development. *American Anthropologist*, 96(3): 540–552.

Ferguson, Anne, Bill Derman, and Richard Mkandawire. 1991. The New Development Rhetoric and Lake Malawi. *Africa* 63(1):1–18.

———. 1993. The Political Ecology of a Fisheries' Collapse: The Case of Lake Malombe, Malawi. Paper prepared for the African Studies Association Annual Meetings, Boston, Mass., December 4–7.

Ferguson, Anne, and Richard Mkandawire. 1993. Common Beans and Farmer Managed Diversity: Regional Variations in Malawi. *Culture and Agriculture Bulletin* 45–46(winter/spring):14–17.

Ferguson, Anne, and Susan Sprecher. 1985. Zimbabwe: Mid-Zambezi Valley Rural Development Project Preparation Report (Main Text and Annexes). No. 119/85 AF-ZIM 10, October.

———. 1987. Women and Plant Genetic Diversity: The Case of Beans in the Central Region of Malawi. Paper presented at the American Anthropological Association Meetings, Chicago, Ill., November 18–22.

———. 1990. Component Breeding: A Strategy for Bean Improvement Where Bean is Grown in Mixtures. In Proceedings of the First SADCC Regional Bean Research Workshop, Mbabane, Swaziland, 4-7 October, 1989. J.B. Smithson, ed. pp. 81-95. CIAT African Workshop Series, No. 6. SADCC/CIAT Regional Programme on Beans in Southern Africa, Arusha, Tanzania, Food and Agriculture Organization of the United Nations.

Ferguson, James. 1994. *The Anti-Politics Machine: "Development," Depoliticization, and Bureaucratic Power in Lesotho.* Minneapolis: University of Minnesota Press.

———. 1996. "Transnational Topographies of Power: Beyond 'the State' and 'Civil Society' in the Study of African Politics." Article Manuscript, April 1996, Mimeo.

Fisiy, Cyprian F. 1992. Power and Privilege in the Administration of Law: Land Law Reforms and Social Differentiation in Cameroon. Research Reports 1992/48, Leiden: African Studies Center.

———. 1995. "Chieftaincy in the Modern State: An Institution at the Crossroads of Democratic Change," *Paideuma* 41:49–62.

Food and Agriculture Organization (United Nations). 1990. Component Breeding: A Strategy for Bean Improvement Where Bean is Grown in Mixtures. In Proceedings of the First SADCC Regional Bean Research Workshop, Mbabane, Swaziland, 4–7 October, 1989. J.B. Smithson, ed. Pp. 81–95. CIAT African Workshop Series, No. 6. SADCC/CIAT Regional Programme on Beans in Southern Africa, Arusha, Tanzania.

Fortes, M., and E. E. Evans-Pritchard. 1987 [1960]. *African Political Systems.* London: KPI Press.

Franco S., E. Nunes, J. Breilh, and A. C. Laurel. 1991. Debates en Medicina Social. Quito: Organización Panamericana de la Salud (OPS)/ALAMES. Serie Desarollo de Recursos Humanos, No. 92.

Frenk, Julio. 1992. Balancing Relevance and Excellence: Organizational Responses to Link Research with Decision Making. *Social Science and Medicine* 35:1397–1404.

Gaillard, Jacques. 1991. *Scientists in the Third World.* Lexington: University of Kentucky Press.

Gaillard, P. 1994. *Ahmadou Ahidjo Patriote et Despote: Batisseur de l'Etat Camerounais.* JALIVRES Collection Destins, Paris.

Galapagos National Park Service. 1997a. The Future of the Galapagos Marine Reserve. Charles Darwin Research Station, Santa Cruz, Galapagos Islands.

———. 1997b. Galapagos National Park Service (GNPS) News Bulletin. Charles Darwin Research Station, Santa Cruz, Galapagos Islands, Ecuador. July 1997.

Garcia, P. 1995. Territorios indigenas y la nueva legislación agraria en el Peru. IWGIA/Racimos de Ungurahui. Lima.

Gasche, Jurg. 1976. Les fondaments de l'organisation sociale des indiens Huitoto et l'illusion exogamique. Actas del XLII Congreso de Americanistas. Volume 2. Paris.

———. 1982. Las comunidades nativas entre la apariencia y la realidad. Revista Amazonia Indigena. COPAL. Lima.

Gellar, Sheldon. 1995. *Senegal: An African Nation Between Islam and the West.* Boulder, Colo.: Westview Press.

GGAOF. 1916. Réglementation forestière. Colonie du Sénégal, Service de l'agriculture et des forêts, Saint-Louis: Imprimerie du Gouvernement. Document containing 1901 Forestry Code.

Glagow, Manfred, Hening Lohmann, Sibylle Nickolmann, Kristen Paul, and Sabine Paul. 1997. *Non-Governmental Organizations in Malawi: Their Contributions for Development and Democratization.* New Brunswick, N.J.: Transaction Publishers.

Goonatilake, Susantha. 1984. *Aborted Discovery: Science and Creativity in the Third World.* London: Zed Books.

Government of Malawi Fisheries Department. 1993. Official Minutes of the Fisheries Department Research Strategy Meeting, Lilongwe. Mimeo.

————. 1994. Participatory Fisheries Management Programme Lake Malombe and Upper Shire River: Status Report. Lilongwe: The Fisheries Department Project Monitoring and Evaluation Unit.

Greene, Michael. 1991. Research for Development. Washington, D.C.: National Academy of Sciences.

Grindle, Merilee S., ed. 1997. *Getting Good Government: Capacity Building in the Public Sectors of Developing Countries.* Cambridge: Harvard Institute for International Development.

Guyer, Jane. 1994. The Spatial Dimensions of Civil Society in Africa: An Anthropologist Looks at Nigeria. In John W. Harbeson, Donals Rothchild, and Naomi Chazan, eds. *Civil Society and the State in Africa.* pp. 215–229. Boulder, Colo.: Lynne Reiner.

Hardin, Garrett. 1968. The Tragedy of the Commons. *Science* 162: 1243–1248.

Harrigan, J. 1991. Malawi. In *Aid and Power: The World Bank and Policy Based Lending.* P. Mosley, J. Harrigan and J.Toye, eds. New York: Routledge.

Henry, Fitzroy J. 1994. Towards Transdisciplinary Research on Diarrhoeal Diseases. *Journal of Diarrhoeal Diseases Research* 12:1–3.

Hermans, J. 1993. Awareness Through the Written Word: The Effect of Basarwa Literature on Policy Decisions in Botswana. Paper presented at the 13th International Congress of Anthropological and Ethnological Sciences, Mexico City, 29 July – 5 August.

Hesseling, Gerti (in collaboration with M. Sypkens Smit). n.d.[circa 1984]. Le Droit Foncier au Sénégal: L'Impact de la Réforme Foncière en Basse Casamance. Mimeo.

Higginbotham, Nick. 1992. Developing Partnerships for Health and Social Science Research: The International Clinical Epidemiology Network (INCLEN) Social Science Component. *Social Science and Medicine* 35:1325–1327.

Hitchcock, R. K., and J. D. Holm. 1993. Bureaucratic Domination of Hunter-Gatherer Societies: A Case Study of the San in Botswana. Development and Change, SAGE, London, Vol. 24 (1993) 305–338.

————. 1995. Grassroots Political Organising among Kalahari Bushmen. IWGIA Document No 3, 1995.

Hobart, Mark, ed. 1993. *An Anthropological Critique of Development: The Growth of Ignorance.* London and New York: Routledge.

Hoben, Allan, P.E. Peters, and D. Rocheleau. 1998. Participation, Civil Society and Foreign Assistance to Africa. In *Africa's Valuable Assets.* Peter Veit, ed. pp. 109–153. Washington, D.C.: World Resources Institute.

Hugon, P. 1968. *Analyse du Developpement en Afrique Noire: L'Exemple du Cameroun*. Paris: PUF.

Hull, T. H. 1994. Institutional constraints to building social science capability in public health research: a case study from Indonesia. *Acta Tropica* 57(2–3):211–227.

Ihonvbere, J. 1994. The Irrelevant State, Ethnicity, and the Quest for Nationhood in Africa. *Ethnic and Racial Studies* 17(1): 43–60.

Janzen, John M. 1978. *The Quest for Therapy: Medical Pluralism in Lower Zaire*. Berkeley: University of California Press.

Jaycox, Edward V.K. 1993. Capacity Building: The Missing Link in African Development. Transcript of address to the African-American Institute Conference, African Capacity Building: Effective and Enduring Partnerships, Reston, Va.: May 20.

Jensen, Axel Martin. 1994. Presentation at the RPTES conference, World Bank, Dakar, Senegal 1–5 November 1994.

Johnson, Terence J. 1972. *Professions and Power*. London: Macmillan.

Johnson, W. 1970. *The Cameroon Federation*. Princeton: Princeton University Press.

Joseph, R. 1978. Economy and Society. In *Gaullist Africa: Cameroon under Ahmadou Ahidjo*. Richard Joseph, ed. pp. 142–161. Enugu, Nigeria: FDP.

Journal of the American Medical Association. 1994. Invited papers from the Second International Congress on Peer Review in Biomedical Publication. 272(2):92–173.

Juma, Calestous. 1989. *The Gene Hunters: Biotechnology and the Scramble for Seeds*. Princeton, N.J.: Princeton University Press.

Karlström, Mikael. 1996. Imagining Democracy: Political Culture and Democratization in Buganda. *Africa* 66(4):485–505.

Kees van Donge, Jan. 1995. Kamuzu's Legacy: The Democratization of Malawi, or Searching for the Rules of the Game in African Politics. *African Affairs* 94: 227–257.

Kelly, Martyn. 1993. Academic Double Standards. *New Scientist* 2 January: 43.

Kelman, Herbert C. 1996. Negotiation as Interactive Problem Solving. *International Negotiation* 1:99–123.

Klein, Rudolf. 1973. *Complaints Against Doctors: A Study in Professional Accountability*. London: Charles Knight.

Kuhn, Thomas S. 1962. *The Structure of Scientific Revolutions.* Chicago: University of Chicago Press.

Kumwenda, J.D.T., S. R. Waddington, S.S. Snapp, R.B. Jones, and M.J. Blackie. 1995. "Soil Fertility Management in the Smallholder Maize Based Cropping Systems of Africa." Paper presented at the Workshop on the Emerging Maize Revolution in Africa: The Role of Technology, Institutions and Policy." East Lansing, Mich.: Michigan State University, July 1–12.

Lee, Kai. 1993. *Compass and Gyroscope: Integrating Science and Politics for the Environment.* Washington, D.C., and Covelo, Calif.: Island Press.

Leonard, David K., and Dale Rogers Marshall, eds. 1982. Institutions of Rural Development for the Poor: Decentralization and Organizational Linkages, Research Series No. 49. Berkeley: Institute of International Studies.

Lerner, D. 1964. *The Passing of Traditional Society.* New York: Free Press.

Le Vine, V. 1986. Leadership and Regime Changes in Perspectives. In *The Political Economy of Cameroon.* Michael G. Schatzberg and I. William Zartman, eds. pp. 20–52. New York: Praeger.

Light, Richard J., and David B. Pillemer. 1984. *Summing Up: The Science of Reviewing Research.* Cambridge: Harvard University Press.

Little, Peter D. 1994. The Link Between Local Participation and Improved Conservation: A Review of Issues and Experiences. In *Natural Connections: Perspectives in Community-Based Conservation.* David Western and R. Michael Wright, eds. pp. 347–372. Washington, D.C.: Island Press.

Long, Norman, ed. 1989. Encounters at the Interface. A Perspective on Social Discontinuities in Rural Development. Agricultural University of Wageningen, Wageningen.

————. 1992. From Paradigm Lost to Paradigm Regained: The Case for an Actor-Oriented Sociology of Development. In *Battlefields of Knowledge: The Interlocking of Theory and Practice in Social Research and Development.* Norman Long and Ann Long, eds. pp. 16–43. London and New York: Routledge.

Long, Norman, and Ann Long, eds. 1992. *Battlefields of Knowledge: The Interlocking of Theory and Practice in Social Research and Development.* London and New York: Routledge.

Lucas, B. Keith. 1963. The Dilemma of Local Government in Africa. In *Essays in Imperial Government.* Kenneth Robinson and Frederick Madden, eds. pp. 193–208. Oxford: Basil Blackwell.

Mabogunje, Akin L. 1982. Profile of the Social Sciences in West Africa. In *Social Sciences and Public Policy in the Developing World.* L.D. Stifel et al., eds. pp. 167–187. Lexington, Mass.: D.C. Heath.

Macdonald, Theodore. 1997. Conflict in the Galapagos Islands: Analysis and Recommendations for Management. Quito, Ecuador: The Charles Darwin Foundation for the Galapagos Islands.

Macdonald, Theodore, S. James Anaya, and Yadira Soto. 1997. Observaciones y recomendaciones sobre el caso del Bloque Samoré: Informe del proyecto en Colombia de la Organización de los Estados Americanos y la Universidad Harvard. Washington, D.C.: Organization of American States.

Mair, Lucy P. 1936. *Native Policies in Africa.* New York: Negro University Press.

Mamdani, Mahmood. 1996. *Citizen and Subject: Contemporary Africa and the Legacy of Late Colonialism.* Princeton, N.J.: Princeton University Press.

Martin, Greg, and M. W. Adams. 1987a. Landraces of *Phaseolus vulgaris* (Fabaceae) in Northern Malawi. I. Regional Variation. *Economic Botany* 41(2):190–203.

———. 1987b. Landraces of *Phaseolus vulgaris* (Fabaceae) in Northern Malawi. II. Generation and Maintenance of Variability. *Economic Botany* 41(2):204–215.

Maybury-Lewis, David. 1996. Local Participation and Cultural Survival: Editorial. *Cultural Survival Quarterly* 20(3):3.

Mazonde, Isaac Ncube. 1996. The Basarwa of Botswana: Leadership, Legitimacy and Participation in Development Sites. *Cultural Survival Quarterly* 20(3):54–56.

McCay, Bonnie M., and James M. Acheson, eds. 1987. *The Question of the Commons: The Culture and Ecology of Communal Resources.* Tucson: University of Arizona Press.

Metcalfe, S. 1994. The Zimbabwe Communal Areas Management Programme for Indigenous Resources (CAMPFIRE). In *Natural Connections: Perspectives in Community Based Conservation.* David Western and R. Michael Wright, eds. Washington D.C.: Island Press.

MINPAT. Sixth Five Year Development Plan. Yaounde: Ministry of Planning and Regional Development.

Morgan, Lynn. 1998. Latin American Social Medicine and the Politics of Theory. In *Building a New Biocultural Synthesis: Political-Economic Perspectives in Biological Anthropology.* A. Goodman and T. Leatherman, eds. pp. 407–424. Ann Arbor: University of Michigan Press.

Mosse, David. 1996. The Social Construction of People's Knowledge in Participatory Rural Development. In *Assessing Participation: A Debate from South Asia.* Sunil and Nicola Bastian, eds. pp. 135–180. Delhi: Konark Publishers.

Moyo, Sam. 1995. *The Land Question in Zimbabwe.* Harare: SAPES Books.

Murphree, M. 1993. Communities as Resource Management Institutions. International Institute for Environment and Development Gatekeeper Series, No. 36. London: IIED.

———. 1997. Congruent Objectives, Competing Interests, and Strategic Compromise: Concept and Process in the Evolution of Zimbabwe's CAMPFIRE Programme. Paper presented to the Conference on Representing Communities: Histories and Politics of Community-Based Resource Management, June 1997. Helen, Georgia, USA.

NADA. 1988. *NADA Review.* Njinikom, Kom.

Nader, Laura. 1996. Introduction. in *Naked Science: Anthropological Inquiry into Boundaries, Power, and Knowledge.* Laura Nader, ed. pp. 1–25. New York: Routledge.

National Research Council. 1992. *Democratization in Africa: African Views, African Voices.* Sahr John Kpundeh, ed. Washington, D.C.: National Academy Press.

Ndongko, W. 1986. The Political Economy of Development in Cameroon: Relations between the State, Indigenous Business, and Foreign Investors. In *The Political Economy of Cameroon.* Michael G. Schatzberg and I. William Zartman, eds. pp. 83–110. New York: Praeger.

Ngaido, Tidiane. 1996. Redefining the Boundaries of Control: Post-Colonial Tenure Policies and Dynamics of Social and Tenure Change in Western Niger. Doctoral Dissertation, University of Wisconsin, Madison.

Nkwi, P. 1976. *Traditional Government and Social Change.* Fribourg, Switzerland: Fribourg University Press.

Obeyesekere, Gananath. 1992. Science, Experimentation, and Clinical Practice in Ayurveda. In *Paths to Asian Medical Knowledge.* C. Leslie and A. Young, eds. pp. 160–176. Berkeley: University of California Press.

ONIC (Colombian National Indian Organization). 1997. Letter to Ricardo Avila, Chief of Staff, General Secretariat, Organization of American States, Washington. Bogota, 16 February 1997.

Ostrom, Elinor. 1990. *Governing the Commons.* Cambridge: Cambridge University Press.

Ouali, Firmin, Paul Kiemdé, and Dénise Yaméogo. 1994. Etude de base sur l'état de la décentralisation au Burkina. Summary report, Commission Nationale de la Décentralisation, Premier Ministère, Burkina Faso, June 1994.

Ouédraogo, Hubert M.G. 1994. Les Coutumes Relatives à la Gestion des Ressources Naturelles au Burkina Faso. FAO, Programme de Cooperation Technique, FAO-LEG: TCP/BKF/2352, Rome, March 1994.

Peluso, Nancy Lee. 1992. *Rich Forests, Poor People: Resource Control and Resistance in Java.* Berkeley: University of California Press.

Perham, Margery. 1960. *Lugard: The Years of Authority, 1898–1945.* London: Collins Press.

Peters, Pauline. 1996. Who's Local Here: The Politics of Participation in Development. *Cultural Survival Quarterly* 20(3):22–25.

Pitt, D. 1970. *Tradition and Economic Progress in Samoa: A Case Study of the Role of Traditional Social Institutions in Economic Development.* Oxford: Clarendon Press.

———. 1976. Development from Below. In *Development from Below.* Pitt, D., ed. pp.7–19. The Hague: Mouton Publishers.

Plato. 1956. *Protagoras and Meno.* WKC Guthrie, transl. London: Penguin Books.

Poats, Susan V., Marianne Schmink, and Anita Spring, eds. 1988. *Gender Issues in Farming Systems Research and Extension.* Boulder, Colo.: Westview Press.

Pottier, Johan. 1993. *Practising Development: Social Science Perspectives.* London and New York: Routledge.

Quan, J. 1993. Report on Socio-Economic Research Strategies. Consultant's Report to the ODA/Fisheries Research and Management Support Project, Malawi. Lilongwe.

Razon-Abad, H. 1996. Politics of Coalition-Building for Democratic Reform. *Cultural Survival Quarterly* 20(3): 45–49.

RdM (République du Mali). 1977. Ordonnance N77-44/CMLN du 12 juillet 1977 portant réorganisation territoriale et administrative de la République du Mali.

———. 1986. Loi No. 86-42/AN-RM Portant Code Forestier. Adopted by the National Assembly 30 January 1986.

———. 1991. Code Electoral. Ordonnance No. 91-074/P-CTSP du 10 octobre 1991.

———. 1994a. Loi No. 94__/AN-RM. Portant organisation de l'exploitation, du transport et du commerce du bois. Assemblée Nationale, RdM.

————. 1994b. Loi No. 94__/. Projet de loi portant principes de constitution et de gestion du domaine des collectivités territoriales décentralisées. Primature, Mission de Décentralisation, RdM, April 1994.

————. 1994c. Loi No. 94__/AN-RM. Fixant les conditions de gestion des ressources forestières. Assemblée Nationale, Republique du Mali.

————. 1994d. Analyse de l'évolution des recettes d'exploitation et de transactions forestières de 1957 à 1990. MDRE, DNEF, RdM, July 1994.

————. 1995. Loi No. 95-034/. Portant code des collectivités territoriales en République du Mali. Adopted 27 January 1995.

RdN (République du Niger). 1992. Projet d'ordonnance portant organisation de la commercialisation et du transport de bois dans les grandes agglomerations, et la fiscalité qui lui est applicable. Ordonnance No. 92-037 du 21 août 1992.

————. 1994. Les marchés ruraux du bois de feu au Niger et l'autogestion locale des ressources naturelles: La problèmatique et les leçons actuelles de l'expérience. Projet Energie II–Energie Domestique, Volet Offre, SEED–CIRAD-Forêt, Ministère de l'Hydraulique et de l'Environnement, Ministère des Mines et de l'Energie, République du Niger.

RdS (République du Sénégal). 1964. Loi No. 64.46 du 17 juin 1964, relative au domaine national. Journal Officiel de la République du Sénégal.

————. 1972. Décret no. 72-636 du 29 mai 1972 relatif aux attributions des chefs de circonscriptions administratives et chefs de village. Journal Officiel de la République du Sénégal, 17 June 1972.

————. 1993. Code Forestier, Loi No. 93-06 du 4 février 1993. Ministère de l'Environnement et de la Protection de la Nature.

————. 1994. Projet de décret portant code forestier (partie réglementaire). Ministère de l'Environnement et de la Protection de la Nature.

Ribeiro, D. 1975. *Fronteras Indigenas de la Civilización.* Mexico: Siglo Veintiuno Editores S.A. Distrito federal de Mexico.

Ribot, Jesse C. 1993. Market-State Relations and Environmental Policy: Limits of State Capacity in Senegal. In *The State and Social Power in Global Environmental Politics.* Ronnie D. Lipschutz and Ken Conca, eds. New York: Columbia University Press. pp. 24–45.

————. 1995a. From Exclusion to Participation: Turning Senegal's Forestry Policy Around? *World Development* 23(9):1587–1599.

————. 1995b. Local Forest Control in Burkina Faso, Mali, Niger, Senegal and The Gambia: A Review and Critique of New Participatory Policies. Africa Region, The World Bank.

————. 1996. Participation Without Representation: Chiefs, Councils and Rural Representation. *Cultural Survival Quarterly* 20(3):40–44. Special Issue on Participation edited by Pauline Peters.

————. 1998. Theorizing Access: Forest Profits along Senegal's Charcoal Commodity Chain. *Development and Change* 29(2):307–341.

————. 1999. Decentralization, Participation, and Accountability in Sahelian Forestry. *Africa* 69(1):23–65.

————. Forthcoming. Forest Rebellion and Local Representation: A Struggle to Participate in Makacoulibantang, Senegal. In *People, Plants and Justice.* Charles Zerner, ed. New York: Columbia University Press.

Richards, Paul. 1993. Cultivation: Knowledge or Performance? In *An Anthropological Critique of Development: The Growth of Ignorance.* Mark Hobart, ed. pp. 63–78. London and New York: Routledge.

Rostow, W. 1962. *The Stages of Economic Growth: Non-Communist Manifesto.* New York: Cambridge University Press.

Roth, Michael. 1994. Critique of Zimbabwe's 1992 Land Act. In *Zimbabwe's Agricultural Revolution.* Mandivamba Rukuni and Carl Eicher, eds. pp. 317–334. Harare: University of Zimbabwe Press.

Salisbury, R. 1970. *Vunamanic: Economic Transformation in Traditional Society.* Berkeley: California University Press.

Santos, F., and F. Barclay, eds. 1994–5. Guia Etnografica de la Alta Amazonia. Volumes 1–2. Quito: FLACSO/IFEA.

Sanz, E., I. Aragón, and A. Méndez. 1995. The function of national journals in disseminating applied science. *Journal of Information Science* 21:319-323.

Schroeder, Richard. 1999. Community Forestry and Conditionality in The Gambia. *Africa* 69(1):1–22.

Schumacher, Edward J. 1975. *Politics, Bureaucracy and Rural Development in Senegal.* Berkeley: University of California Press.

Schumpeter, J. A. 1943. *Capitalism, Socialism and Democracy.* London: Geo. Allen & Unwin.

Scoones, Ian. 1996. *Hazards and Opportunities: Farming Livelihoods in Dryland Africa: Lessons from Zimbabwe.* London and Atlantic Highlands, N.J.: Zed Books.

Shapin, Steven. 1995. Here and Everywhere: Sociology of Scientific Knowledge. *Annual Review of Sociology* 21:289–321.

Silverman, M., and P. H. Gulliver, eds. 1992. *Approaching the Past: Historical Anthropology Through Irish Case Studies*. New York: Columbia University Press.

Sivaramakrishnan, K. 1996. Participatory Forestry in Bengal: Competing Narratives, Statemaking and Development. *Cultural Survival Quarterly* 20(3): 35–39.

Smith, R. 1983. Las Comunidades Nativas y el Mito del Gran Vacio Amazonico. Lima: AIDESEP.

Smith, Richard C. 1997. Can Goliath and David Have a Happy Marriage? Petroleum Development and Long-Term Management of Indigenous Territories in the Peruvian Amazon. Paper presented at the Conference on Representing Communities: Histories and Politics of Community-Based Resource Management, June 1997, Helen, Georgia, organized by J. P. Brosius, A. L. Tsing, and C. Zerner.

Snapp, S. S. 1995. Improving Fertilizer Efficiency with Small Additions of High Quality Organic Inputs. In Report on the First Meeting of the Network Working Group. Soil Fertility Research Network for Maize Based Farming Systems in Selected Countries of Southern Africa. S. R. Waddington, ed. Lilongwe, Malawi: The Rockefeller Foundation Southern African Agricultural Sciences Program.

Spierenburg, Marja. 1995. The Role of the Mhondoro Cult in the Struggle for Control over Land in Dande (Northern Zimbabwe): Social Commentaries and the Influence of Adherents. Center for Applied Social Sciences, University of Zimbabwe, Harare, and Amsterdam School for Social Science Research, Amsterdam, October 1995.

Stavenhagen, R. 1994. Indigenous Rights: Some Conceptual Problems. In *Indigenous Peoples' Experiences with Self-Government*. W. Assies and J. Hoekema, eds. Copenhagen: IWGIA/University of Amsterdam.

Stepan, Nancy. 1981. *Beginnings of Brazilian Science: Oswaldo Cruz, Medical Research and Policy, 1890–1920*. New York: Science History Publications.

Stifel, Laurence D., Ralph K. Davidson, and James S. Coleman, eds. 1982. *Social Sciences and Public Policy in the Developing World*. pp. ix–xix, 57–82. Lexington, Mass.: D.C. Heath.

Stirrat, R.L. 1996. The New Orthodoxy and Old Truths: Participation, Empowerment and Other Buzz Words. In *Assessing Participation: A Debate from South Asia*. Sunil and Nicola Bastian, eds. pp. 67–92. Konark Publishers.

Suret-Canale, Jean. 1966. La fin de la chefferie en Guinée. *Journal of African History*, 7(3):459–493.

————. 1970. The Fouta-Djalon Chieftaincy. In *West African Chiefs: Their Changing Status under Colonial Rule and Independence*. Michael Crowder and Obaro Kikme, eds. pp. 79–97. New York and Ile-Ife, Nigeria: Africana Publishing Corporation and University of Ife Press.

Susser, Mervyn, and Alfred Yankauer. 1993. Prior, Duplicate, Repetitive, Fragmented, and Redundant Publication and Editorial Decisions. *American Journal of Public Health* 83:792–793.

Tambiah, Stanley. 1990. *Magic, Science, Religion, and the Scope of Rationality*. Cambridge: Cambridge University Press.

Tavares de Pinho, A. 1993. Burkina Faso: Legislation des forêts et de la faune. Rapport interimaire a des fins de discussion, FAO, Rome, December 1993.

Thomson, Jamie, and Chéibane Coulibaly. 1994. Decentralization in the Sahel: Regional Synthesis. SAH/D (94) 427, Regional Conference on Land Tenure and Decentralization in the Sahel, Praia, Cape Verde, CILSS, OECD, Club du Sahel, January 1994.

Thurairaja, Valentine. 1993. "Lake Malawi Conservation of Biodiversity, Issues and Problems. Final report for the GEF Unit of UNEP, Nairobi.

Trostle, James. 1992. Introduction. Research Capacity Building in International Health: Definitions, Evaluations, and Strategies for Success. *Social Science and Medicine* 35:1321–1324.

————. 1993. Why Publish? Differences in Institutional Incentives to Disseminate Research Findings. Manuscript presented at the HIID Research Retreat, Kennebunkport, Maine. 3 May.

Trostle, James, and Jonathon Simon. 1992. Building Applied Health Research Capacity in Less-Developed Countries: Problems Encountered by the ADDR Project. *Social Science and Medicine* 35:1379–1387.

Trostle, James, Johannes Sommerfeld, and Jonathon Simon. 1997. Strengthening Human Resource Capacity in Developing Countries: Who Are the Actors? What Are their Actions? In *Getting Good Government: Capacity Building in Developing Countries*. Merilee S. Grindle, ed. pp. 63–93. Cambridge, Mass.: Harvard Institute for International Development.

UNESCO. 1997. World Heritage Committee Galapagos Statement. Paris, UNESCO, 23–28 June.

Universo (El). 1996. Seguirá pesca en Galápagos. Guayaquil: *El Universo*, 19 noviembre 1996.

Uphoff, Norman T. 1991. Fitting Projects to People. In *Putting People First: Sociological Variables in Rural Development*. M. Cernea, ed. pp. 359–395. New York: Oxford University Press for the World Bank.

———. 1992. *Learning from Gal Oya: Possibilities for Participatory Development and Post-Newtonian Social Science.* Ithaca: Cornell University Press.

Useem, John, Ruth H. Useem, and Florence E. McCarthy. 1979. Linkages Between the Scientific Communities of Less Developed and Developed Nations: A Case Study of the Philippines. In *Bonds without Bondage: Explorations in Transcultural Interactions.* Krishna Kumar, ed. pp. 33–61. Honolulu: East-West Center.

Valle de Aquino, T., A. Manduca, J. Sales, and E. Soares. 1996. La Economía de los Kaxinawa del Rio Jordão. in *Amazonía: Economía indígena y mercado.* Quito: COICA/Oxfam América.

Vaughan, Megan. 1991. *Curing Their Ills: Colonial Power and African Illness.* Stanford: Stanford University Press.

Viteri Gualinga, Carlos. 1977. Nuevos retos del movimiento indigena amazonico. Paper presented at the III Jornadas Amazonicas, organized by CEDIME, July, 1977, Puyo, Ecuador.

Vlassoff, Carol, and Lenore Manderson. 1994. Evaluating Agency Initiatives: Building Social Science Capability in Tropical Disease Research. *Acta Tropica* 57:103–122

von Vollenhoven, J. 1920. *Une âme du chef.* Paris: Librarie Plon.

Watts, Michael J. 1993. Idioms of Land and Labor: Producing Politics and Rice in Senegambia. In *Land in African Agrarian Systems.* Thomas J. Bassett and Donald E. Crummey, eds. pp. 157–221. Madison: University of Wisconsin Press.

World Bank. 1994. Poverty Assessment. Yaounde, Cameroon.

———. 1996. *The World Bank Participation Sourcebook.* Washington, D.C.: The World Bank.

Zemsky, Robert, ed. 1998. *Policy Perspectives.* Special issue. 7(4), March. Philadelphia: University of Pennsylvania.

Zielinski, Christopher. 1995. New Equities of Information in an Electronic Age. *British Medical Journal* 310(6993):1480–1481.

Subject Index

agency, 6, 11, 14, 19, 46, 80, 105, 114, 116, 122, 141, 150–151, 153, 174, 191

aid (see donors), 6, 8, 11, 30, 34, 57–58, 60, 69–70, 91–92, 195

Amazon, 61–196

Amazonia, 61, 63, 75–76

biomedical research, 12, 157–159

blueprint approach, 124

Botswana, 10–11, 77–80, 82–87, 89–94

bottom-up approach, 129

Cameroon, 13, 59, 175–181, 183–185, 188, 190, 192–193, 196

CAMPFIRE (Communal Areas Management Program for Indigenous Resources), 123–124, 128–132, 150–152

chiefs, 35–40, 45, 51, 53–54, 57–59, 62–63, 85, 91, 184

citizens, 32, 34, 52–53, 56, 82, 99, 138, 149

civic organization/bodies, 107

civic science, 151

civil society, 6, 8, 18–19, 28, 30, 32–33, 69, 97, 190–191, 196

Colombia, 11, 95–97, 110–114, 117, 119

colonial rule, 2, 51, 53

colonialism, 32

common lands, 20, 22

common property, 20, 24, 99–102, 144

commons, 20, 44, 100

community, 6–11, 13, 17–18, 22–24, 27, 29–33, 35, 37–40, 42, 44, 47–48, 50–52, 54–59, 61–64, 68, 70–74, 76–78, 83–85, 98–101, 105, 107, 110, 112–113, 117, 120, 125, 130–131, 138, 145–146, 148–149, 159, 164, 168, 172, 181–183, 188–190, 193–196

consultation, 38, 65, 96–98, 110–113, 115–119, 145, 177, 186

cooperatives, 34, 38–39, 41–42, 45, 48, 57–59, 107

decentralization, 29–31, 34, 36–38, 40, 44–45, 50, 53–56, 59–60

democracy/democratic governance, 15–19, 28, 34, 98, 113, 123, 149

development, 1–10, 12–22, 24–33, 35, 39, 41, 44, 51, 53, 57, 61–196

donors (see aid), 3, 8, 45–46, 69, 77, 86, 94, 141, 144, 146, 150, 154, 159, 161, 163, 165, 170–172

forest, 10, 16, 23–24, 29, 31, 34–35, 37, 41–42, 44–49, 51–54, 57, 60–61, 65, 73, 191

forest policy, 23

forest service, 34, 41–42, 44–47, 49, 51–54, 60

forestry, 9, 18, 21, 23, 27, 29, 31, 33–34, 40–41, 43, 45–46, 48–53, 56, 60

Galapagos, 11, 96–101, 103–108, 119

ILO Convention #169, 112, 119

India, 9, 15, 28, 164

indigenous groups, 10, 61, 63–66, 112–113

indigenous knowledge, 1, 4, 13, 148

indigenous organizations, 62, 64, 66–67, 69–70, 73, 75–76, 117

indigenous peoples, 5, 61–196

indigenous rights, 30, 64, 75, 111, 113–114

knowledge, 1–6, 11–13, 31, 57, 67, 70–71, 74, 87, 94–95, 121–124, 126, 129, 132–133, 135–136, 138, 140, 142, 144, 146, 148–151, 157–161, 164, 166, 168, 172, 174, 195

land tenure, 16, 22, 34, 57, 114, 190

leadership, 11, 22, 27, 51, 63, 69–70, 107, 127, 180, 183–184, 187, 190, 192–193

local knowledge, 1, 4–5, 57, 123, 129, 132, 136, 148, 151, 172, 195

Malawi, 12, 121, 123, 133–150, 154–155, 173

NGO, 7–9, 13–15, 17, 25–27, 73, 82–83, 86, 94, 130, 141, 150

nongovernmental organization, 7–8, 15

panchayat, 22, 24

participation, 1–14, 28–34, 36–41, 44–47, 49–50, 52–57, 62, 64, 66, 68–69, 75, 86, 95–100, 105–106, 109–110, 113, 115, 118–119, 123, 129, 131–133, 147–150, 173, 175–176, 181–182, 186–188, 195–196

participatory development, 1, 6–8, 10, 13, 19, 28, 30, 33, 35

patronage, 9, 11, 18, 24, 27

policy, 2–3, 16, 23, 36, 44, 51, 55, 57–59, 65, 76, 78, 81–83, 85, 101, 114, 126, 130, 138, 143, 145, 151, 164, 171–172, 174, 176–180

representation, 7, 9–10, 18, 29, 31, 33–35, 38, 40, 44, 47, 54, 58, 62, 68–69, 87, 91, 94, 122, 129, 164, 170, 178, 181

representatives, 3, 13, 16–18, 20, 27, 31, 36, 38, 40, 42, 45–46, 48, 51, 55, 57, 59, 64–65, 67–68, 77–78, 82, 85, 89–90, 94, 106, 108, 112, 116–119, 127, 188

resettlement, 88, 122–125, 127–128

Sahel, 29, 31, 34–35, 56

scientific knowledge, 3, 12, 122–124, 133, 140, 158

scientific method, 157

scientific research, 132, 135, 157, 159–160, 162, 164, 169–170, 173

spokesperson, 8

state, 2–3, 8–11, 15–19, 22–24, 26, 29–38, 40, 45–46, 49–51, 54–55, 57–59, 62, 64, 68–69, 76, 93, 100–102, 112, 115, 118, 120, 123, 126, 133–135, 140, 144, 146, 149, 151, 162, 164, 166, 170, 180, 184, 186, 189, 191–192, 194, 196

sustainable development, 95, 122, 150, 186, 195

top-down development, 30

training, 71, 135, 137, 139, 143, 163–165, 174, 182, 191

West Africa, 9, 33, 49, 57, 59

World Bank, 56–57, 95, 146–147, 155, 162, 174

Zimbabwe, 12, 121–126, 129–130, 152

AUTHOR INDEX

Acheson, James M.,103

Adamolekun, Lapido, 56

Adams, M. W. 136, 153

African Development Fund, 152

Agrawal, Arun, 4–5, 14, 158

Ahluwalia, Meenakshi, 9

Alexandre, Pierre, 32, 35–36, 52, 58

Anaya, S. James, 96, 116, 120

Applied Diarrheal Disease Research Project (ADDR), 160–162, 165–166, 168–174

Ayeh, Eric, 136

Baland, Jean-Marie, 57

Banerji, Debaba, r172

Barclay, F., 61–62

Barnes-McConnell, Patricia, 136

Bassett, Thomas J., 50

Bayart, F., 178–179, 194

Bell, R. H., V.145

Benavides, M, 10–11, 13, 61, 74

Berg, Eliot J., 174

BKF (Government of Burkina Faso), 36, 41–42

Bland, S. J., R. 148

Botswana Government, 78–80, 82–85, 89, 91, 93

Bratton, Michael, 152

Brokensha, D., 4

Bromley, Daniel W., 103

Buell, Raymond Leslie, 32, 35, 49, 51–52, 57–58

Cernea, M., 57, 195

Chambers, Robert, 4, 12, 137, 160

Chapin, Mac, 67

Chauveau, Jean-Pierre, 57

Child, Graham, 18, 57, 73, 152, 174, 187, 191

Chirif, A., 61, 65

Chirwa, W. C., 138

COICA, 62, 75

Colombian National Indian Organization (ONIC), 111, 114–115, 117

Conyers, Diana, 56

Coulibaly, Cheibane, 56

Coulter, G. W., 154

Cowan, L. Gray, 35, 49, 58–59

Crowder, Michael, 58

Cruise-O'Brien, Donald, 58–59

Crummey, Donald E., 50

Davis, Shelton H., 61, 133, 137

Derman, B., 11, 121, 146, 149, 152, 154–155

Deschamps, Hubert 35

Diallo, Mahamadou A., 37–38, 49, 59

Donda., S. J., 145, 148

Downs, Charles R., 50

Drinkwater, Michael, 152

Elbow, Kent M., 59

Escobar, Arturo, 3, 12, 121–122, 151

Evans-Pritchard, E. E., 58

Eyinga, A., 178

Fairhead, James, 5, 53

Feldstein, Hilary Sims, 135

Ferguson, James, 164

Fisiy, Cyprian F., 35, 37, 50, 58–59

Food and Agriculture Organization (FAO) (United Nations), 41, 125, 143, 146, 152

Fortes, M., 58

Franco, S., 167

Frenk, Julio, 163

Galapagos National Park Service, 99, 107–108

Garcia, P., 65

Gasche, Jurg, 63, 75

Gellar, Sheldon, 49

Glagow, Manfred, 138

Goonatilake, Susantha, 172

Greene, Michael, 160

Grindle, Merilee S., 174

Gulliver, P. H., 8

Guyer, Jane, 58

Hardin, Garrett, 100

Harrigan, J., 138

Henry, Fitzroy J., 57, 161

Hermans, J., 79

Hesseling, Gerti, 37, 39, 49–50

Higginbotham, Nick, 160

Hitchcock, R. K., 91–92

Hobart, Mark, 5

Hoben, Allan, 7

Holm, J. D., 91–92

Hugon, P., 176

Hull, T. H., 169

Ihonvbere, J., 180, 188

Ikime, Obaro, 58

Janzen, John M., 162

Jaycox, Edward V. K., 174

Johnson, Terence J., 162, 183

Joseph, R. 176, 178

Journal of the American Medical Association, 169

Juma, Calestous, 139

Kees van Donge, Jan, 138

Kelly, Martyn, 159

Kelman, Hebert C., 114

Klein, Rudolf, 162

Kuhn, Thomas S., 1, 12

Kumwenda, J. D. T., 141

Le Vine, V., 178

Leach, Melissa, 53

Lee, Kai, 151

Leonard, David K., 56

Lerner, D., 196

Mabogunje, Akin L.,163

Macdonald, Theodore, 11, 95–96, 99–100, 116, 120

Mair, Lucy P., 32

Mamdani, Mahmood, 29, 32–33, 35, 37, 50–51

Manderson, Lenore, 160

Marshall, Dale Rogers, 56

Martin, Greg, 136, 153

Maybury-Lewis, David, 7

Mazonde, Isaac Ncube, 10–11, 13, 58, 77

McCay, Bonnie M., 103

Metcalfe, S., 129, 152

Mkandawire, Richard, 137, 146, 149, 154–155

Morgan, Lynn, 167

Mosse, David, 6

Moyo, Sam, 152

Murphree, M., 152

NADA, 175, 180, 184–188, 190, 192–194

Nader, Laura, 158

National Research Council, 57–58

Ndongko, W., 177

Ngaido, Tidiane, 36–37

Nkwi, P., 13, 175, 181–182, 185

Obeyesekere, Gananath, 158

Ostrom, Elinor, 100, 103

Ouali, Firmin, 35, 37, 44, 49

Ouédraogo, Hubert M. G., 35, 54

Pacey, Arnold, 137

Pariona, M., 74

Peluso, Nancy Lee, 57

Perham, Margery, 32, 35

Peters, Pauline, 1, 14, 56

Pillemer, David B., 170

Pitt, D., 195–196

Plato, 157

Platteau, Jean-Philippe, 57

Poats, Susan V., 135

Pottier, Johan, 1

Quan, J., 148, 154

Razon-Abad, H., 10

RdM (République du Mali), 36, 38, 45, 49

RdN (République du Niger), 37

RdS (République du Sénégal), 36–38, 49

Reyna, S. P., 50

Ribeiro, D., 61

Ribot, Jesse C., 7, 9, 13, 29, 31–32, 37, 40, 48–49, 52–53, 58–59

Richards, Paul, 5

Roth, Michael, 152

Sales, J., 48

Santos, F., 61–62

Sanz, E., 169

Schmink, Marianne, 135

Schroeder, Richard, 32

Schumacher, Edward J., 49, 58

Schumpeter, J. A., 59

Scoones, Ian, 152

Shapin, Steven, 158

Silverman, M., 8

Simon, Jonathan, 129, 161, 173

Sivaramakrishnan, K., 10

Smith, R., 56, 61, 65, 119

Snapp, S. S., 141

Soto, Yadira, 96, 116, 120

Spierenburg, Marja, 35, 37, 54, 58

Sprecher, Susan, 139–140

Spring, Anita, 135

Stavenhagen, R., 65

Stepan, Nancy, 170–171

Stifel, Laurence, D. 163

Stirrat, R. L., 1

Suret-Canale, Jean, 35, 52, 58

Susser, Mervyn, 173

Tambiah, Stanley, 160

Tavares de Pinho, A., 41

Thomson, Jamie, 56

Thrupp, Lori Ann, 137

Thurairaja, Valentine, 155

Trostle, James, 12, 157, 160–161, 169, 173

UNESCO, 95–96, 104, 162

Universo, (El), 106

Uphoff, Norman T., 12, 57, 160, 177, 186

Valle de Aquino, T. 75

Vaughan, Megan, 51, 57

Vlassoff, Carol, 160

von Vollenhoven, J. 51, 57

Warren, D. M., 4

Watts, Michael J., 50, 56

Werner, O., 4

World Bank, 56–57, 95, 146–147, 155, 162, 174

Yankauer, Alfred, 173

Zemsky, Robert, 159

Zielinski, Christopher, 170